Refashioning Bill Gibb for the 21st Century

Refashioning Bill Gibb for the 21st Century

Edited by Shane Strachan and Josephine Steed

BLOOMSBURY VISUAL ARTS
LONDON · NEW YORK · OXFORD · NEW DELHI · SYDNEY

BLOOMSBURY VISUAL ARTS
Bloomsbury Publishing Plc, 50 Bedford Square, London, WC1B 3DP, UK
Bloomsbury Publishing Inc, 1385 Broadway, New York, NY 10018, USA
Bloomsbury Publishing Ireland, 29 Earlsfort Terrace, Dublin 2, D02 AY28, Ireland

BLOOMSBURY, BLOOMSBURY VISUAL ARTS and the Diana logo are trademarks
of Bloomsbury Publishing Plc

First published in Great Britain 2026

Copyright © Shane Strachan, Josephine Steed and contributors, 2026

Shane Strachan, Josephine Steed and contributors have asserted their right under the Copyright, Designs and Patents Act, 1988, to be identified as Authors of this work.

For legal purposes the Acknowledgements on p. xix constitute an extension of this copyright page.

Cover design: Adriana Brioso
Cover image: Blue lurex dress, 1973. Aberdeen Archives Gallery and Museums (AAGM) Collection: ABDMS071537. © Bill Gibb Trust.
Frontispiece: @Vintage_Egyptologist (Colleen Darnell) on Instagram, 2021.
Photographed by Mennatullah Hossam.

All rights reserved. No part of this publication may be: i) reproduced or transmitted in any form, electronic or mechanical, including photocopying, recording or by means of any information storage or retrieval system without prior permission in writing from the publishers; or ii) used or reproduced in any way for the training, development or operation of artificial intelligence (AI) technologies, including generative AI technologies. The rights holders expressly reserve this publication from the text and data mining exception as per Article 4(3) of the Digital Single Market Directive (EU) 2019/790.

Bloomsbury Publishing Plc does not have any control over, or responsibility for, any third-party websites referred to or in this book. All internet addresses given in this book were correct at the time of going to press. The author and publisher regret any inconvenience caused if addresses have changed or sites have ceased to exist, but can accept no responsibility for any such changes.

A catalogue record for this book is available from the British Library.

A catalog record for this book is available from the Library of Congress.

ISBN: PB: 978-1-3504-4462-1
HB: 978-1-3504-4463-8
ePDF: 978-1-3504-4464-5
ePub: 978-1-3504-4465-2

Typeset by RefineCatch Limited, Bungay, Suffolk
Printed and bound in India

For product safety related questions contact productsafety@bloomsbury.com.

To find out more about our authors and books visit www.bloomsbury.com
and sign up for our newsletters.

Figure 0.1 (facing page) *Blue lurex dress, 1973. Aberdeen Archives Gallery and Museums (AAGM) Collection: ABDMS071537. © Bill Gibb Trust.*

Contents

List of Illustrations viii
Foreword, Dame Zandra Rhodes, Fashion and Textile Designer xvi
Acknowledgements xix

Introduction
   Shane Strachan, University of Aberdeen, UK and Josephine Steed, Robert Gordon University, UK 1

Part One Gibb's Design Process: Influences and Collaborations 9

1   An interview with Bill Gibb's sisters 11

2   Disciplined flamboyance: Gibb's drawing and design process
    Christine Rew, Former Manager of Aberdeen Archives, Gallery and Museums Service, UK 19

3   Britain's fashion education revolution: Bricolage and Historicism in the work of Bill Gibb
    Marie McLoughlin, University of Brighton, UK 35

4   Folkloric revivals and exoticism in fashion: Bill Gibb and the vanguard of designers in 1960s–1970s France
    Elizabeth Fischer, University of Art and Design HEAD - Genève, Switzerland 49

5   An interview with Kaffe Fassett, Artist 63

6   Gibb's knitwear in the 1970s: collaboration, innovation and 'slow' fashion
    Josephine Steed, Robert Gordon University, UK 71

Part Two Gibb's Fashion Legacy 85

7 The show must go on: was Bill Gibb the greatest showman?
Iain R. Webb, Kingston University, UK 89

8 Souvenirs of style: a web of memory association
NJ Stevenson, London College of Fashion, University of the Arts London, UK 103

9 An interview with Morna Annandale of Aberdeen Archives, Gallery and Museums 115

10 Restyled and reimagined: exploring Bill Gibb's digital legacy on Instagram
Madeleine Marcella-Hood, Christina Reid and Peter Reid, Robert Gordon University, UK 119

11 From Gibb to Gucci: how folklore fashions comfort in turbulent times
Karen Cross, Robert Gordon University, UK 130

Part Three Reinterpreting Gibb Today 143

12 Bill Gibb through the lens of cultural appropriation
Jeena Sharma, Fashion Journalist 145

13 Addressing climate change through Bill Gibb's design legacy
Lynn Wilson, University of Glasgow, UK 157

14 An interview with Giles Deacon, Fashion Designer 168

15 Exploring Gibb's design process within fashion education
Shane Strachan, University of Aberdeen, UK and Josephine Steed, Robert Gordon University, UK 173

16 The Bill Gibb Line: creative crossovers in fashion and poetry
Shane Strachan, University of Aberdeen, UK 186

Notes 201
Selected References 222
List of Contributors 223
Index 228

Illustrations

0.1	Blue lurex dress, 1973. Aberdeen Archives Gallery and Museums (AAGM) Collection: ABDMS071537. © Bill Gibb Trust.	v
0.2	Model Jill Harley wearing a Bill Gibb printed satin outfit with leather trim at the fashion show at Les Ambassadeurs, London, 27th October 1972. Photo by Mike Lawn/Fox Photos/Hulton Archive/Getty Images.	xvi
0.3	Woollen printed scarf with Bill Gibb signature, mid-1970s. AAGM Collections: ABDMS093606.	4
0.4	Detail from drawing of dress and caped coat; mid-late 1960s. AAGM Collections: ABDMS070938.	8
0.5 and 0.6	Dress for Baccarat in 1969 combines patterned prints, checks and florals with leather thongs. AAGM Collections: ABDMS023985.	83
0.7	Multidrawing of coats, tops and knickerbockers; Autumn/Winter 1972. AAGM Collections: ABDMS070169.	87
0.8	Black and gold knitted jacket and top with pleated gold metallic skirt for Autumn/Winter 1974. AAGM Collections: ABDMS015707 and ABDMS015708.	142
0.9	Lynn Wilson, Josephine Steed, Morna Annandale, Shane Strachan, Karen Cross, Madeleine Marcella-Hood and Christine Rew viewing the Bill Gibb archive at AAGM's Treasure Hub.	223
0.10	Detail from woollen printed scarf with Bill Gibb signature, mid-1970s. AAGM Collections: ABDMS093606.	236
1.1	Gibb's drawing of his grandmother from his St Martin's submission portfolio in 1962. AAGM Collections: ABDMS082324.	12
1.2	Gibb with his father and mother in London, *c.*1962. Courtesy of Patricia Davidson.	13
1.3	Marlyn, Patsy and Janet on Patsy's wedding day in 1969 joined by two flower girls, all dressed in original Gibb designs. Courtesy of Patricia Davidson.	16
1.4	Gibb with sisters Patsy and Janet in Scotland in 1987. Courtesy of Patricia Davidson.	17

2.1	A drawing from one of Gibb's Fraserburgh Academy schoolbooks *c.*1958 when he was 15 years old. Courtesy of Bill Gibb Trust. Photo by Mike Davidson.	20
2.2	1982 drawing of dress for Harrods and Amanda Bishop's Carven boutique in Jeddah, Saudi Arabia. AAGM Collections: ABDMS070412.	20
2.3	1968 drawing of jersey trouser suits for the Alice Paul boutique. AAGM archive: ABDMS067446.	21
2.4	Drawing of dress commission for 'Gudrun', *c.*1970. AAGM Collections: ABDMS070470.	22
2.5	Detail from 1969 dress for Baccarat combining patterned prints, checks, and florals with leather thongs. AAGM Collections: ABDMS023985.	22
2.6	Drawing of jacket and skirt outfit with fabric swatch for the Autumn/Winter 1970 Collection. AAGM Collections: ABDMS067683.	24
2.7	Multidrawing of jackets and coats for Autumn/Winter 1976 knitting collection. AAGM Collections: ABDMS067101.	24
2.8	Drawing of apron dress with fabric swatches for Spring/Summer 1977 Collection. AAGM Collections: ABDMS067481.	26
2.9	Multidrawing of eleven 1972 outfit designs including dresses, tops and skirts. AAGM Collections: ABDMS070163.	28
2.10	Multidrawing of evening wear for Autumn/Winter 1977/78 collection. AAGM archive: ABDMS067616.	29
2.11	Multidrawing of wool crêpe tops, skirts and dresses for Autumn/Winter 1976/77 collection. AAGM Collections: ABDMS067521.	30
2.12	Drawing of dress with fabric swatches for Autumn/Winter 1976/77 collection. AAGM Collections: ABDMS067522.	30
2.13	Drawing of blouse and skirt for the Autumn 1973 collection with bee embellishments. AAGM Collections: ABDMS070176.	31
2.14	Drawing of bee pocket design for the Autumn/Winter 1979 couture knitting collection. AAGM Collections: ABDMS070554.	31
2.15	Drawing of wedding dress commission for actress Susan George for her marriage to actor Simon MacCorkindale on 22 December 1984. AAGM Collections: ABDMS067614.	32
2.16	Drawing of men's jacket and trousers with fabric swatches for Reid and Taylor 1979 promotion. AAGM Collections: ABDMS067627.	34
2.17	Drawing of detachable-hooded fur duffle coat with fur swatches for Hockley Autumn/Winter 1983/84 fur collection. AAGM: ABDMS035559.	34

3.1	Muriel Pemberton's 'Pink & Plum' fashion campaign for Emcar in *Honey* magazine, 1963.	36
3.2	Watercolour of Bill Gibb by Muriel Pemberton, c.1964. Courtesy of Chris Beetles.	36
3.3	Gibb's painting of Henry VIII and Anne Boleyn marked 'Very Good' by his Fraserburgh Academy art teacher, Robert Duthie. AAGM Collections: ABDMS082324.	37
3.4	Early fashion drawings included in Gibb's portfolio for St Martin's School of Art. AAGM Collections: ABDMS082324.	37
3.5	The front cover of Gibb's portfolio for St Martin's School of Art. AAGM Collections: ABDMS082324.	38
3.6	Drawing of coat and trousers in 1968 for Judy Brittain, British *Vogue* magazine's knitting editor. AAGM Collections: ABDMS067675.	43
3.7	Examples of traditional Italian womenswear sketched by Gibb for his Royal College of Art portfolio submission. AAGM Collections: ABDMS081998.	44
3.8	Examples of traditional Italian menswear also sketched by Gibb for his portfolio. AAGM Collections: ABDMS081998.	44
3.9	Example page (997) from *Zur Geschichte Der Kostüme* (1890) by Louis Braun. This copy is held by Central Saint Martins which Gibb would have used during his time at St Martin's. Courtesy of Judy Willcocks, CSM.	45
3.10	Detail of 1970s printed cotton dress featuring chevron braid. Courtesy of Kerry Taylor Auctions.	46
3.11	Installation view of Gibb's 1970 'Dress of the Year' shown alongside *Vogue* article as part of the Tartan exhibition at V&A Dundee. Photograph by Ruth Clark, courtesy of V&A Dundee.	47
4.1	Autumn/Winter 1977 design featuring sequin embellishment by Jakob Schlaepfer as part of a 'Happy Birthday Bill Gibb' magazine advertisement special. Photo: Retro AdArchives / Alamy.	51
4.2 and 4.3	Two of Gibb's designs for the Embroidery Industry of Vorarlberg in Austria featuring embroidery by Arnold Blotter and Herman Bosch. AAGM Collections: ABDMS054220 and ABDMS054217.	55
4.4	Illustration of Bashkir women's woollen garment, jackets and shirts based on designs from the Budapest Ethnographic Museum. From Max Tilke's *The Costumes of Eastern Europe* (London: Ernest Benn, 1926), 76.	56
4.5	Illustration by Colin Barnes in Issue 30 of *Textiles Suisses* (1977) of Gibb garment featuring multicoloured embroidery on tartan wool by Jakob Schlaepfer.	58

4.6	Further illustration by Barnes in *Textiles Suisses* of a Gibb evening dress featuring silver and sequin embroidery on flame chiffon by Jakob Schlaepfer.	58
5.1	Drawing of Kaffe Fassett included in Gibb's portfolio submission to the Royal College of Art in 1966. AAGM Collections: ABDMS081998.	63
5.2	Egyptian-inspired drawings which decorated Gibb's childhood bedroom. Courtesy of Patricia Davidson.	65
5.3	Detail from 1975 'Moon and Buddha' knitwear collection. AAGM Collections: ABDMS023893. Photo by Mike Davidson.	69
6.1	Hand-knitting sample by Kaffe Fassett for the Autumn/Winter 1976 Byzantine collection with instructions for translating to machine knitting. AAGM Collections: ABDMS067474.	73
6.2 and 6.3	Caramel and mint patterned knitted jacket made with the synthetic Courtelle and Lurex yarns, 1981. AAGM Collections: ABDMS024230.	75
6.4 and 6.5	Machine-knit kimono from the 'Moon and Buddha' collection, 1975. AAGM Collections: ABDMS015722.	76
6.6	Missoni's Spring/Summer 2011 collection at Milan Fashion Week in September 2010. Photo: DPA Picture Alliance Archive / Alamy.	77
6.7	Drawing of top and skirt for *The Daily Telegraph* Autumn/Winter 1982 pattern offer. AAGM Collections: ABDMS070419.	79
6.8 and 6.9	Black throw with multicoloured fringing and coat dress with electric-blue trim from the Autumn/Winter 1976 Byzantine knitwear collection. AAGM Collections: ABDMS023987 and ABDMS023986.	81
7.1	*Daily Mirror* fashion editor Lesley Ebbetts in a Qiana jersey dress with shell motif from Gibb's 1973 collection ahead of his 1977 retrospective.	90
7.2	Cindy White backstage at the Royal Albert Hall in 1977 wearing a lurex dress from Gibb's 1973 collection. Photo: Niall McInerney / Bloomsbury Fashion Photography Archive.	91
7.3	Gibb travelling with Kate Franklin. Courtesy of Iain R. Webb.	93
7.4	Autumn/Winter 1977 Ready to Wear show at the Hyde Park Hotel. The dress features embroidery by Swiss company Jakob Schlaepfer. Photo: Tim Jenkins/WWD/Penske Media via Getty Images.	94
7.5	Gibb backstage at the Oriental Club ahead of his April 1972 show. Photo: Evening Standard/Hulton Archive/Getty Images.	98
7.6	Kate Moss arriving at Louis Vuitton Menswear Fall/Winter 2015–16 in the 'Lovat' print dress from Gibb's Spring/Summer 1974 collection and a 'Gibb for Philip Hockley' fox fur and suede coat. Photo: Pierre Suu/GC Images.	100

7.7	Drawing of top and skirt with map print for High Summer 1971 collection. AAGM Collection: ABDMS067520.	101
7.8	Detail from 1971 Bill Gibb for Baccarat ensemble: satin printed with red and grey sixteenth-century world map. Courtesy of Kerry Taylor Auctions.	101
8.1	Bill Gibb for Baccarat suede dress made for Liz Taylor in *Billy: Bill Gibb's Moment in Time*, Fashion and Textile Museum, 2008. Courtesy of NJ Stevenson.	105
8.2	Custom-made wedding dress made for Irene Andrae, Fashion and Textile Museum, 2008.	108
8.3	Section featuring Gibb's sisters' wedding dresses alongside Tessa Dahl's pink taffeta dress. Courtesy of NJ Stevenson.	109
8.4	Cut out of Clive Boursnell show photography. Courtesy of NJ Stevenson.	111
8.5	Adel Rootstein mannequin wearing gold lace dress custom-made for Meg Wynn Owen. Courtesy of NJ Stevenson.	111
8.6	Image of whole gallery at the Fashion and Textile Museum showing Adel Rootstein mannequin on swing wearing leather outfit. Courtesy of NJ Stevenson.	113
9.1 and 9.2	Red wool dress with cream trim from Autumn 1973 collection. AAGM Collections: ABDMS076368.	116
9.3 and 9.4	Marbled leather suit jacket and satin skirt (1973) once worn by actress Charlotte Rampling. AAGM Collections: ABDMS095712.1-3.	117
10.1	@LauraKitty (Laura McLaws Helms) on Instagram, 2018.	121
10.2	@LauraKitty (Laura McLaws Helms) on Instagram, 2016. Photographed by Lisa Candela.	121
10.3 and 10.4	@VintageFelix (Felix Gaona) on Instagram, 2019.	124
10.5 and 10.6	@Karen_VintageBoutique (Karen Stott) on Instagram, 2024.	125
10.7	@PretaVintage (Nicola Chinn) on Instagram, 2017.	126
10.8	@Karen_VintageBoutique (Karen Stott) on Instagram, 2017.	126
10.9	@Vintage_Egyptologist (Colleen Darnell) on Instagram, 2021. Photographed by Mennatullah Hossam.	127
10.10 and 10.11	@TimelessVixen (Lauren Lepire) on Instagram 2023. Modelled by Lauren Lepire. Photographed by Douglas Walker.	128
11.1	Cream Qiana jersey top and skirt, 1973. AAGM Collections: ABDMS093638.	131
11.2	Dolman sleeve silk dress, 1973. AAGM Collections: ABDMS071568.	131
11.3	Gucci Fall/Winter 2008/09, Milan Fashion Week. Photo by Venturelli/WireImage via Getty.	134
11.4	Drawing of fur coats by Bill Gibb, 1974. AAGM Collections: ABDMS067059.	134
11.5	Drawing of layered lace dress by Bill Gibb, 1977. AAGM Collections: ABDMS067593.	135

11.6	Gucci Fall/Winter 2020, Milan Fashion Week. Photo by WWD/Penske Media via Getty Images.	135
11.7	Multidrawing of dresses, tops and skirts, 1972. AAGM Collections: ABDMS067453.	137
11.8	Gucci Fall/Winter 2020, Milan Fashion Week. Photo by WWD/Penske Media via Getty Images.	137
11.9	Gucci Spring/Summer 2020, Milan Fashion Week. Photo by WWD/Penske Media via Getty Images.	138
11.10	Drawing of cardigan and leggings for Couture Knitting collection by Bill Gibb, 1979. AAGM Collections: ABDMS070558.	138
11.11	Gucci Fall/Winter 2018, Milan Fashion Week. Photo by Davide Maestri/WWD/Penske Media via Getty Images.	139
11.12	Byzantine coat dress by Bill Gibb, Autumn/Winter 1976. AAGM Collections: ABDMS023986.	139
11.13	Gucci Spring/Summer 2020, Milan Fashion Week. Photo by WWD/Penske Media via Getty Images.	140
11.14	Drawing of pleated jacket and dress by Bill Gibb, 1976. AAGM Collections: ABDMS035647.	140
12.1 and 12.2	Sketches of Middle Eastern and Indian design from Gibb's submission portfolio to the Royal College of Art. AAGM Collections: ABDMS081998.	147
12.3	Sketches of Persian motifs from Gibb's submission portfolio to the Royal College of Art. AAGM Collections: ABDMS081998.	149
12.4	Pharrell Williams with models wearing his Fall/Winter 2024 menswear collection for Louis Vuitton at Paris Fashion Week. Photo: Francois Durand/Getty Images.	151
12.5	Detail from Gibb's 'Tana' dress worn by Sandie Shaw in 1972. Photo by Ruth Clark, courtesy of V&A Dundee.	152
12.6	Disco singer Asha Puthli wearing one of her Gibb dresses in Germany in 1976. Photo: Schweigmann/United Archives via Getty Images.	154
12.7	Printed silk kimono (1977) on display as part of *Kimono* exhibition at V&A Dundee in 2024. The print was designed by Janet Taylor for Bill Gibb to commemorate the Silver Jubilee of Queen Elizabeth II. Photo by Ruth Clark, courtesy of V&A Dundee.	155
13.1	Detail of bee buttons on black dress sleeve from 1972 collection. AAGM Collections: ABDMS015726.	158
13.2	Bee tin once owned by Bill Gibb. AAGM Collections: ABDMS082315.	158
13.3 and 13.4	Green woollen cape with orange trim for the Autumn/Winter 1977–78 Scottish Collection. AAGM Collections: ABDMS076724.	159

13.5 and 13.6	Cream, green and pink silk kimono-shape wrap with rose print including bee surrounded by hand-sewn sequins. AAGM Collections: ABDMS015711.	160
13.7	Drawing of 1981 kimono coat in collaboration with Deacon Knitwear for a fashion show for the manufacturer Courtaulds. AAGM Collections: ABDMS070369.	162
13.8	Bee print deigned by Sally MacLachlan printed on black leather skirt suit from 1972 collection. AAGM Collections: ABDMS071550.	164
13.9	Circular Economy Wardrobe diagram from Lynn Wilson, '"Private sufficiency, public luxury": an exploration of consumer clothing circularity' in Marylyn Carrigan et al. (eds), *Research Handbook on Ethical Consumption* (Edward Elgar Publishing, 2023): 312–26.	166
14.1	Chestnut leather suit with silver chrysanthemum print by Sally MacLachlan and chrysanthemum buttons, 1972. AAGM Collection: ABDMS015704.	169
15.1	Shane Strachan performing at *The Bill Gibb Line* exhibition. Photo by Grant Anderson for Look Again.	174
15.2	Gray's F&TD Students explore the Bill Gibb archive at AAGM's Aberdeen Treasure Hub. Photo by Shane Strachan.	176
15.3	Shane Strachan wearing Charlotte Rose Scoular's design. Photo by Grant Anderson for Look Again.	179
15.4	Megan Davies wearing Catherine Macdonald. Photo by Fergus O'Connor (Robert Gordon University).	180
15.5	Shane Strachan wearing Sarah Walker and Samantha Macdonald. Photo by Graeme Roger.	180
15.6	Shane Strachan wearing Kimberley Monaghan and Kirstie Noble. Photo by Graeme Roger.	182
15.7	Finlay Rintoul wearing Catriona Battensby. Photo by Fergus O'Connor (Robert Gordon University).	182
15.8	Simulation development of a 1970s Bill Gibb yellow, orange and blue shell print wrap dress from Central Saint Martins' Museum and Study Collection. Courtesy of Lucie Shilton.	183
15.9	Blender software rendering of 1970s Bill Gibb coat dress with enamel bee buttons from Central Saint Martins' Museum and Study Collection. Courtesy of Lucie Shilton.	184
16.1	Detail from multidrawing of 1971 designs including the 'map dress' described at start of poem. AAGM Collections: ABDMS067450. The print is featured in Figure 7.8.	188
16.2	Drawing of pleated kimono from the Spring/Summer 1977 collection. AAGM Collections: ABDMS035670.	190

16.3	Singer and songwriter Linda Lewis backstage at Gibb's 1977 retrospective. Photo: Niall McInerney / Bloomsbury Fashion Photography Archive.	193
16.4	Model wearing knitwear from Gibb's 1977 A/W Scottish Collection at the Royal Albert Hall. Photo: Niall McInerney / Bloomsbury Fashion Photography Archive.	193
16.5	Drawing of embroidered dress for Spring/Summer 1979 collection. AAGM Collections: ABDMS035724.	197
16.6	Portrait of Bill Gibb in 1966 by Kaffe Fassett, painted in egg tempera. Courtesy of Kaffe Fassett.	200

Foreword

When I think of Bill Gibb, a flood of memories sweep through my mind – memories of an extraordinary designer, of imaginative and fantastical garments, and of the vibrant 1970s and 1980s British fashion scene, an era defined by an explosion of creativity that I am so grateful to have been a part of.

I first got to know Bill when he, Jean Muir and I were chosen by Anne Knight as the three independent designers featured in Odyssey at Fortnum & Mason – a spectacular boutique space. Later, in October 1972, Bill, Jean, John Bates and I shared the spotlight in a fashion show at Les Ambassadeurs Club in Park Lane. Bill was a constant presence at the fashion parties of the time, always bringing his wonderful sense of humour and ability to make us laugh. He was not just a remarkable talent but also a deeply lovable person.

Figure 0.2 *Model Jill Harley wearing a Bill Gibb printed satin outfit with leather trim at the fashion show at Les Ambassadeurs, London, 27th October 1972. Photo by Mike Lawn/Fox Photos/Hulton Archive/Getty Images.*

Bill was a true visionary who forged totally new looks. Whether drawing inspiration from his Scottish heritage or delving into historical research, his garments always told stories. Each piece was imbued with emotional depth and a captivating sense of fantasy.

One of Bill's most remarkable collaborations was with his then-boyfriend, the artist Kaffe Fassett. Together, they created incredibly innovative pieces that blended knitwear and tweed in ways that were groundbreaking.

It was a personal joy for me that the Fashion and Textile Museum, which I founded, hosted Bill's first retrospective in 2008: *Bill Gibb's Moment in Time*, curated by NJ Stevenson.

It is my great privilege to introduce this book, which celebrates Bill Gibb's enduring legacy. The essays inside reaffirm his relevance and his influence on fashion today.

With love and admiration,

Zandra Rhodes

Acknowledgements

The editors and publisher gratefully acknowledge the permission granted to reproduce the copyright material in this book. We would especially like to thank the family of Bill Gibb for approving the reproduction of his designs through the Bill Gibb Trust, and for their wider support towards the publication.

We are also grateful to Aberdeen Archives, Gallery and Museums (AAGM) for their support with this project. All images provided by Aberdeen City Council (Archives, Gallery and Museums Collection) are signified by 'AAGM Collections' followed by the object identifier.

We would also like to thank all the contributors who have been with us on this journey from the initial academic symposium in 2021 through to the publication of this volume, as well as the additional contributors who have joined us since and the family, friends, collaborators and admirers of Gibb who have contributed to interviews throughout.

Thanks also to our own friends and family, and to colleagues at our respective institutions – Gray's School of Art (Robert Gordon University, Aberdeen) and the University of Aberdeen – who have supported us throughout the editorial process.

Every effort has been made to trace copyright holders and to obtain their permission for the use of copyright material. However, if any have been inadvertently overlooked, the publishers will be pleased, if notified of any omissions, to make the necessary arrangement at the first opportunity. Some third-party copyrighted material displayed in the pages of this book are done so on the basis of 'fair dealing for the purposes of criticism and review' or 'fair use for the purposes of teaching, criticism, scholarship or research' only in accordance with international copyright laws and is not intended to infringe upon the ownership rights of the original owners.

Introduction:
Bill Gibb: ahead of his time?
Shane Strachan and Josephine Steed

Featuring contributions from renowned scholars, curators, journalists and creatives, this publication is the first book on British fashion designer Bill Gibb since 2008 and takes a fresh approach to exploring and evaluating his creative legacy in relation to contemporary concerns.

Born in the North East of Scotland and brought up on his family's farm, Bill Gibb (1943–88) went on to be one of the most innovative designers of twentieth-century British fashion. However, due to his short career and untimely death at only 44, his contribution and legacy to contemporary culture, fashion and design history is largely unknown to younger generations of artists and designers. A contemporary of fashion legends including Dame Zandra Rhodes, Ossie Clark and Jean Muir, Gibb's unique designs captured the essence of the 1970s with his love of mixing patterns, colour and textures which brought a new vibrancy and excitement onto the British design scene. His work attracted the attention of celebrities including Bianca Jagger, Twiggy, Lulu and Joan Collins and more latterly Kate Moss and Rita Ora, whilst also inspiring later designers including Giles Deacon, John Galliano and Vivienne Westwood. From his sketches to toiles, textile samples to finished garments, his collections give an unparalleled insight into the inner workings of one of Britain's much-loved, yet unsung designers – innovative designs which have often been described as 'ahead' of their time.[1]

Since his untimely death in January 1988, there is a sense of 'What if?' in many articles written about Gibb that suggest he would have had a glorious comeback if only he'd lived longer, or if only he'd worked in a different country than Britain where he was ultimately underrated, undervalued and under-supported even though he did so much for British fashion design and manufacturing.[2] As journalist Alice Fisher explained in a 2023 *Observer* article, 'Gibb was ahead of his time in taking great pride in having all of his designs manufactured in the UK'.[3] This more sustainable approach than many of his contemporaries (and many designers since) is just one of the contemporary issues Gibb has resonance with which makes him a particularly suitable area of study for modern-day fashion researchers, designers and students.

In November 2008, fashion writer Suzy Menkes published an article in *The New York Times* titled, 'Bill Gibb: A bittersweet story of a forgotten designer', which states the Scottish designer 'left a legacy that current students should rush to view' in a new exhibition at the Fashion and Textiles Museum in London titled 'Billy: Bill Gibb's Moment in Time', curated by fashion researcher NJ Stevenson. Menkes continues, 'Seeing is believing. And the wild mix of geometry and flowers, the patina of patterns, the magic carpets of knitting and the Renaissance fantasies that Gibb created in just one fecund decade make a stunning display'.[4] It is curious Menkes should label Gibb 'forgotten' in both the title and the article ('a forgotten fashion hero') given her mention of the 'slew of current designers' inspired by Gibb like John Galliano, who had contributed to Iain R. Webb's book *Bill Gibb: Fashion and Fantasy*, published by V&A just the month before. On top of this, a year-long exhibition curated by Webb, 'Bill Gibb: A Personal Journey', opened three months later at Fashion Museum Bath – yet another sign that Gibb was actively being *remembered* at this time on a significant scale.

However, even in his own lifetime, Gibb was portrayed in the media as someone in danger of slipping out of public consciousness. Regardless of being named Designer of the Year by British *Vogue* in 1970 for his trendsetting bohemian designs, creating one-off commissions for global stars like Elizabeth Taylor and Twiggy, and holding the largest solo fashion show for a British designer at the time – a packed out ten-year retrospective at the Royal Albert Hall in 1977 – he was described as a 'former highflier' as soon as 1984 in an *Observer* article titled 'Where are they now?' which focused more on his financial struggles in the late 1970s and early 1980s than his creativity and work.[5]

Yet, while 'forgotten' may suggest otherwise, at the end of her 2008 article Menkes claims that Gibb 'holds a place in fashion history – even if it was too wild and wondrous territory for most mortals to inhabit'.[6] This adds to the sense that Gibb was not only ahead of his time with his otherworldly designs, but that he actually created *timeless* garments, arguably achieved through a postmodern collaging of lines, patterns and embellishments from various periods and cultures.

It comes as no surprise then that we appear to be in another peak phase of 'rediscovering' Bill Gibb. This book's ambition to 'refashion' the designer for the twenty-first century came out of a 2021 symposium coordinated by Gray's School of Art (Robert Gordon University) and Aberdeen Archives, Gallery and Museums (AAGM) titled 'Fashion, Fantasy and Collaboration: The Legacy of Bill Gibb', which invited speakers to reflect on Gibb's life and works and their relevance to contemporary audiences, such as the growing interest in his work on social media sites like Instagram and the increasingly high bids his clothes fetch in online auctions due to their rarity and excellent craftsmanship. The idea to host the symposium was the result of a 2018–20 interdisciplinary collaboration between creative writer Shane Strachan, cultural catalyst organization Look Again Aberdeen, RGU Art & Heritage Collections, and the Fashion and Textile Design department at Gray's involving their third-year students. This collaboration culminated in *The Bill Gibb Line*, a spoken word podcast, film and exhibition which sought to tell Gibb's story to new audiences through new fashion-show poems performed by Strachan while wearing student-designed garments inspired by Gibb.

Building on the momentum of *The Bill Gibb Line* and the symposium, *Refashioning Bill Gibb for the 21st Century* is a groundbreaking book which redefines Gibb's outstanding contribution to twentieth-century fashion design by exploring different perspectives of his work together with over 100 beautiful reproductions – many newly digitized – of fashion illustrations, patterns and garments from AAGM which holds the largest collection of his work. Across three sections exploring Gibb's design process, influences and collaborations, his fashion legacy, and reinterpretations of Gibb for today's world, new perspectives on the designer are provided by NYC-based fashion journalist Jeena Sharma, fashion historian Marie McLoughlin, Geneva-based academic Elizabeth Fischer and various Scottish fashion researchers, alongside new material from fashion commentator Iain R. Webb, curator NJ Stevenson, and Christine Rew, curator and author of *Bill Gibb, The Golden Boy of British Fashion* at Aberdeen Art Gallery (2003).[7] Fresh evaluations are made on his continued contribution through the lenses of cultural appropriation versus appreciation, sustainability, textile collaborations, the impact of social media on his legacy for new audiences and his folkloric fashion ethos in relation to contemporary society to name but a few.

Throughout, the book interviews provide personal insights into Gibb by those closest to him as well as those who have discovered his work since his untimely death. The first of these is a moving interview with Gibb's three younger sisters reminiscing and reflecting on their memories of their beloved brother. Kaffe Fassett, his long-term collaborator and friend, then shares a firsthand account of how he and Gibb worked together during the early years of his career, their collaborative knitted textile innovations and finding inspiration from museum collections and their travels together. AAGM curator Morna Annandale provides examples of how personal stories related to donated Gibb garments bring new light to his designs, and British fashion designer Giles Deacon provides further insight into Gibb's legacy and how his naturalistic approach to fashion validated Deacon's own individual design process.

Given Gibb's fascinating farm boy to fashion designer story has been covered in previous publications by Webb and Rew, in the spirit of innovation, we invite readers to engage with Gibb's story in new ways, not only through the personal interviews with his family and collaborators, but also the narrative poems from *The Bill Gibb Line* which run through this book charting his career highs and lows. These are all collaged from verbatim material found in newspapers and magazines from the 1960s to 1980s, including the voices and perspectives of fashion reviewers, models and Gibb himself, and this poetic process is explored in the final chapter.

This book has been created through a shared interest and love of Bill Gibb by all the contributors – as one of his sisters remarks in the opening interview, Gibb was both 'an ordinary man' and 'an extraordinary man'. We hope the book brings a whole new audience to Gibb's work and staves off any possibility of him being forgotten for generations to come.

Figure 0.3 *Woollen printed scarf with Bill Gibb signature, mid-1970s. AAGM Collections: ABDMS093606.*

Bill Gibb: A Timeline

This timeline expands on that included in Christine Rew's 2003 publication *Bill Gibb: The Golden Boy of British Fashion* (Aberdeen: Aberdeen Art Gallery, 2003).

1943 – Born William Elphinstone Gibb on 23 January in Aberdeenshire, Scotland.
1958 – Talent spotted by his Fraserburgh Academy art teacher Robert Duthie.
    Wins a local WRI costume-design competition aged 15.
1962 – Begins studies at St Martin's School of Art in London under Muriel Pemberton.
1966 – Meets artist Kaffe Fassett.
    Awarded a scholarship for postgraduate study at Royal College of Art under Janey Ironside.
1967 – One of six designers selected for the Yardley London Look award in New York.
    Collection ordered by Bendels.
    Research tour of America with Kaffe Fassett.
    Leaves postgraduate study at Royal College of Art after first year.

1968 – Forms Alice Paul boutique off Kensington High Street.
    Visit to Scotland with Kaffe Fassett.
1969 – Joins Monty Black's Baccarat as a designer.
    Pop star Lulu marries Maurice Gibb from the Bee Gees in a Bill Gibb wedding dress.
1970 – Renaissance collection based on tapestry fabrics.
    Named Designer of the Year by *Vogue*.
    Dress from tartan and checks collection chosen by Beatrix Miller, editor of *Vogue*, as Dress of the Year for the Museum of Costume in Bath.
    Designs the 'Renaissance' dress for model Twiggy for the *Daily Mirror* Fashion Celebrity dinner.
    Bill Gibb Room opens in November at Harrods.
1971 – Commission from the Austrian Embroidery Federation.
    Peru travel special for *Vogue*.
    Twiggy wears a Bill Gibb design for the Los Angeles premiere of *The Boyfriend*.
    Baccarat dress by Bill Gibb made for actress Elizabeth Taylor.
1972 – Forms Bill Gibb Limited with Kathleen (Kate) Franklin and backing from Lovable.
    First solo collection launched at the Oriental Club in London. Filmed for the BBC.
    Printed leather and sequin outfit featured in *British Vogue*. Photo by Clive Arrowsmith.
    Takes part in a fashion show alongside John Bates (for Jean Varon), Jean Muir and Zandra Rhodes at Les Ambassadeurs Club in Park Lane, London.
    Shows his designs in Aberdeen at three catwalks events at the Royal Darroch Hotel sponsored by *The Press and Journal* and the Aberdeen District Milk Board.
1973 – Takes part in Modefest in Trogir, Yugoslavia.
    Takes part in 'Designs in Fashion' fashion show organized by the British Overseas Trade Board held at the Royal College of Art.
    Indian-American singer Asha Puthli wears a Bill Gibb dress on the cover of her self-titled debut album, photographed by Mick Rock.
1974 – Lovable collapses in America and the promoter Bryan Morrison joins Kate and Bill to form a new company, Bill Gibb Limited.
    Nail varnish licensing promotion with Nailoid.
    Knitting pack offer for *The Sunday Times*.
    Collaboration with Fassett for a full knitwear collection inspired by their trip to Morocco as part of Gibb's Autumn/Winter collection.
1975 – Opens first shop in Bond Street.
    Porcelain collection.
    Moon and Buddha collection.
1976 – Byzantine collection.

Menswear promotion for Reid and Taylor.

Tobago travel special for *Vogue*.

Article in the *Daily Express* by writer Helena Matheopoulos refers to Gibb's work as 'the museum pieces of the future'.

Takes part in a televised ITV 'Best in Fashion' fashion show at Chatsworth House, Derbyshire UK.

1977 – Flowers and Lace collection.

Scottish collection.

Ten-year retrospective at the Royal Albert Hall.

Fiji travel special for *Vogue*.

Spring/Summer 1977 collection incorporates Japanese-inspired kimono designs.

Invited to participate in a Best of Fashion Show at the British Embassy in Paris.

Stages an in-flight fashion show en route to Paris from London for executives and sponsors on the new Air France Airbus.

1978 – Opens shop in Madison Avenue, New York in May.

Company goes into receivership and is bought by Alfred and Philip Fox.

Launches ready-to-wear and a couture collection in October.

Actress Joan Collins wears Gibb's Qiana dress in the film *The Stud*.

1979 – Backers withdraw, and company goes into receivership.

Cue collection for Austin Reed launched.

Menswear promotion for Reid and Taylor.

Designs for Harrods and other London shops.

A Fashion Spectacular catwalk show in aid of Cancer Research.

Benson & Hedges Silk Cut promotion with Liberty's of London; a pattern for Bill's silk kimono and trousers available to readers of the *Daily Mail*.

One of seven designers alongside Zandra Rhodes invited to design a pattern for *Cosmopolitan* readers.

1980 – Starts a series of exclusive patterns for *The Daily Telegraph*.

Works with Annette Carol on exclusive knitwear collection for Harrods.

Sale of fashion drawings 1967–78 at the Sloane International Gallery.

Takes part as one of the designers in *A Faerie Tale* at the Park Lane Hotel in London.

1981 – Silk daywear collection for Chapter II.

Courtelle knitwear collection for Bill Gibb at Harrods.

Design trip to Hong Kong for Harrods.

Designs Tessa Dahl's (actor, author and daughter of Roald Dahl) wedding dress.

1982 – Promotion for the Silk Commission at the Guild Hall, London.

1984 – Sportswear collection.
1985 – Re-launch with support from the Government's Business Expansion Scheme.
Bronze Age collection, his first major collection since 1979.
Silk Sensation promotion for the European Commission for the Promotion of Silk.
Bride of the Year promotion with the *Daily Mirror*.
1986 – Rose collection.
Mail order collection in collaboration with John Bates; the Designer Club.
Pattern for *Woman & Home's* Diamond Jubilee issue.
1987 – Produces *Hollywood Knits*, a book of knitting patterns based on film star photographs.
Harris Tweed Designer collection.
Mail order offer for *Woman's Journal*.
Continues to design for private clients.
1988 – Dies of cancer in London on 3 January, aged 44.

*

1989 – St Martin's merges with Central School of Art and Design in 1989 to become Central Saint Martins (CSM).
1997 – Aberdeen City Council purchases over 2,000 of Bill Gibb's original fashion drawings and related items.
2003 – Publication of Christine Rew's *Bill Gibb: The Golden Boy of British Fashion* alongside first retrospective exhibition held at Aberdeen Art Gallery.
2008 – 'Billy: Bill Gibb's Moment in Time' is opened by Twiggy at the Fashion and Textiles Museum in London.
Publication of Iain R. Webb's *Bill Gibb: Fashion and Fantasy*.
2009 – Exhibition of 'Bill Gibb: A Personal Journey' at Fashion Museum Bath.
2018 – European Fashion Heritage Association describes Gibb as one of the best examples of 'romantic eclecticism'.
2019 – Opening of Shane Strachan's, *The Bill Gibb Line* exhibition at Look Again Aberdeen.
British celebrity Rita Ora is captured in the press wearing Gibb knitwear from his 1976 Byzantine Collection.
2020 – Opening of *The Bill Gibb Line* expanded exhibition at Aberdeen Art Gallery.
2021 – 'Fashion, Fantasy and Collaboration: The Legacy of Bill Gibb' symposium held online.
2023 – Gibb's tartan and fair-isle inspired garment from 1970 on display as part of the Tartan exhibition at V&A, Dundee, Scotland.
2024 – Gibb's printed silk kimono from 1977 on display as part of Kimono exhibition at V&A Dundee, Scotland.

The Hansom Cab Inn, 15 February 1967

In a pub at the top of Earl's Court Road
the barmaids' fancy dress suggests
we've entered the Edwardian era.
Oh please! We're the fashion forward press –
we'll have no trips to the past, dears.

At the start of the show, we're thrown:
who dares cut a coat in a sweeping curve
before dropping plumb-straight to the hem?
Who pairs lilac and camel in check?
And mushroom shoulders on a plain white dress?

We sigh with relief at trousers caught
harem-style in tight anklets – exotic!
We're simply sick of mini-skirts
and feel the pinch on these draughty days,
but are lower hem-lines here to stay?

What novel treatment of traditional tweed –
amethyst and white with inverted pleats.
And witness the birth of the kilted suit:
a tartan skirt and brief bolero
in MacMillan rainbow hues.

As voile flowers in powder blue,
we hunt for seed pearls
embroidered on collar and cuff,
but on a little black chiffon shift
we cannot miss the sleeves' huge puff.

These gay boutique clothes
are for young (but not kooky!) clients
who crave individuality.
Down in hard-bitten London town we rave:
Bill Gibb's name has been made.

Poem inspired by:
Anonymous, 'Buchan Fashion Designer Makes Experts Sit Up', *The Press and Journal*, 16 February 1967: 1.

Figure 0.4 *Detail from drawing of dress and caped coat; mid-late 1960s. AAGM Collections: ABDMS070938.*

Part One

Gibb's Design Process: Influences and Collaborations

This section begins with an interview with Bill Gibb's sisters providing insight into his childhood and the influence of being brought up in the North East of Scotland within a farming family and community. The sisters reflect on Gibb's early interests in drawing and design and his love of black-and-white films and historical costume which inspired many of his later collections. The sisters also describe the challenges of his move to London to study at St Martin's and how he retained a connection to his Scottish roots and his family throughout his career.

The following chapter by Christine Rew discusses Gibb's disciplined approach to designing and construction where drawing skills were one of his greatest strengths. Rew provides unique insight into Gibb's creative talent and design process through her extensive knowledge of the archive of over 2,000 illustrations and other artefacts held at Aberdeen Archives, Gallery and Museums.

Gibb's fashion design education at St Martin's in the 1960s is the subject of Marie McLoughlin's chapter. It explores how, under the tutelage of Muriel Pemberton, the founder and head of the Department of Dress and Fashion Design, Gibb developed his unique mixing of different historical styles and techniques to create something new through Bricolage – a magpie approach of experimentation and collaboration which not only informed and influenced his own work but that of later alumni of St Martin's like Galliano and McQueen who built their own design process of mixing old and new styles.

Elizabeth Fischer discusses Gibb within the context of French fashion world in the 1960s and 1970s especially the work of influential designers such as Kenzo Takada, Jules-François Crahay and Yves Saint Laurent. Similarly influenced by folkloric revivals, Gibb's design approach is compared with how they incorporated a range of design aspects from other cultures within their work, alongside drawing from their own cultural backgrounds. Fischer also touches on their design processes in reference to cultural appropriation which is explored further in Karen Cross's chapter in Part 2 and Jeena Sharma's in Part 3.

An interview with Kaffe Fassett follows which provides a firsthand account of how he and Gibb collaborated and inspired one another, as well as sought out inspirations from museum collections and travels together. Fassett's discussion of their evolving knitwear collaborations leads into Josephine Steed's chapter on Gibb's 1970s knitwear collections, where Gibb has been described as having made a significant contribution, leaving a legacy on the knitwear industry which is still evident today. Steed reflects on the changes in society as the 1960s ended where the revival of making your own fashion garments which emerged in the 1970s led to a more democratic, inclusive and slow-design approach.

1

An interview with Bill Gibb's sisters

This interview with Bill Gibb's younger sisters – Patricia (Patsy), Janet and Marlyn – was originally conducted by Josephine Steed, Shane Strachan and Rachel Thibbotumunuwe (Learning Manager at AAGM) for the 2021 symposium, 'Fashion, Fantasy and Collaboration: The Legacy of Bill Gibb'. All three sisters still live in rural areas of the North East of Scotland where Gibb was born and raised.

Patsy: I'm Patsy Davidson, the eldest sister of the three girls.

Janet: Hello, I'm Janet Arnott, originally Janet Gibb and I'm the middle sister of Billy.

Marlyn: Hello I'm Marlyn. I'm the youngest of the three girls and the one that's supposed to most look like Billy.

Patsy: The fashion world, not only in couture wear, but in the high street shops – influences of Billy are everywhere, with appliques and butterflies, bees, flowers, and jackets, sweaters . . . Even when you go out shopping, you'll have a look at the things and you say, 'Gosh, that could be a Billy influence there'. These details in his clothes that sometimes we never noticed until Billy died really. I think he would have been humbled to see the many designers like Galliano and McQueen who have been inspired by various ideas of Billy's.

Janet: He started drawing from a very early age and he would watch our granny who used to sit there with pen to paper doing landscapes at that time. You would always see him sketching and he amazed everybody by the work he did when he was really young. Certainly, he amazed us, but his inspiration came from watching old films – black and white films – and costume design. Things like Maid Marion and Robin Hood. He paid attention to the extravagant designs and costumes and he had a great affinity with the human form, especially the female form. He liked to get a hold of us and then try out the bedspreads and the curtains, and he would always be draping the fabric to see how it would flow from the body, and that was the beginning of him trying to be the designer that he became.

Figure 1.1 *Gibb's drawing of his grandmother from his St Martin's submission portfolio in 1962. AAGM Collections: ABDMS082324.*

Patsy: I remember at the end of a school term, there was a fancy dress ball which was held at the Station Hotel in Fraserburgh and it just was right up Billy's street. He dressed up as Dracula with the huge collar and blood dripping down the sides of his face. His partner at the time was in a virginal white dress, with a very white face and the two indents in her neck. Because I was just 15, he persuaded mam and dad to let me go, and so I got dressed up as the Queen of Sheba. Lo and behold, we went into this wonderful ball and of course Billy won first prize, his partner second prize, and I got third. It was fabulous.

Janet: It was his art teacher at Fraserburgh Academy, Bob Duthie, that really saw in him the potential that far exceeded anything that he had come across in a local boy before. He invited mam and dad in to have a chat about this talented lad and suggested that St Martin's would be the place I think for him to go to.

Marlyn: He was only 19 when he went to St Martin's. That must have been so difficult. At that time, you didn't go far – you didn't go the length of yourself then – and after a few months there he was awful homesick. He wanted to come home – he spoke differently, he acted differently, he missed the sea, he missed the land, he missed family. So it was extremely challenging for Billy. Mam and dad were so concerned that he might give up that they actually flew to London because Miss Pemberton, the Head of Dress at St Martin's, was concerned that Billy would give up and she thought, 'What a shame', because he was so brilliant. His designs were so brilliant, but he couldn't master the making of the clothes. That was his biggest problem. He couldn't and that was part of the course, so I think following a heart-to-heart with mam and dad and Miss Pemberton, he was encouraged to stay there and try and make the most of it and I think encouraged to meet people. He was very likeable, but Billy was also very shy as well.

He went on to graduate top of the class, did very well and he also won a scholarship to the Royal College of Art, so it was worth his while being encouraged to carry on. It would have been such a disappointment had he not.

Figure 1.2 *Gibb with his father and mother in London, c.1962. Courtesy of Patricia Davidson.*

Patsy: The times we went to London in his heyday, he was hard up as a church mouse. If you went in carrying a packet of chocolate biscuits he was delighted to see you. I was a nanny in New York for a couple of years for a family of five children and I saved up all my days off so that when Billy came to visit, he came for three whole weeks. We did some wonderful things, but one particular incident sticks in my mind. We were going out for the evening to the Peppermint Lounge, which was really the 'in place' in New York in the Sixties where like The Beatles went and so forth, and we had to be in evening dress, but the licensing law, you had to be 21 and I says, 'Billy I'm 17. I'll never ever get into somewhere like the Peppermint Lounge', but by the time Billy had my hair up in a French twist, the makeup on, and everything else – I had a little black dress and what have you. And so we queued at the door and Billy says, 'You go first,' and though I just walked right in, the doorman stopped Billy to ask him for his ID. He needed to get out his passport to show that he was old enough, and when we got inside we just fell about laughing. It was just so much fun. He just was a delight to be with.

Even if you went out for a walk with Billy, he would have seen different shades in the tree with the sunlight shining through, and along the beach, especially the Fraserburgh Beach after the tide had gone back out, how it left the sand with all the ripples and the different colours you could see in the pebbles. He could see the browns and golds and everything. Things that we didn't. We just took for granted things like that and never noticed it, but Billy did and I think that his combination of pattern on pattern, mixing checks with other contrasting designs was innovative and refreshingly different. I think that stunned the fashion world and his attention to detail was second to none. I mean, he was absolutely fastidious, whether it was buttons, bows, beads, feathers – everything had to be perfect and accessorized. I remember going to some of his shows and everything right down to the shoes, the headdress – he oversaw every girl before she went out onto the catwalk.

I think Billy was always a Romantic and I'm sure every lady that has ever worn a Bill Gibb outfit felt a million bucks because it was a bespoke outfit and, back then, nobody else would have an outfit like it. Billy often said about his clothes that they were fluid lines that move with your body. Twiggy was one of his favourite models, but Billy didn't design for the skinny. He designed for any shape and, as Billy once said, 'I'm really nae caring if you hang it on the wall, as long as it's something that you like.'

Marlyn: He was ahead of his time. I think the lines are still very much wearable today. We went to the Royal Albert Hall which was the big show. I think every star in creation was there, every celebrity – you name them, they were there. Then they were all wearing Billy's clothes on the catwalk and everything. After that, there was a party at the San Lorenzo, which we all went to. It was absolutely surreal, but you were mixing with these people, having dinner and a glass of champagne as they always seem to drink. It was just fantastic. I remember another time at the San Lorenzo with Billy and there was Bianca Jagger and she was sitting having lunch and she cried, 'Bill, Bill, darling, Bill' – they always went 'Bill, darling!' and over she came. I'll never forget the look on her face. She looked at Billy so adoringly as much to say, 'You make me feel so wonderful with your clothes'. I mean, it was just amazing.

And Twiggy and Justin came up and stayed in the farm with us. She was just an everyday person really, Twiggy. She was fun to be around, washed the dishes when we had supper and that. So we met loads and loads of celebrities through Billy and a lot kept in touch. I mean I had a letter from Twiggy about a couple of years ago. She was coming up to Aberdeen and I had written to her, and I had lovely reply back from her. 'Fond memories', always 'fond memories' all the time. So we met lots of people. Very exciting for us coming from the country, I can tell you.

Janet: When we went to the big show at the Royal Albert Hall, I think we really couldn't believe it. This whole building was set aside for Bill Gibb and then all these stars came in and he was just so well received. But he was always shy Billy. He hated putting himself up front and being the centre of attention and he burned so much adrenaline getting ready for a show. That particular show, he really thought that his company had bitten off more than they should have, and they were giving him a greater accolade than he felt he deserved, because that was Billy.

When the shows were passed, he became burned out, exhausted, but waiting for the reviews to come out and of course this would always be the deciding factor on how well we would go forward to the next collection. A show left him delighted but drained with the amount of work and thought – if he couldn't get the cutters to make the right cut or the pattern makers to create the way that he saw it, he just . . . you know he was fastidious about little intricate details and design detail – all important. I always said that rather than him understanding the wearer of his designs, I think he looked for the wearer that would understand his design.

Patsy: When mum and I went down to London for my wedding dress, Billy had sketched a rough idea of what would suit my figure and he was probably quite right. I'm not saying it was what I had as an idea as a wedding dress, but I thought, 'Oh well, we'll just go with the flow'. Being a young bride-to-be, there's so many other things happening: the wedding, the flowers, the cakes, whatever . . . I was working and time just wore on and, before I realized it, the wedding day was getting nearer and nearer. The dress had finally arrived a couple of days beforehand, and Nives Losani, his wonderful Italian seamstress was still stitching on petals the night before the wedding, and even on the day of the wedding. Nives, being Italian, she said, 'You have to have a piece of horse's hair stitched into the hem for good luck,' she says. So dad went out to the field – just as well he had horses – came back with a bit of mane from the horse and it was duly stitched in to the hem of the dress.

Janet: When it came to my wedding dress, the design – the paper it's designed on – he's written on it, 'I've given in to you with your wanting a waisted dress,' because Patsy's had been more like an Empire line and I thought, 'No, I need a waisted dress'. He did have a set idea about what he wanted to do, so he wasn't keen on designing this waisted dress. In the end he did, but the train he attached to my dress was 20-feet long so I had to have it twice over my arm to carry all night. You could see the marks of carrying this heavy train, but he definitely had skills.

Figure 1.3 *Marlyn, Patsy and Janet on Patsy's wedding day in 1969 joined by two flower girls, all dressed in original Gibb designs. Courtesy of Patricia Davidson.*

Marlyn: Speaking of wedding dresses, I'd gone to London and had a few bits of material pinned to me – 'Oh, that's fine. You'll look fab!' he said. It arrived the night before my wedding. I never had a veil made – nothing! Nives got up at five o'clock in the morning and made the veil and that was that.

I remember one of the times when he was ill in the last year of his life and he'd come back home for a visit. I have three daughters and he was out with a camera and still putting scarves onto my daughters like he did with us when we were little. It was the same flowing floaty style. He thought a woman should be a woman. That was Billy's style.

Janet: He definitely brought out the femininity in women and we loved it. Not just me personally – all women. He made you feel feminine and on donning one of those dresses with the gossamer skirts flying out, you just . . . you know, there were few occasions for you ever to wear such gowns. It was sad when the power dressing Eighties came in really, because the call for that type of extravagant gown was lost, and the cost became prohibitive of course because people were now onto more wearable, everyday type of outfits and there wasn't such a demand for that.

Figure 1.4 *Gibb with sisters Patsy and Janet in Scotland in 1987. Courtesy of Patricia Davidson.*

Patsy: Our mam is in a nursing home in Fraserburgh and I said what was happening and I says, 'Is there anything mam that you would like to add you think?', and she said when Billy was really ill and was dying in St Stephen's Hospital, mam stayed in one of the rooms there. During his last few days, Billy asked her, 'Mam, do you think I've let you down with my life?' It was always that kind of insecurity about him, which was really, really sad and she says, 'Billy, we're so proud of what you have achieved in your life' and assured him that his legacy in the fashion world would be remembered for generations to come, and a sort of smile came across his face. I thought, poor soul – even right till the end, he was still unsure of himself, and the wonderful talent that he had.

Janet: Well, I was just going to add to that – at the same time that Billy was in London, we went down for that two–three days to be with him and he did the *Hollywood Knits* book and on the cover he wrote, 'To the knitter of the family'. So I thought, 'Right, well, now which one will I choose?', so I took the Loretta Young cardigan. I said, 'I've got to get this done so I can get it finished and take it down to London and let him see that.' I got the buttons sewn on at the last minute. I took it out of my bag to show him and he was so poorly then – really poorly – but he managed to help trail the garment out of the bag and he says, 'Oh, you finished it.' I says I did, and he says, 'You've put on the wrong buttons.' And I just thought – the designer never left him. I wasn't disappointed he said that because his mind was still focused on the garment. I remember thinking that he was an ordinary man, but he was an extraordinary man. So . . . memories.

Marlyn: Lots of memories. Lots of memories.

Following this interview, Bill Gibb's mother Jessie sadly passed away in April 2022. In November 2024, Bill's three sisters joined with his three brothers to unveil the completion of Bill Gibb Court in Fraserburgh, a new housing development in his name on the site of the old secondary school he attended.

2

Disciplined flamboyance: Gibb's drawing and design process

Christine Rew

'Sitting down in front of a blank sheet of paper is one of the most frightening things I know,' Bill Gibb told *Vogue* magazine.[1] Yet Gibb's drawing ability was one of his great strengths. He usually began by working through concepts with a series of small figures drawn over the page, giving the impression of someone who had to quickly capture all the ideas in his head on paper. These preliminary drawings were subsequently refined to become a finished sketch: a dense and impeccably illustrated record of how the garment would look with detailed notes, proposed colour schemes and fabric sketches. In 1997 Aberdeen City Council purchased a significant archive of over 2,000 of his original fashion sketches and related ephemera which together provide an unparalleled glimpse into his creative talent, balancing a love of glamour and fantasy with a disciplined approach to designing.[2]

Early years

His mother recalls that as a child he was always drawing; that artistic urge to create never left him and he was still designing right up to his death in 1988. Born into a farming community in north Aberdeenshire, Gibb was brought up primarily by his maternal grandparents and was inspired by his grandmother, Evelyn Reid, a talented amateur artist who painted landscapes. She sparked his interest in drawing which he combined with his fascination with history. He was always 'scribbling in the backs of books – historical figures, costumes,' he told Brenda Polan later and filled his teenage jotters with accurate images of outfits, accessories and shoes copied from history books and drawings of imaginary scenes, including a brightly coloured medieval court.[3] The women wear flowing gowns with cinched-in high waists, a theme that was to emerge later in Gibb's 1970 Renaissance collection. A series of drawings dating to around 1960 feature glamorous evening wear inspired by his love of romance and film star sophistication. A bright green dress with snug bodice and an impossibly small waist echoes a mermaid with its fishtail skirt; a bride wears a bouffant skirt of layered net and a slim-fitting vivid pink dress with layers of tulle is teamed with bright blue gloves (Figure 2.1). These are the seeds of Gibb's continuing love of fantasy, extravagance and luxury which he later applied so brilliantly to his 1980s fantasy gowns (Figure 2.2). As the eldest of four brothers, Gibb would have been expected to take over the family farm. However, as his grandmother told the *People's Journal*: 'When he grew older and was ready to take up a career, the one thing he determined on was getting to a London art school.'[4] With his family's support, in 1962 he accepted a place to study at St Martin's School of Art in London, now Central Saint Martins.

Gibb's portfolio and sketches from his time at both St Martin's School of Art and the Royal College of Art, where he was awarded a scholarship in 1966, evidence a continued love of historical costume,

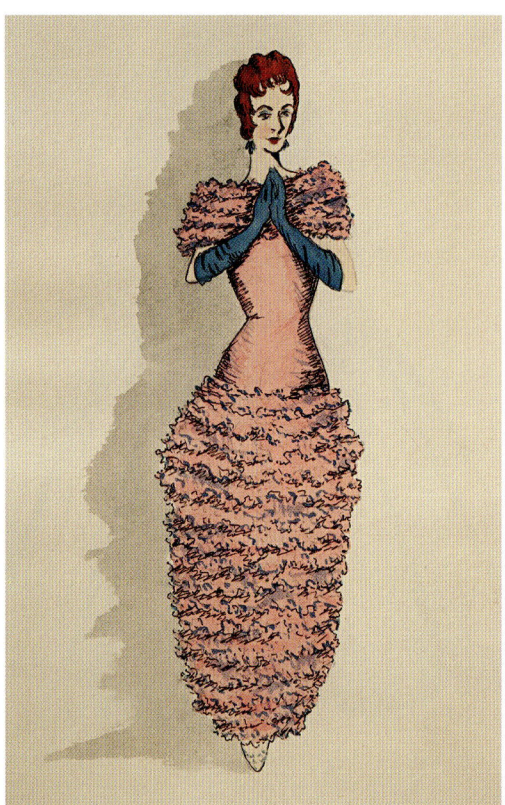

Figure 2.1 *A drawing from one of Gibb's Fraserburgh Academy schoolbooks c.1958 when he was 15 years old. Courtesy of the Bill Gibb Trust. Photo by Mike Davidson.*

Figure 2.2 *1982 drawing of dress for Harrods and Amanda Bishop's Carven boutique in Jeddah, Saudi Arabia. AAGM Collections: ABDMS070412.*

especially the Byzantine and Renaissance eras, along with drawings and notes for folk dress and traditional costume from Europe and East Asia. He would pick up many of these themes later in his career, yet most of his fashion designs from this period tend towards the mainstream: smart suits, clean-cut jackets and flared trousers (Figure 2.3 and Figure 3.6).

Starting out

Gibb was selected in 1967 to participate in the Yardley 'London Look Award' in New York. He was unsuccessful in the competition; however, Henri Bendel commissioned his collection for their stores.

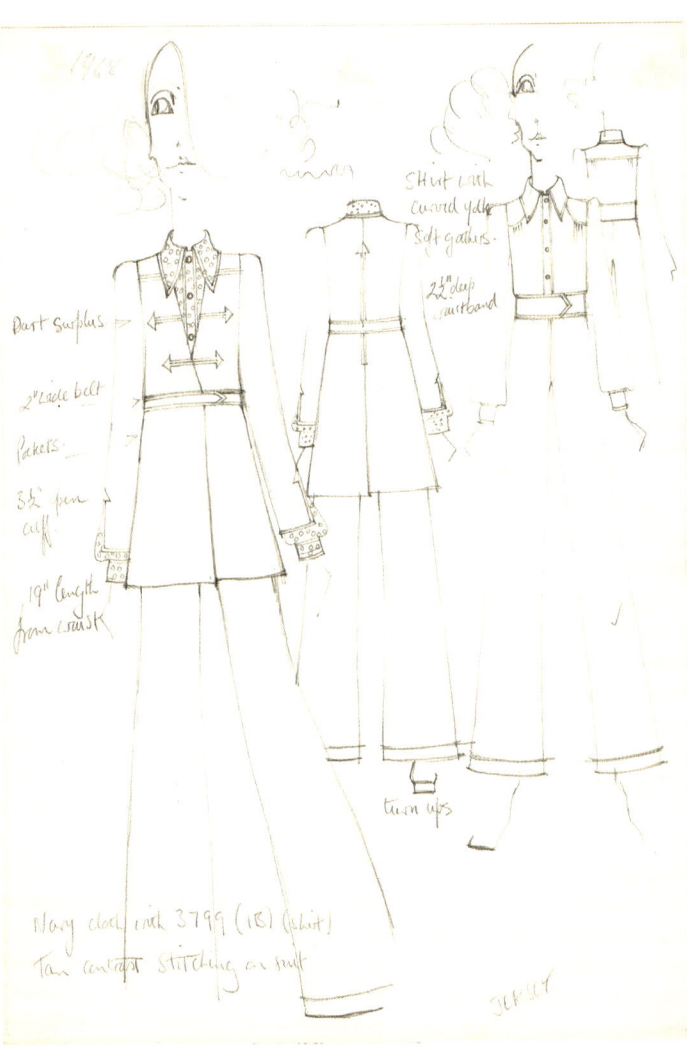

Figure 2.3 *1968 drawing of jersey trouser suits for the Alice Paul boutiquLe. AAGM archive: ABDMS067446.*

On his return to London, he gave up his place at the Royal College of Art and established a boutique in Kensington, Alice Paul, with sisters Annie and Alice Russell. They arranged the business side and marketing, with Gibb providing the designs. The sketches reveal a continuing strand of minimalism and structured designs with blocks of colour, and his love of embellishment, top stitching, trimmings and fastenings were also established at this period. Drawings specify fabrics and construction along with design details and back views, a trait which he continued throughout his career. A drawing for a 1968 trouser suit (Figure 2.3), for instance, states that the jacket will have a 2″ belt and 3½″ open cuff with blouse sleeve cuff terminating 19″ from the waist; the fabric is navy cloth with tan contrast stitching.

Alice Paul was successful, but short lived, closing in 1969. Monty Black, who founded the British fashion house and distributor Baccarat with his wife Clare, offered Gibb a contract to work with him on a freelance basis. His initial pared-back designs quickly morphed into a new approach when he began to experiment with combining multiple patterns and fabrics in a single garment. In his 1969 collection of 'Gypsy Dresses' for Baccarat he pioneered an innovative use of mixing geometric and chequerboard

Figure 2.4 *Drawing of dress commission for 'Gudrun', c.1970. AAGM Collections: ABDMS070470.*

Figure 2.5 *Detail from 1969 dress for Baccarat combining patterned prints, checks, and florals with leather thongs. AAGM Collections: ABDMS023985.*

patterns with floral prints and stripes and multiple trimmings. These dresses were a mash-up of influences: the hippie culture which he and artist Kaffe Fassett (who he met in the mid-1960s) had encountered in America, combined with references to European folk costume and the Renaissance period (figures 2.4 and 2.5). They also show an emerging love of combining tight bodices and a high waistline with capacious, billowing skirts first seen in his childhood medieval court drawings.

Gibb's designs felt right for the time, mirroring a change in society and politics as the 1960s ended – a decade that had seen the rise of a youthful, popular culture symbolized by the iconic miniskirts promoted by Mary Quant. Now a new generation of designers was emerging, among them Ossie Clark, Zandra Rhodes, Janice Wainwright, Marion Foale and Sally Tuffin, who like Gibb, were art-school trained. Their lyrical designs appealed to young women seeking individuality as fashion became a form of self-expression. 'Replacing the worn-out dress roles of the past, women were pleasing themselves with the originality and variety of their appearance, seldom conforming to anyone else's idea of what elegant meant' commented Georgina Howell in her survey of fashion from *Vogue* magazine.[5] Ernestine Carter also reflected in the *Sunday Times* that hippie culture had 'opened the door to an independent make-your-own look, a rebellion against orthodox maxims of taste, a happy anarchy of pattern, textures and colours.'[6] Linda Grant writing in *Stella* magazine summed up the changing mood: 'the only rule was that you must not look anything like your mother, who had outrageously started to wear her skirts an inch or two above the knee'.[7]

When Judy Brittain of *Vogue* magazine suggested that Fassett design knitwear to complement Gibb's garments, a new look emerged. British *Vogue* ran a coloured spread in its January 1970 edition, entitled 'Glorious Confusion', with striking photographs by Sarah Moon. Overnight, Gibb became Britain's brightest young talent and his creations went on to influence the high street and designer fashions for much of the 1970s. The drawings for this collection are on A3-size paper; most are black and white, some inked in with fabric swatches attached. The look is innocent and the garments original. The entire collection featured jackets, skirts and trousers in soft vegetable-dyed tartans, reminiscent of the Aberdeenshire countryside, or dogtooth check fabric, teamed with matching intarsia knits by Fassett (Figure 2.6). The designs were also photographed for the *Sunday Times* by Patrick Lichfield, including a high-waisted dress and trousers which were made up in black, brown and cream checked Madras cotton paired with one of Fassett's knits described as a 'black knitted spencer, patterned in brown and cream, front-laced, the sleeves and hem deeply fringed'.[8] *Vogue* chose him as 'Designer of the Year' and the editor, Beatrix Miller selected a patterned ensemble with a knife-pleated skirt as 'Dress of the Year' for the collection held by the Fashion Museum in Bath. Gibb's signature style was now established: a blend of romance, glamour, fantasy and fun, incorporating handcrafting and textile techniques and traditional idioms from other countries and historical periods. These spirited designs were based on a disciplined approach to designing and construction and a clear vision.

Figure 2.6 *Drawing of jacket and skirt outfit with fabric swatch for the Autumn/Winter 1970 Collection. AAGM Collections: ABDMS067683.*

Figure 2.7 *Multidrawing of jackets and coats for Autumn/Winter 1976 knitting collection. AAGM Collections: ABDMS067101.*

An evolving drawing style

In the early 1960s, his sketches present rather traditional individual figures with inked-in facial features and a variety of hairstyles. By the time he left the Royal College of Art in 1967, Gibb's drawing style had developed, with the faces of his figures becoming more oblique and partially described, the right side remaining blank; the appearance is also more girlish with big hairdos and heavy eye make-up. There are some similarities in his drawings at this time to contemporary fashion illustration, including Veronica Papworth's stylized drawings with vacant-eyed models which accompanied her weekly fashion columns for the *Sunday Express*.[9] Likewise, he would have known the baby-doll figures with long limbs and huge round eyes, underlined with kohl, in the early Biba mail-order catalogues.[10] It is likely that Gibb's technique also drew inspiration from Bobby Hillson's drawing style. She worked as a fashion illustrator for British *Vogue*, the *Observer* and the *Sunday Times* before joining the teaching staff of the Fashion diploma course at St Martin's School of Art and was a tutor throughout Gibb's period of study there.[11]

By the time Gibb launched his own business in 1972 his drawing style had matured and was established. Although some earlier drawings were on foolscap or A2 paper and occasionally he used A5 paper (the Autumn 1973 collection for instance), by the mid-1970s he always drew on A4 notepads. Throughout his career these designs were stored in ring binders, his preferred method of organizing drawings – both the multi-image sketches and finished drawings. Gibb customized the front cover of the binders with cards and images such as ancient jewellery. A picture of female film stars adorns the cover of the binder holding drawings for private clients, whilst another has a pastel-coloured print of a unicorn. Gibb preferred to use black Pentel pens for sketching, as did many of his contemporaries including Ossie Clark and John Bates. Occasionally he drew with blue Biro pens and would use coloured Pentel pens sparingly to highlight design details.

The finished sketches show figures which are detailed and well-ordered with clumpy shoes and either a left- or front-facing profile (figures 2.4 and 2.6). Gibb usually favoured a small, neat headline and where hair is drawn, it is long and flowing as it escapes at the nape of the neck from a snood, turban or hat. Clark's design drawings from the same period are more fluid, with rather nebulous figures filling the page so fully that their foreheads and hairlines run off the page. His floaty, flounced skirts are hinted at, with sweeping lines, whilst he pays more attention to details such as buttons, floral trims, pintucks and gathered yokes.[12] These drawings imply how the final garments will look, whereas the precision of Gibb's illustrate a finalized outfit.

Gibb started designing each of his distinctive collections with a silhouette which is repeated and refined across his multi-image concept sketches. Whereas Jean Muir, known for her mastery of intricate cutting and fluid, unfussy garments, told *Vogue* that: 'Each collection is a natural development from my last one . . . Jersey is always the beginning – and colours which are specially dyed for me.'[13] Examples of her sketches held in the collections of the Victoria and Albert Museum are impressionistic and freely drawn in black felt tip or pencil.[14] Like Gibb she attached swatches of fabric, sometimes using coloured pencil to indicate the shading of the garment and annotated the sketches with directions for her workroom team. In the same issue of *Vogue,* Maureen Baker of Susan Small told readers: 'When I start planning a collection I know the type of things I want to do but the final versions are quite unlike the preliminary sketches – it's not until you start working with the fabric that an idea takes shape.'[15] This approach is unlike Gibb's, as his final designs can be traced back with ease to his initial multi-image sketches.

The posture and hairstyles of his figures changed with time, notably from the late 1970s when they become more formulaic and lacking in spirit, possibly reflecting his own mood as he reacted to the failure of his business in both 1978 and 1979. These later models have a more sophisticated stance with a sharp angular profile, hollowed cheekbones and pouting lips, sometimes coloured bright red. When Gibb's health deteriorated in the 1980s, leading to lower energy levels, he fell back on using photocopied sheets of blank body outlines, adding in the garment designs. This allowed him to continue designing until the end of his life.

Drawing and design process

'A collection is three months solid graft. Picking the fabrics, making 200 rough sketches, and boiling them down to 50 or 60, then turning them into reality' he told *Vogue*.[16] Gibb acknowledged that his most successful collections had a theme: 'I always work on a theme because I know there must be discipline.'[17]

Figure 2.8 *Drawing of apron dress with fabric swatches for Spring/Summer 1977 Collection. AAGM Collections: ABDMS067481.*

He collaborated closely with Fassett on the themes, with each collection featuring his colourful patterned knitwear alongside Gibb's silhouettes. A shell motif, applied to the garments as embroidery or beadwork, appears throughout his 1973 collection. The Byzantine collection of 1976 took a series of cream arches on a black background as its starting point (Figure 2.7). Fassett also designed an intarsia mosaic pattern of red, purple, blue and pink. Both patterns appeared in the knitwear and could be worn as co-ordinates or individually. The 1978 Scottish collection was inspired by tartan fabric and the 'Paisley pattern', derived from the traditional Persian teardrop motif, the *boteh*, adopted by Victorian textile producers in the Scottish town of Paisley. This was his last themed collection for seven years.

Starting with multi-image sketches, Gibb worked through a collection's theme, honing his initial ideas and experimenting with cut and fastenings:

> Maybe after doing fifty small sketches in one day I will think: well that's the mood I'm going into, and then I'll wonder if the colour is going to be green or blue or whatever. Yes: I do try consciously to be original, to look for a feeling, but as you say, I must watch out that what I'm doing is not becoming too eccentric.[18]

One multi-image drawing for his nature-inspired 1972 collection has eleven tiny, detailed costumes across the page, only four of which are marked up for progressing. Gibb has scribbled notes to himself ('felt with embroidery – cabbage perhaps') and references to animals in a natural history book he consulted for inspiration; elsewhere he lists numerous plants, including Bluebell, Ribwort Plantain, Ghost Orchid, Field Bindweed and Spreading Bellflower, sourced from 'The Plant Kingdom' (Figure 2.9). These ideas became his first solo collection with screen-printed leathers, salamander images created from snakeskin appliquéd onto wool suits and fantasy dresses such as the Snow Owl dress.[19] 'I get interested in *all* aspects of design' he told *Designer* magazine 'and for me 'less' sometimes means 'more'. I might be sitting there with a sheet of paper and get a wonderful silhouette rather than the details. Or I could go the other way and focus on pure adornment. It really depends on the mood of the moment, what I would call the sixth sense syndrome.'[20]

By the mid-1970s his method was more organized, with multi-images appearing on the page in two horizontal rows of four or five figures as ideas evolved (Figure 2.10). More detailed figures emerged as he refined his concepts; design elements were adjusted, improved, or discarded. From these multi-image sheets of around 250 to 300 miniature designs, possibly forty to fifty complete ensembles were chosen in conjunction with his business partner Kate Franklin (with whom he formed Bill Gibb Limited in 1972). Each collection included day dresses, coats, jackets, skirts, trousers, knitwear and evening wear, all reflecting the chosen theme and available in one of two colourways. For example, a drawing from the autumn collection 1973 lists twelve coats (ten for day and two for evening), eight suits and eight dresses for day and eight suits and six dresses for evening wear along with six 'fantasy' gowns and a selection of seven knitted jackets, 'classic tight long-sleeved jumpers' and

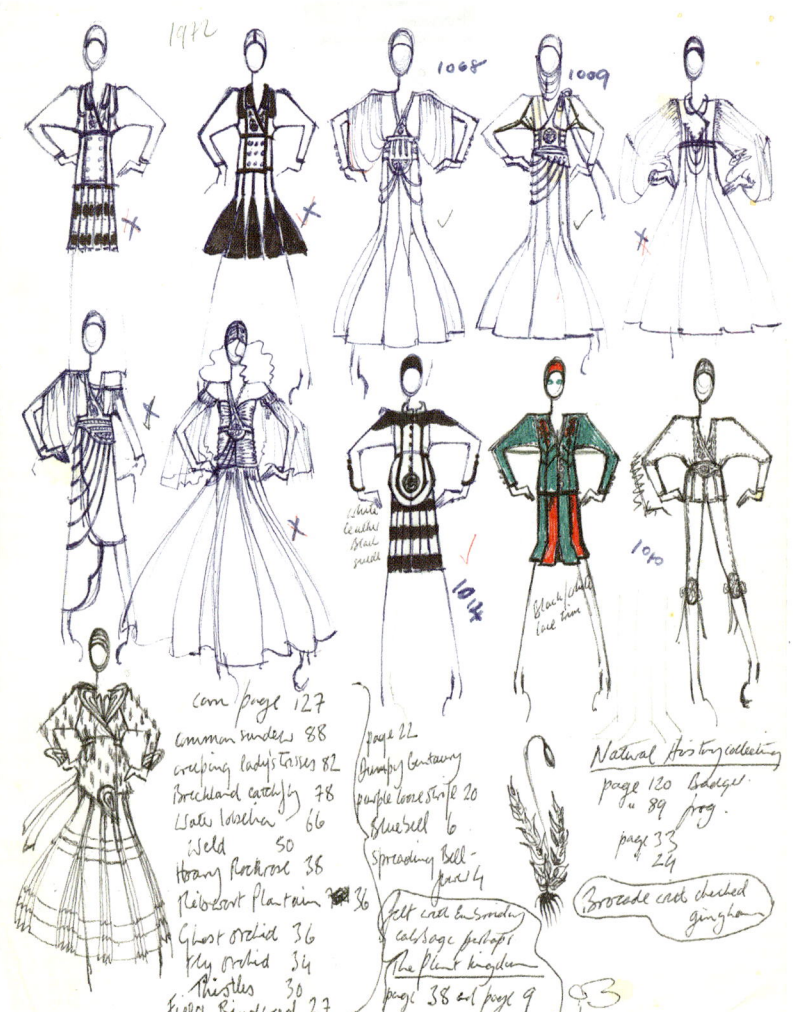

Figure 2.9
Multidrawing of eleven 1972 outfit designs including dresses, tops and skirts. AAGM Collections: ABDMS070163.

coats.[21] Together they would decide whether a particular design would appeal to clients and how it might sit within the collection's theme. The practical aspects of making were also considered. Moreover, Gibb had other aspirations – he wanted to surprise and delight his customers: 'I am always being accused of gilding the lily, but I love rich fabrics, embroidery and colours. Clothes have to go on living for a very long time; they must be worth keeping. They must never stop thrilling their owners.'[22]

The selected drawings were then worked up as finished sketches (figures 2.11 and 2.12). Although he had frequently employed colour to flesh out pattern and texture when designing for Alice Paul and Baccarat in the 1960s, in later drawings colour is kept simply for inking-in details. This practice

Figure 2.10 *Multidrawing of evening wear for Autumn/Winter 1977/78 collection. AAGM archive: ABDMS067616.*

allowed the fabrics, which were chosen after much research and deliberation, to lead the final colour scheme. Small swatches were pinned on to the design sheet, along with colour notes, pieces of trimming fabric or samples of knitting. The finished drawings provided sufficient detail for the pattern cutters to work directly. Each drawing shows a front view specifying fastenings, pocket flaps, belts, trim or beadwork. A back view is included, usually in the top right-hand corner, illustrating how the garment should be cut and details of any embellishment (figures 2.8 and 2.12). If a jacket or coat was to be removed during the catwalk show, the blouse or top underneath is also illustrated and can be cross-referenced with its own individual sketch. These finished sketches have an enduring appeal and his private clients were delighted to receive them as gifts, signed in Gibb's distinctive handwriting. During

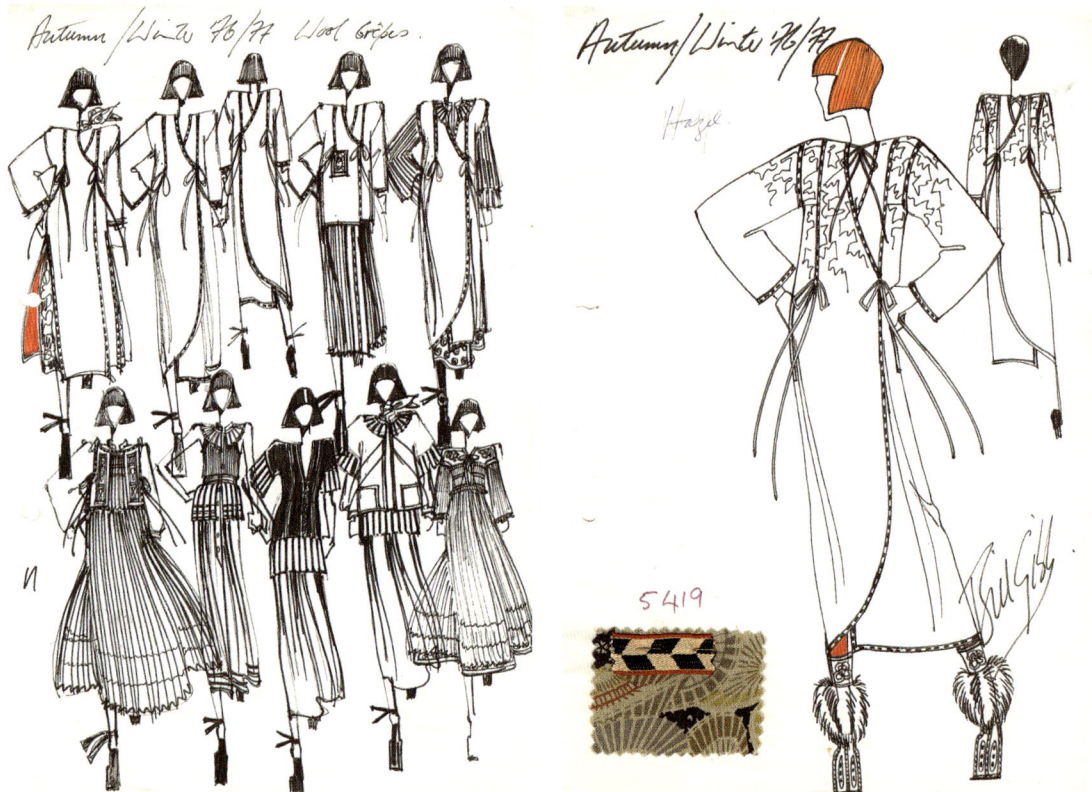

Figure 2.11 *Multidrawing of wool crêpe tops, skirts and dresses for Autumn/Winter 1976/77 collection. AAGM Collections: ABDMS067521.*

Figure 2.12 *Drawing of dress with fabric swatches for Autumn/Winter 1976/77 collection. AAGM Collections: ABDMS067522.*

a period of financial difficulty for the business in the late 1970s, several were framed and sold through a commercial gallery in London.

Bee for Bill

One design feature was closely associated with Gibb and appeared throughout his collections: the bee. Originally it was designed by Fassett as a round bumble brooch, enamelled in several colours to complement the shades of each collection's knits. Jackie McGlone recalls how she met Gibb in 1972. He gave her 'one of his enamelled "Bee" brooches. I still have it and often think of him when I look at it, although I would never wear it for fear of losing it.'[23] Norman Parkinson's photo of him for *Vogue* shows Gibb holding a large cream cushion with thirty-three embroidered bees, one for each year of his life, made by Nives Losani, his pattern cutter, as a birthday present.[24] As he had told *Vogue* the year

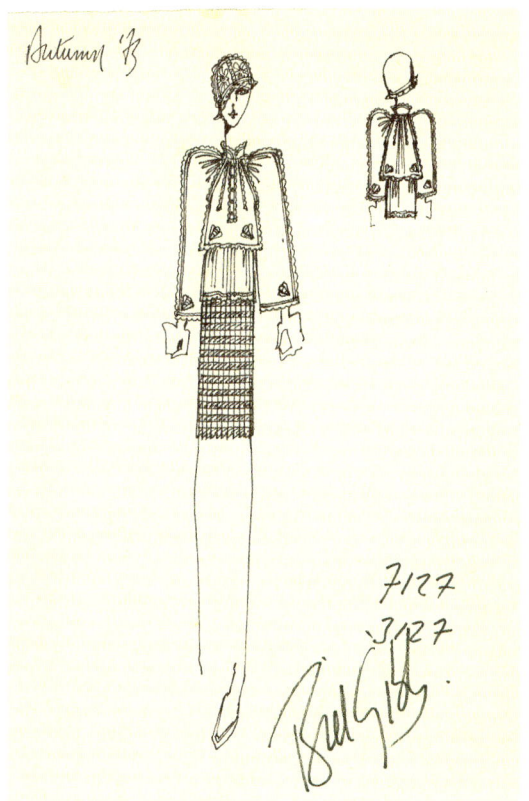 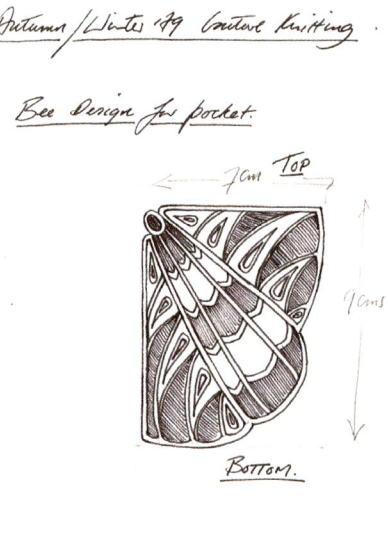

Figure 2.13 *Drawing of blouse and skirt for the Autumn 1973 collection with bee embellishments. AAGM Collections: ABDMS070176.*

Figure 2.14 *Drawing of bee pocket design for the Autumn/Winter 1979 couture knitting collection. AAGM Collections: ABDMS070554.*

before, ever since fashion columnist Ernestine Carter remarked 'Bee for Bill' he was associated with the image and his clients came to expect the motif in his collections.[25] Gibb took this motif and incorporated it into his designs as his branding. In the early 1970s the drawings show a plump bumble bee with rounded wings which was embroidered on the waistbands, pockets and dress yokes, including his Autumn 1973 and Winter 1974 collections (Figure 2.13). Two years later the drawings reveal a slimmer bee with elongated wings embroidered on the pockets of his coats and jackets and adapted as delicate beadwork on evening wear. By 1978 the bee has developed broader wings, spread across dress bodices, yokes and shoulders and sometimes appearing as a more figurative insect on dress pockets (Figure 2.14). Only the wings appear on his casualwear collection for Harrods in 1981: a V-shape wing motif adorns sweatshirts, and a similar embellishment trims the pockets of jeans.[26] In 1985 he launched the Bronze Age collection with a new symbol, a scroll designed by Rachel Leach. The mood had moved away from the glamour and fantasy with which Gibb was associated and he hoped to make a comeback with this new collection inspired by ancient history: the bee was no longer applicable.

Collaboration

Once designing was complete Gibb collaborated with others – pattern cutters, machinists, embroiderers and tailors to turn his ideas into reality. Whilst he knew the look he wanted to achieve, he depended on his workroom team, described as a 'Renaissance atelier' by Carter, to make it possible.[27] He persuaded Albert Purton to move from Baccarat when he set up Bill Gibb Ltd in 1972. Purton was responsible for the clever tailoring and sumptuous leather suits in many of Gibb's collections. Peter

Figure 2.15 *Drawing of wedding dress commission for actress Susan George for her marriage to actor Simon MacCorkindale on 22 December 1984. AAGM Collections: ABDMS067614.*

Wright also worked as a cutter, as did freelancer Pauline Parsons. From 1975 she made many of his lavish evening gowns and some bridal dresses for private clients and celebrities (Figure 2.15). Losani, an Italian seamstress who answered an advert for help to make up his Alice Paul designs, was a key figure in the team, staying with him for seventeen years. Photocopied drawings, annotated with notes, trimmings and fabric swatches were passed to the pattern cutters. Each drawing had a unique four-digit reference number indicating the season and type of garment. The first digit is a garment identifier – 1 for jacket, 2 for trousers, 3 for skirt, 4 for top or blouse, 5 for dress and so on. The garment's sequence in the collection was identified by the last digit, running in ascending order, with the remaining numbers indicating year and season (figures 2.8, 2.12 and 2.13). By studying these detailed drawings and discussing the style in detail, the cutters were able to make a paper pattern, estimate the fabric required and cut out the garment. Losani recalled that this was 'crucial in building a dress and solving small and large problems of wearability'.[28] Parsons often made a part toile, or calico pattern, before cutting, whilst Losani cut directly.

Gibb's skill lay not only in the intelligent cut and construction of the garments but in his choice of fabrics and colour palettes. Swatches on the drawings range from printed velvets, furs and tweeds to smooth satins, printed silks and Qiana jersey, his preferred choice for evening wear. Finding the right fabric was important, working in harmony with Fassett's complex, intensely patterned knits to achieve the collage of pattern, texture and beauty he desired. Small print fabrics with floral motifs, many designed by Susan Collier and Sarah Campbell for Liberty, appear in his early collections. He also commissioned individually hand-printed fabrics. The 1972 collection featured silk-screen printed chrysanthemum leathers by Sally MacLachlan, who also created the ornithological prints used in his voluminous smock dresses. Piero Boboli of Rustichiana likewise printed intricate designs on a variety of fabrics for him. Abstract, marbled, exotic animal and floral prints were commissioned from textile designers Sue Kemp, Bob and Ellen Ashley and Janet Taylor. She collaborated with Gibb throughout the 1970s creating hand-printed silks for day and evening wear and abstract silk scarves designed to be worn with the self-coloured skirts and tweeds of his 1978 ready-to-wear collection. Elaborate beadwork and embroidery was commissioned from Lesley Hogger and her team at Spangles in Covent Garden, London, who specialized in high quality craft beadwork. Dress yokes, collars, shoulder inserts and pockets were sent to Spangles with the design mapped out. The beading was worked by hand using a tambouring technique to secure the beads and sequins, then returned to Gibb's workshop for incorporating into the clothes.

After the company went into receivership in 1979, Gibb diversified, working on several pocket projects including a series of dressmaking patterns for the *Daily Telegraph* and knitwear collaborations with Fassett for magazines such as *Homes and Gardens* and *Woman's Journal.* Licensing ventures and capsule collections for Harrods, Herschelle, Philip Hockley furs and Emelle followed and these, along with promotions for the likes of Wella, the Silk Council and the Harris Tweed Federation, entailed

Figure 2.16 *Drawing of men's jacket and trousers with fabric swatches for Reid and Taylor 1979 promotion. AAGM Collections: ABDMS067627.*

Figure 2.17 *Drawing of detachable-hooded fur duffle coat with fur swatches for Hockley Autumn/Winter 1983/84 fur collection. AAGM: ABDMS035559.*

designing to a remit, restricting his more extravagant instincts (figures 2.16 and 2.17). He found it difficult to adapt to the impact of economic recession and the changing fashion industry; the drawings from this period, whilst still exact, lack the sparkle and liveliness of his earlier work, reflecting his more cautious frame of mind.

Gibb designed for a self-poised woman who desired individuality combined with shapes which were undemanding. 'I design with a discriminating woman in mind,' he said, 'probably a career woman with great style and confidence, a woman on the move and in the know, with a vibrant personality to carry the clothes off.'[29] The drawings demonstrate that most garments had a simple underlying construction, relying on the drape of the fabric, along with hand-crafted embellishment, to achieve impact. He is best known for his fantasy creations, eclectic colour sense, love of texture and innovative garment layering. However, it was Gibb's underlying mastery of cut and construction that made it possible to blend his romantic concoctions with stylish daywear so successfully.

3

Britain's fashion education revolution: Bricolage and Historicism in the work of Bill Gibb

Marie McLoughlin

Bricolage, putting together existing things to make something new, and Historicism, a plundering of the past, were a hallmark of British high fashion at the end of the twentieth century; in contrast, Japanese and Belgian design often used the architectural language of space and form. Gibb was one of the first to use bricolage and historicism as a design methodology. It was an approach informed by his design education, with these methods present in Gibb's work from his earliest student days. The unique curriculum at St Martin's not only fostered this approach in Gibb, but it also gave rise to a lyrical and romantic period in British fashion spearheaded by him.

Gibb's fashion education began at St Martin's School of Art in 1962. After Gibb's death, St Martin's amalgamated with Central School of Art and Design in 1989 to become Central Saint Martins (CSM). The origins and ethos of the two schools were very different. St Martin's claimed to be the oldest art school in London with links to Hogarth's drawing schools in St Martin's Lane, although its formal records only go back to 1854. Central School of Arts and Crafts (later changed to Design) was founded much later in 1896, and drew upon the teachings of William Morris; indeed his daughter May taught embroidery there. These distinctions are important. When Gibb was at St Martin's it was still very much an art school, offering no design subjects other than fashion. Muriel Pemberton, the founder and head of the Department of Dress and Fashion Design, had arrived there in 1931, to teach an evening class in fashion illustration. In 1947 Pemberton had illustrated both Dior's New Look and the wedding of Princess Elizabeth (later Queen Elizabeth II) for the national press. In 1963, when Gibb would have known her, Pemberton was featured in *Honey* magazine showing her designs for Emcar in her signature colour scheme of pink and maroon (Figure 3.1). As a member of the Royal Watercolour Society she exhibited regularly at the Royal Academy and sometimes painted her students, including Gibb (Figure 3.2). Pemberton was still Head of Department when I was a student there in 1970.

So, the St Martin's fashion course was in an art school and run by a well-respected artist. Fashion studies there were closer to performance art than to the artisanal craftmanship courses in technical colleges. The prospectuses of the early 1960s describe the fashion course as: 'The study of dress design comprises instruction in creative design, the history of costume, methods of production, flat pattern cutting, modelling, fitting, sketching, study of colour and texture.' The 'history of costume' was clearly a very important part of the course. It was also important to Gibb. In the archives of Aberdeen Art Gallery there are drawings from Bill Gibb's years at St Martin's and from his application portfolio, work done whilst he was a schoolboy at Fraserburgh Academy. A small gouache painting of Henry VIII and Anne Boleyn at Hampton Court Palace is signed W Gibb. It appears to be dated 10.2.59, which means it was painted when Gibb was just 16 and has been marked 'very good' by his teacher,

Figure 3.1 *Muriel Pemberton's 'Pink & Plum' fashion campaign for Emcar in* Honey *magazine, 1963.*

Figure 3.2 *Watercolour of Bill Gibb by Muriel Pemberton, c.1964. Courtesy of Chris Beetles.*

Figure 3.3 *Gibb's painting of Henry VIII and Anne Boleyn marked 'Very Good' by his Fraserburgh Academy art teacher, Robert Duthie. AAGM Collections: ABDMS082324.*

Figure 3.4 *Early fashion drawings included in Gibb's portfolio for St Martin's School of Art. AAGM Collections: ABDMS082324.*

Bob Duthie. The painting is dominated by the capacious and elaborate dress of Boleyn shown in purples and blue (Figure 3.3). This clear love of drawing, painting and historic dress was a good fit for a prospective St Martin's student. The pink 'Fashion Folio' is only A3 in size (Figure 3.5), much smaller than the one he was later to submit to the Royal College of Art (RCA) but contains 30 or 40 drawings of all kinds. The thoughtfully designed cover, already showing the invention and embellishment that became his hallmark, suggests this was a very earnest bid for a place on the St Martin's fashion course, the largest in the country and already highly regarded. Gibb's fashion designs (Figure 3.4) in the portfolio do not reflect contemporary fashion trends of the 1960s. They echo neither the post-war, full-skirted Dior-inspired fashions of the 1950s, nor the pared back youthquake designs of the 1960s. They are more like the fashion designs of fifty years earlier, as seen in the French fashion magazine *Gazette du Bon Ton* – a sign that Gibb's work was to be part of changing the future direction of fashion by looking to the past.

Fashion education in the 1960s

Given Gibb stayed on at Fraserburgh Academy after 16 he must have had his sights on higher education of some kind. The usual options at 18 were university or teacher training college. The reforms of the British Government's 1944 Butler Education Act (1945 in Scotland) had raised the school leaving age from fourteen and guaranteed free higher education to the most able. For the first time working-class children were able to go to universities. Art education had fallen behind these reforms and was rarely seen as an option for bright students like Gibb. This was about to change. The Coldstream Report of 1960 recommended the biggest shakeup of art education since 1852. These changes, unpopular with many, repositioned art education in the United Kingdom away from the local art school which had few entry requirements and from where, after four years of study, gifted students might apply to the Royal College of Art, to better, but fewer, art school courses, creating a tier of art education that was the academic equal of universities. These changes would favour bright, talented students like Gibb. A new art school degree, of three years duration, would be offered by a carefully vetted number of art schools. The addition of historical studies and a written element in the final examination would raise the status of art and design to that of an academic discipline. Coincidentally successful students would also receive a mandatory grant of paid fees and means tested maintenance payments, as university students did.

Figure 3.5 *The front cover of Gibb's portfolio for St Martin's School of Art. AAGM Collections: ABDMS082324.*

Against the backdrop of these far-reaching changes Bob Duthie advised George and Jessie Gibb to send their son over 500 miles away to attend a college not just in London, but at its very centre, on the edge of Soho, London's red-light district. Duthie must have felt that this gave Gibb the best chance of a career in fashion, for which he clearly showed an aptitude. However, at this time the top fashion designers had rarely come through an art school route. London couturiers, like Norman Hartnell and Hardy Amies, usually came from a similar background to their customers and had learned their trade through informal apprenticeships in elite fashion houses. What Duthie was recommending was high risk and, even with the government help available at that time, not without costs. There is a tendency to view Gibb as a shy and unworldly farm boy with an exceptional gift who was guided by his art master. That is undoubtedly true, but it overlooks the degree of tenacity it took on Gibb's part to make such a major transition to study something as ephemeral and uncertain as fashion. This would have required a good deal of determination and self-belief.

Previously art schools had offered a two-part qualification. A certificate after two years of general study followed by specialization in a chosen subject for a further two years leading to a NDD, the National Design Diploma. NDD graduates could apply to the Royal College of Art for further study. Coldstream's proposal was that there would now be a one-year Pre-Diploma course, later called a Foundation course, at a local art school, in general art and design subjects then students would apply to one of the DipAD (Diploma in Art and Design) colleges to study a specialist art or design subject. So, there would still be four years of study but the final qualification, the Diploma in Art and Design, would be of degree level. Like university study this usually meant the student would need to be away from home. All DipAD students were to be at least 18 years of age and have a university entry level general education of five 'O' levels and two 'A' levels in addition to a portfolio. An allowance had been made in the rules that the formal qualifications could be waived if the portfolio was exceptional. The transition from NDD courses to DipAD courses was not smooth. Just over 100 colleges had offered the NDD qualification. After a very rapid review, only twenty-nine colleges were recognized as able to offer the DipAD. Pemberton served on the board looking at courses for Dress and Textiles, only seven were recognized as able to offer degree level education in Dress and Fashion. Competition for places would be fierce.

This was clearly a massive step for a shy young man from Aberdeenshire. Gibb went to London in 1962 and studied for four years at St Martin's before he qualified in 1966. This was not unusual. Pemberton created a category of students in the Dress department called 'Special Students': those students who had not done a Foundation course for whatever reason, often overseas students, would spend a preparatory year studying in the department before embarking on the degree course, thus fulfilling the four years of art school study recommended. Howard Tangye, an Australian who later became Head of Womenswear at CSM was one such graduate. Tangye has spoken warmly of Gibb who was his external examiner when he graduated in the early 1970s. To be offered this important role so soon after his own graduation indicates just how highly Gibb was regarded by his alma mater.

One of the reasons why so many colleges did not reach the standard required to award a degree-level qualification was that they were not able to provide the complementary historical studies element needed. Many did not even have a library. The aim was for art students to have an academic liberal studies education. However, the response of some colleges was to introduce an inflexible regime of art history classes, with no option of design or dress history, and written exams, including at Hornsey, one of the few colleges to offer Fashion at DipAD. This led to student protests at several colleges, most notably at Hornsey. The Coldstream committee reconvened to investigate the unrest. Nicolas Pevsner, the committee member with responsibility for this new academic element sympathized, saying 'The textile student needs little Giotto, (or a little will go a long way).'[1] Some complementary studies were already embedded in the curriculum at St Martin's. The artist Jo Brocklehurst, a fashion student during the 1940s, recalled visits to the opera. Fashion students had traditionally spent lengthy periods studying in the V&A, especially in the dress and textile departments. A massive increase in the number of students post-war had created pressure on space in St Martin's Charing Cross Road. The neighbouring building was leased for the expanding fashion department, but a suggestion in the management minutes was that fashion students could spend more time in the V&A, whilst Fine Art students could go to draw at the zoo. At this time students expected tuition at classes every day plus two or three evenings a week. The idea of self-directed study, away from the college, was some way in the future. The fact that fashion students had always spent time in the V&A had roots in Pemberton's own design education.

The development of Muriel Pemberton's syllabus

In the 1920s Pemberton had won a painting scholarship to the RCA, but she realized that a girl from Burslem in the Potteries without a private income would struggle to earn a living from painting alone. She decided to swap to the less prestigious Design School and to specialize in Fashion, notwithstanding that this was not a subject the school offered. She was asked to write her own syllabus within the Design School curriculum; it had to feature observational and technical drawing, history, specialist technical skills and an understanding of the contemporary marketplace. This outline was to form the framework of the course she would slowly create at St Martin's. 'Observational drawings' took the form of costume life classes at St Martin's. They served two purposes; one was to prepare students for a possible career in fashion illustration, something at which Pemberton excelled, and which had been her first class at St Martin's. And secondly to embed in students a grasp of anatomy so that, when designing, an understanding of the proportions between neck and waist, shoulder and elbow and so on, would be instinctive. With the coming of the DipAD the 1963 prospectus shows a doubling of the

Dress and Fashion staff. Most were part-time, a deliberate policy of Pemberton's who liked to use lecturers who were also working in the fashion industry, whether in design, pattern cutting, tailoring or even flower making. There was one new permanent member of staff, her very capable deputy Elizabeth Suter, who, significantly, was a noted illustrator for *The Times* and *The Telegraph*. She documented the Paris couture shows at a time when photographers or sketch artists were forbidden, quickly sketching from memory as she left a show. I recall her calling students together to describe the details of the latest couture shows, this at a time when Paris held extraordinary influence, embargoing images of its latest designs until its customers had received their orders. These customers would include stores buying a toile or pattern to allow them to reproduce designs under licence. The 1963 prospectus is also the first appearance of a whole new department of Liberal Studies, sometimes called Complementary Studies: a department that provided the theoretical element we would today call 'historical and cultural studies', and which gave the new qualification the academic rigour that was lacking in the NDD. Interestingly, two names in that staff list, Ronald Wilson and Pauline Stevenson, were actually fashion history lecturers based in the V&A.

It is clear from the 1963 prospectus that, of the key elements of Pemberton's earlier RCA syllabus, drawing and history studies were prioritized in the preparations for the new course. Gibb's application portfolio indicates that these should be subjects where he would feel most at home. This makes it all the more surprising that, after a few months at St Martin's, Gibb returned home, homesick and not wanting to continue his studies. Pemberton intervened and spoke to his parents who flew down to London to talk to her. His sisters say that one of the reasons he wanted to leave was that he struggled with the actual making of the clothes. Marilyn said, 'His designs were so brilliant, but he couldn't master the making of the clothes. That was his biggest problem. He couldn't and that was part of the course.' It was part of the course but not the most important part.

In fashion design education there had been a longstanding battle, with Pemberton at the forefront, of whether fashion courses should be in the art academy, alongside painting and other design disciplines, or in the technical school where crafts such as tailoring and sewing were taught. Traditionally the London 'Trade schools', such as London College of Fashion, had given girls the craft skills for the West End workrooms of court dressmakers. Very rarely could these girls attain the role of designer which was seen as the prerogative of middle-class students with 'taste'. This battle is clearly played out in the papers from the Board of Trade and the Board of Education in the 1930s. Pemberton, a government examiner for the Board of Education, steadfastly argued for a broader more academic education for her students and a comparison of the St Martin's curriculum and that of Trade schools is shown in the papers in the National Archive. So being able to sew and make clothes well was not a requirement for a designer in Pemberton's eyes.

But being able to design and cut a pattern was. This is where Pemberton imported another of the strands of the syllabus she had written, which had enabled her to become the first ever RCA fashion graduate. As pattern cutting was not taught at the college, Pemberton found a well-regarded pattern cutting school in nearby Knightsbridge. The Katinka School had advertised in *Vogue* from the 1920s where it described itself 'as a Court Dressmaker specialising in embroidery'. Émigrés highly skilled in needlecrafts, especially embroidery, had arrived in London following the Russian Revolution. It is likely that Katinka had those origins too. What we do know is that, by the 1930s, its principal was Natalie Bray, a pattern cutter who had worked for Paris couturier Lucien Lelong. He is best remembered now as the wartime head of the *Chambre Syndicale de la Couture* who, during the war, employed two young designers, Christian Dior and Pierre Cardin. Going through Gibb's papers in the Aberdeen Art Gallery archive it was delightful to find his copy of Natalie Bray's *Dress Pattern Designing: The Basic Principles of Cut and Fit*. I had the same pattern cutting tutor as Gibb, Vera South, and remember being sent out to buy my own copy before I started classes. Like Gibb I kept it, as have many of my contemporaries. By the standards of the 1960s, with simple straight up and down tabard style dresses and miniskirts, it was old fashioned, even archaic, showing how to create elaborate bias-cut flounces and so on. This was not the drape method of pattern cutting or 'modelling', of placing and pinning cloth onto mannequins, but was the method needed for fitted or tailored clothes. Flat pattern cutting was the mathematical manipulation of a 'basic block', a cardboard pattern that would give a close fit. Darts and seams could be repositioned. Sections could be cut on the bias or the straight grain; fullness could be added by pleats or gathers but the surface area of the basic block could not be reduced. Later adjustments could be made on the dress stand but an understanding of mathematics and basic algebra was needed to turn the flat pattern into something that could be used to create a three-dimensional garment. It was unforgiving, but Gibb clearly mastered it as a design from 1968 demonstrates (Figure 3.6).

The detailed measurements on this page suggest that this garment was made, it was not just a design sketch. Christine Rew, late of Aberdeen Archives, Gallery & Museums, writing in *Costume* in 1994 stated: 'He was meticulous in his attention to detail: most dresses had no darts, utilising the cut and drape of the fabric and seams for fit.'[2] This is not the work of someone who could not master the making of clothes. This drawing is detailed: it is really a 'technical drawing' showing a complete understanding of the structure of garment making. It could be made by a technician today.

Bricolage and Historicism

Study in the V&A, not only in the galleries but in the library too, were an important part of the Dress and Fashion course at St Martin's. The government's Department of Practical Art and its Superintendent Henry Cole had used profits from the Great Exhibition of 1851 and the patronage of Prince Albert to transform some boggy ground in South Kensington into a centre of excellence for the study of the sciences and applied arts. Cole created the South Kensington Museum, now known as the Victoria &

Figure 3.6 *Drawing of coat and trousers in 1968 for Judy Brittain, British* Vogue *magazine's knitting editor. AAGM Collections: ABDMS067675.*

Albert Museum (V&A); The National Art Training School, now known as the Royal College of Art; The National Art Library, still housed at the V&A; and the Normal School of Science, which became Imperial College and the Science Museum. The Royal College of Music and the Albert Hall completed this set of outstanding centres of learning and practice. Money was also given to small local art schools, as recorded by St Martin's in 1854. The applied arts collection at the V&A was amassed with the declared intention of improving the quality of British 'arts and manufactures' which were seen as poorly designed compared to other countries, especially France. Items of excellence were collected from all periods and places and made available for students and industry to study. It was hoped a more discerning consumer could be cultivated too. Determined efforts were made to attract people of all clsses to the new museum, with late night openings – thanks to gas lighting – and a café.

When Pemberton was a student at the RCA it was still sharing premises with the V&A. When Gibb and his fellow students spent hours studying and drawing in the V&A, they were following a well-trodden path created by Cole a hundred years earlier. Concepts of cultural appropriation would have been as alien to Gibb in the 1960s as they would have been to Pemberton in the 1920s. Cole's intention was that all world knowledge in the applied arts be brought together to be used as inspiration by young designers. Sketchbook drawings in the Aberdeen archive, which appear to have been mounted for inclusion in Gibb's RCA application portfolio, show how a designer would have studied construction details and silhouettes from other cultures (figures 3.7 and 3.8). The library of the V&A would hold

Figure 3.7 *Examples of traditional Italian womenswear sketched by Gibb for his Royal College of Art portfolio submission. AAGM Collections: ABDMS081998.*

Figure 3.8 *Examples of traditional Italian menswear also sketched by Gibb for his portfolio. AAGM Collections: ABDMS081998.*

ethnographic books of costumes. Zandra Rhodes, writing in her autobiography *The Art of Zandra Rhodes* (1984) tells of how frustrating it was that her textile designs were cut into for the minimalist fashion of the 1960s.[3] She discovered an early twentieth-century book by German ethnographer Max Tilke, *Costume Patterns and Designs* (first published Berlin, 1922). These designs enabled Rhodes to design garments which used large intact panels of her prints. There was a rare copy of another Max Tilke book, *Costumes of Eastern Europe,* in the Special Collection of St Martin's Library. Gibb may have seen it. However, his folk costume drawings appear to be closer in style to those in a large collection of fashion plates from the end of the nineteenth century he could also have seen, *Zur Geschichte Der Kostume,* which are now in the CSM Museum and Archive (Figure 3.9). These resources were there for the benefit of fashion students rather than anthropologists. Tilke, writing in *Costumes of Eastern Europe* in 1925, wrote 'my chief aim is to offer fashion artists and dress designers new inspiration'.[4]

Figure 3.9 *Example page (997) from* Zur Geschichte Der Kostüme *(1890) by Louis Braun. This copy is held by Central Saint Martins which Gibb would have used during his time at St Martin's. Courtesy of Judy Willcocks, CSM.*

The use of these types of sources is treated more warily today. There is a debate about when inspiration strays into cultural appropriation. Also, quite rightly, there is unease and scrutiny around institutions built using the profits of the slave trade or collections that reflect exploitation by a colonial occupying power. South Kensington was built half a century after Britain had abolished the slave trade; slavery in America ended just as the V&A prepared to open its doors. The V&A's holdings were purchased or donated rather than spoils of war. The adoption of motifs and techniques, whether from other periods or other cultures, was one of the founding principles of the museum as described earlier. Admittedly many students browsed the collections like children in a sweet shop, picking and mixing anything that caught their fancy with little emphasis on academic scholarship. But they also took those shapes and motifs and mixed them with other ideas: they did not claim them as their own. There is a chevron braid, pinned into Gibb's St Martin's notebook, that became a *leitmotif* in his work in the 1970s. It can be seen on the 'Renaissance' dress he made for Twiggy for the Daily Mirror Fashion Celebrity dinner of October 1970 (now in the V&A collection) and in a ready-to-wear printed cotton dress, carrying his 'Bill Gibb' label, of the same year (Figure 3.10). Twiggy's more elaborate bespoke

Figure 3.10 *Detail of 1970s printed cotton dress featuring chevron braid. Courtesy of Kerry Taylor Auctions.*

dress mixed historic shaping, a print of a Holbein painting, figured fabrics and passementerie (trimmings), including patterned braid tassels and covered buttons. Many of Gibb's contemporaries were less inventive in their use of other cultures. Laura Ashley used Regency era styles made up in the small prints taken from the Indian block printed muslins that would have been familiar to Jane Austen. Thea Porter imported exotic textiles, first for interiors then as ethnic clothing. Biba embraced first an Art Nouveau style aesthetic and then an Art Deco one; and Ossie Clark created romantic variations of 1930s tea-gowns in crepe and chiffon. The reworking of traditional designs from past cultures did not start with designers in the 1960s; rather it has a long tradition in British culture, so much so it is no longer perceived as 'other'. Liberty prints, Paisley shawls, kimonos and the quintessential British country house style of chintz and floral patterns, are all inspired by textiles from the Indian sub-continent and elsewhere, and all pre-date the founding of the V&A. Gibb's nostalgia was less literal than that of other designers in the 1960s. His designs evoked a mythical past of fairytale princesses, ethereal fabrics and exquisite embroidery.

Figure 3.11 *Installation view of Gibb's 1970 'Dress of the Year' shown alongside* Vogue *article as part of the Tartan exhibition at V&A Dundee. Photograph by Ruth Clark, courtesy of V&A Dundee.*

The important point is that Gibb used a *mélange* of different styles and techniques to create something new: Bricolage. He used textiles designed especially for him and also Liberty prints. His magpie approach not only informed and influenced his own work but also that of later renowned St Martin's alumni like Galliano and McQueen who were able to build on a design process that mixed old and new styles, and a variety of media, that Gibb had pioneered. Galliano stated: 'British Designers are storytellers, fairytale tellers, dreamers and I think this was really the essence of the romance behind Bill Gibb.'[5]

Gibb is much credited for his skill at mixing different textures and patterns, such as checks and florals. He would already be familiar with Scottish clothing which happily mixes Fair Isle knits and tartan kilts. Gibb's partnership with Kaffe Fassett, himself inspired by Scottish woollens, led to a reworking of these traditional designs, with Fassett designing the knits and Gibb, often using Liberty fabrics, reinterpreting the pleated, swirling skirts. The famous Sarah Moon images, displayed in the *Vogue* January 1970 story titled 'Glorious Confusion', still looked fresh when it was exhibited at the 2023 V&A Dundee exhibition of 'Tartan' (Figure 3.11). They sum up both this collaboration and Gibb's Scottishness. This outfit was chosen for the Fashion Museum Bath by *Vogue* editor Beatrix Miller as the 1970 Dress of the Year. For many this fixed Gibb in the public mind as the Scottish magician who could mix pleats, tartans and checks in Liberty's Varuna wool and top it with a riotously coloured Fassett-knitted Fair Isle waistcoat. From here on, Gibb's work was expected to be multi-layered with artisanal detailing.

Speaking to *Vogue* after Gibb's death, Pemberton said: 'He was a tremendously talented and sensitive student, of gentle disposition, with a fine appreciation of texture – of delicate, gossamer fabrics as well as weighty, thick ones – and a great feel for mixtures.'[6] These rich mixtures can be seen as the results of the joyous use of Historicism and Bricolage in his work, all spurred on by his interest in history from a young age through to the unique set of circumstances at St Martin's where Pemberton's guidance and ready access to the V&A had an undoubtable influence on Gibb's pioneering designs.

4

Folkloric revivals and exoticism in fashion: Bill Gibb and the vanguard of designers in 1960s–1970s France

Elizabeth Fischer

The 1960s ushered in an era in which ready-to-wear clothing and new fashion capitals emerged, challenging the long-standing hierarchies upheld by Parisian 'haute couture'. A generation of young designers in Europe, who hadn't been trained in traditional couture and openly rejected its diktats, responded to the aspirations of a younger population with lower spending power but a high degree of fashion awareness – it was all about style, 'a certain way of living rather than a certain way of dressing'.[1] More casual and innovative fashions, geared to the lifestyles of the post-war generations, were devised by a group of designers who were essentially young people designing for their peers.

To survive, at all levels the fashion industry had to respond to the aspirations of the twenty-somethings, now their main clientele. A survey conducted in 1963 by the French Ministry of Economy confirmed that the highest rate of clothing consumption per capita was held by men and women between 15 to 20 years of age to a far greater extent than by any other generation.[2] Department stores dedicated corners to 'young fashions', offering head-to-toe outfits selling a 'look' and lifestyle more than just clothes. Independent boutiques retailing designer fashion as well as industrially manufactured garments were opening in Paris and all over suburban France, displaying their wares in bohemian or fantasy settings directly inspired by London's Carnaby Street.[3] The name immediately became a byword in French-language media for anything young and hip referencing London's 'swinging' styles from the 1960s onwards – 'the most comical, funny aspect of these fashions which are all the rage whether on Carnaby Street or in Saint-Germain des Prés' as chronicled by a Swiss fashion reporter in

1971[4] – even when London's fashionable scene moved to other streets and neighbourhoods. The French writer François Bon recalls buying his first pair of flared jeans as a teenager in a small-town store in Poitiers: 'On the record sleeve of the Beatles' "Abbey Road", [. . .] Harrison wore flared jeans and we became one of them, their equal, with a single slap of our belt buckles'.[5] They connected F. Bon to the modern youth enthralled by the lodestars of British pop music.

London emerged as the capital of a fashion revolution which swept over the Western world and was reported on internationally. Designers from the Continent flocked to the city to observe what was going on as 'England had suddenly become the trendsetter for avant-garde fashions'.[6] The Swiss couturier Heinz W. Riva imported the miniskirt to a shocked catholic Italy on opening his namesake house in Rome in 1966–67, after a stint in London.[7] In March 1972 the *Journal de Genève*, a major French-language Swiss newspaper, announced the launch of Bill Gibb's label in an article comparing the expensive couture of Hardy Amies and Norman Hartnell to the youthful, affordable and highly exportable designs by Mary Quant: 'another young designer, a man, Bill Gibb, is launching his own brand on the market, showing his first collection in April. The celebrity Twiggy will wear outfits designed by him in Ken Russell's forthcoming movie "The Boyfriend", in which she will be starring.'[8] There are no further mentions of the Scottish designer in this main Swiss newspaper, although British fashion is regularly featured with Quant stealing the limelight in most instances. As Swiss textile manufacturers supplied fashion designers all over the world with elaborate and exclusive fabrics, such as Jakob Schlaepfer for Gibb (Figure 4.1),[9] their corporation's trade journal, *Textiles Suisses*, never failed to feature shops retailing Swiss wares in Europe and the Americas, as well as the designs made out of the precious material. Hence the Swiss media was regularly informed of design trends across the Channel.

Aware of losing ground, haute couture creators set up ready-to-wear lines called 'prêt-à-porter des couturiers' to distinguish them from their new competitors. However, 'couture was not the best launching pad from which to create fashions for other young people'.[10] The 'couturiers' Pierre Cardin, Paco Rabanne and André Courrèges, who operated in both segments, advocated what the latter heralded as 'couture future' which resolutely turned its back on any inspiration from the past. Modern silhouettes were linear, sharp, and mirrored the most avant-garde forays of science and spatial exploration. The Japanese designer Kenzo Takada remembers beholding a vision in the streets of Paris on his arrival in 1965: a couple of cosmonauts, alighting not from the moon but straight from Courrèges.[11] Yves Saint Laurent founded his couture ready-to-wear 'Rive Gauche' line in 1966, supported by Didier Grumbach, head of the C. Mendès garment manufacture. That year his feminine tuxedo suit created a stir. Courrèges had presented trousers for women, for day and evening wear, in 1962 and in his spring 1965 'bomb' collection so dubbed by the French press. However, the British women designer duo Foale and Tuffin had been designing feminine pant suits right from the outset of the 1960s:

Courrège's endorsement went a long way toward advancing the acceptance of pants for all occasions, which had become widespread by the end of the 1960s. In August 1964, London's Tuffin and Foale reported on their trouser suits: 'We had a big battle with buyers over them, till Paris did them. Now they're screaming for them.'[12]

Designer Betsy Johnson said of their pant suits: 'The cut was incredible, the best I've ever seen. I'm sure Saint Laurent was influenced by them.'[13] Rive Gauche boutiques spanned cities all over the world, opening in September 1969 in London on New Bond Street. Saint Laurent was accompanied by his muse Louise (aka Loulou) Fitzgerald de la Falaise. Born in England in 1947 of a French aristocrat and an Anglo-Irish mother who modelled for Schiaparelli, she told French *Vogue* that she much preferred London's atmosphere and British youth to the French and wished she could spend half the year in

Figure 4.1 *Autumn/Winter 1977 design featuring sequin embellishment by Jakob Schlaepfer as part of a 'Happy Birthday Bill Gibb' magazine advertisement special. Photo: Retro AdArchives / Alamy.*

England. She was pictured wearing fashions by Ossie Clark and vintage accessories found at an antique market in Kings Road.[14] From 1972 Loulou was one of Saint Laurent's main collaborators, in charge of the brand's accessories, jewellery and knitwear. Thus the couturier had a firsthand source reporting back on the London scene.

Fashion became a melting pot of trends and inspirations, as travel by plane became more affordable for a larger part of the population. What started out as soul-searching trips undertaken by hippies to India or Nepal at the end of the 1960s turned into all-inclusive holiday package deals for middle-class families shepherded in charter flights to picture perfect warmer climates by the 1970s. Exotic places became idealized postcards. Folklore and ethnic customs inspired a good number of fashion designers both in France and Britain who tended to layer various cultural references in a single collection – authentic or reinvented Indian blouses, North-African djellabas, Eastern kaftans, moujik trousers, Afghan sheepskin coats, Peruvian ponchos, Irish and Scandinavian knits, 'Gypsy' skirts, Romanian embroidered blouses: it seemed like the entire world could be casually plundered. Specific aspects of given cultures were thus essentialized by the so-called tourist gaze, collected as signs 'often visually objectified and captured to be reproduced, recaptured and reformulated over time, space' and in products such as fashion.[15] This attitude was mirrored in the extremely popular French DIY crafts magazine *100 Idées*, founded in 1972.[16] The editorial team 'invented' craft projects every month derived from indigenous traditions, sourced all around the world including Europe, which were the subject of in-depth reports. Armchair travel allowed readers to partake in an infinite variety of activities to enhance their home and wardrobe. 'Vrai, simple, beau' was the catchphrase of *100 Idées* which saw itself as a champion of disappearing crafts.

Contrary to Courrèges' credo, this multicultural imaginary was often combined with a nostalgia for vintage garments, country skirts and smocks, retro nightwear and lingerie worn as dresses – a practice inherited from hippie styling as if generic-looking peasants had moved to town: 'The embroidered peasant look has reached epidemic proportions in France and looks as if it will do the same in England. Now you can find the clothes to make up this look without having to hunt round the antique markets.'[17] Specific references to former twentieth-century styles and earlier Western dress would also appear in collections.

Drawing inspiration from foreign textile traditions or ethnic and folkloric costumes was by far not a novelty in French fashion. At the beginning of the twentieth century, Fortuny, Callot Soeurs and Babani integrated, or fully replicated, antique and/or Eastern fabrics in their designs. Poiret, Lanvin, Paquin and Patou turned to Eastern Europe (where they had travelled) or to the Middle East for the cut and ornamentation of garments. The Japanese kimono fascinated painters and designers alike, as did harem-pants, pyjamas and kaftans. Non-Western influences definitely enriched Parisian fashionable styles before the First World War and endured for the entire twentieth century.[18] Foreign designers wishing to acquire their induction in fashion came to Paris, bringing their own heritage to French fashion houses and craftspeople.[19]

This essay will focus on the specific approaches of Bill Gibb, Kenzo Takada (1939–2020), Jules-François Crahay (1917–88) and Yves Saint Laurent (1936–2008) among others, to infusing their fashions with ethnic sources. This aspect of their design process raises the question of cultural appropriation, an issue which has sparked important and heated debates of late. During the 1960s and 1970s, it was not perceived in these terms, neither in fashion nor other design, artistic or cultural fields. Rather, it was experienced as akin to the hippie's pluriethnic trends in dress, borrowing foreign elements as a countercultural stance to bourgeois norms. The ethnic elements were equated with authenticity and naturalism. However, this was fraught with contradiction: appreciation of the Other's dress and ornaments was not accompanied by a preoccupation with the plight of native peoples or of indigenous minorities. It reflected an aesthetically driven and casual pluriethnicity, adopting the guise but not the cause.[20] 'The late 1960s and early 1970s [...] were another period in which a naturalism that came from hippie counterculture became fashionable – although the *naturalness* was itself simulated and in any case even the natural may easily be a pose, consciously manipulated.'[21] The same can be said of the ethnic borrowings which at the time were perceived as a form of appreciation rather than of appropriation.

Bill Gibb: '... a bit medieval, a bit of nature, something ethnic ...'

As the designer Giles Deacon explained to Iain R. Webb in 2007, Bill Gibb's design process involved 'getting all these quite random things from here, from there – a bit medieval, a bit of nature, something ethnic. He turned it all around and there it goes, down the catwalk. These are very artful clothes.'[22] Gibb borrowed design elements from cultures around the world, notably Eastern and European folk dress. He was particularly deft at translating his vision of craft-oriented influences into texture, weave, knit (with Kaffe Fassett) and pattern, all of which were greatly enhanced by the voluminous surfaces of fabric he favoured in his cuts.[23]

Gibb nourished his inspiration with regular visits to the British Museum and the V&A, as well as with costume research: 'I surround myself with books [...] Bellini to Bosch to Erté to a history of the plant kingdom.'[24] Elizabethan, Renaissance and Pre-Raphaelite iconographic influences would regularly surface throughout his career, as well as aspects of his own Scottish background. He applied black-and-white lining braid to the various edges and main seams of a dress as an ingenious way to highlight structure and achieve unity in his eclectic mix of colours, textures, patterns and shapes – 'one of the greatest little tricks of the game'.[25]

Another unifying factor can be traced to the characteristic British sense of fantasy, the specific genre which emerged in Victorian and Edwardian society. From a Continental point of view, fantasy is intimately linked to the British imaginary, as illustrated by the opening ceremony of the 2012

Olympic Games in London, entitled 'The Isle of Wonder' in reference to Shakespeare's 'The Tempest'. Broadcast worldwide, thirty minutes of the show celebrated Britain's faerie heritage, testimony that fantasy runs permanently through every strata of British society.[26] Gibb's vision of women in billowing attire, referencing a medieval and Pre-Raphaelite imaginary as idealized through the prism of Victorian British fantasy, imbued his creations with a unique flavour, qualified as 'strange garments which draw the attention' in an authoritative French fashion dictionary.[27] In the exhibition catalogue *Hippie Chic*, Bill Gibb's work is included in the section 'Fantasy Hippie'.[28] This flavour had absolutely no equivalent in French fashions of his time. His inspirations from nature and things past were rooted in his own upbringing and family environment. They were truly lived and embodied in his designs, not mere borrowings meant to diversify his collections; this is particularly evident when his design process is compared with that of Kenzo, Crahay and Saint Laurent based on their differing design approaches and how these were shaped by their own diverse backgrounds.

Kenzo: 'The world is beautiful'

After training at Bunka College of Fashion in Tokyo, Kenzo Takada embarked on a year-long round boat trip in 1964–65 to France, with stopovers in Hong Kong, Saigon, Singapore, Colombo, Djibouti and Alexandria. These cities 'made as many visual impacts that have had an enduring influence on me. This boat journey, my first trip, was the most extraordinary in all my life and has nourished all my collections ever since.'[29] He thus acquired a taste for travel and foreign cultures early on.

Arriving in Marseille, he headed to Paris and immediately toured several European cities. Milano, Florence, Rome, Munich, Madrid made lasting impressions on him, as well as London which he visited twice a year after founding his own label.[30] He kept up this habit of travelling to immerse himself in various cultures throughout his career, cultivating his motto, 'The world is beautiful'. His fascination with ethnic dress was steeped in firsthand encounters and a sincere and joyful admiration for the incredible diversity of world cultures. He would send studio assistants on field trips to document folkloric dress and artisanal craft techniques. His inspirations ranged from South America to Europe and to Asia, layered with various peasant and folkloric styles. He reinterpreted the venerated Japanese subject of flowers in fabric (especially cotton and silk) and knitting, through Romanian and other Eastern European traditions during the 1970s, in a wide variety of hues and sizes.

He playfully experimented with knits, inventing unusual vegetal and animal motifs, pairing plunging necklines with puffed sleeves or oversized layers of tunics, jackets and scarves. Contrary to Gibb and Fassett, his knits were less textured and did not play on subtle variations in tone and hue. He favoured vibrant colour schemes and bold, clashing shapes: 'To anything classic I add the unexpected. A touch of excess, an air of folklore, and a palette of highly unusual colours.'[31]

In 1982–83, Kenzo showed voluminous tiered dresses with wide sleeves made out of lengths of decorative ribbons sewn one to another. These fantastic outfits were reminiscent of the collection Gibb produced some ten years earlier in 1971 for the Embroidery Industry of Vorarlberg in Austria. He had stitched together row upon row of embroidery trimming samples, producing swathes of patchworked fabric shaped into voluminous skirts and puffed-sleeved blouses (figures 4.2 and 4.3). Incidentally, the designs were a sell-out in Japan.[32] The styles in Kenzo's 1982–83 collection are reminiscent of Gibb's 1970–71 'Renaissance Costume Splendour' satin and appliquéd outfits for Baccarat. Both Kenzo and Gibb could at once highlight the sheer beauty and quality of materials while creating show-stopping silhouettes.

Similar to Gibb's fashion education, Kenzo's mix of indigenous textile crafts and folkloric dress was fuelled early on by his discovery of the ethnographic plates of the cut and patterns of traditional European and 'Oriental' dress published by the German costume designer and cultural historian Max Karl Tilke (1869–1942). These books, first published in German in the 1920s, have been re-editioned in various languages ever since despite later criticism of Tilke's methodology and lack of scientific rigour. They are a staple of any fashion library, still used for design reference. It confirmed Kenzo in the idea

Figures 4.2 and 4.3 *Two of Gibb's designs for the Embroidery Industry of Vorarlberg in Austria featuring embroidery by Arnold Blotter and Herman Bosch. AAGM Collections: ABDMS054220 and ABDMS054217.*

Figure 4.4 *Illustration of Bashkir women's woollen garment, jackets and shirts based on designs from the Budapest Ethnographic Museum. From Max Tilke's* The Costumes of Eastern Europe *(London: Ernest Benn, 1926), 76.*

that 'all the world's folklores can join hands; my inspiration fits into the order of things'.[33] The flat diagrammatic rendering of the garments in Tilke's costume plates (Figure 4.4) convinced Kenzo that the main techniques of popular dress were like a patchwork: an assembling of geometric shapes akin to the cut of the kimono. His early cotton and knit collections clearly reflect these schematic designs.

The foundation for Kenzo's unfettered silhouettes was the traditional cut of the Japanese kimono which he re-evaluated following a trip to his native country: 'When I opened shop, I had no idea what was my identity. Naming the brand Kenzo enabled me to think things over. How was I different? I pondered on what was Japanese dress, and investigated the kimono, on how to offer it here. I worked on flat cuts.'[34] In his 1971–72 Autumn/Winter collection, he applied a square-shaped straight cut: 'I called it "anti-couture" in contrast to the traditional Parisian technique closely following the body's curves. I deliberately wished to develop unstructured shapes, undefined, to introduce more width, something new and different, based on the technique of the kimono.'[35] Long straight flat pleats could enlarge his garments to fit several body sizes. He eliminated fastenings such as zippers and buttons in favour of adjustable straps, ties and belts. He omitted inner linings so as to remove unnecessary bulk. Instead, he lined sleeve ends, hemlines, collars and belts with vibrant contrasting bands of colour, recalling the decoration of 'haori' kimono coats. This finishing detail highlighted the structure of Kenzo's designs as did Gibb's signature black-and-white trimming braid. The generous amount of fabric used by both designers for their garments ideally set off the surface patterns, decorations and colour schemes.

Just like Kenzo Takada, Gibb was keenly aware of his own roots and his textile and dress heritage. These reappeared constantly in his work, from the earthy Aberdeenshire colours and Scottish tartans of his breakthrough 1970 collection through to his Autumn/Winter 1977 'Scottish collection' produced a decade into his professional career, as explicitly mentioned in *Swiss Textiles* (figures 4.5 and 4.6) in a review of London Fashions:

> In his exciting and very beautiful new Autumn 1977 collection, this Scottish designer has highlighted Swiss embroidery on his homeland's tartans, an unusual combination which resulted in original and very effective daywear designs. He used embroidered tweed insets on fur coats and jackets, worn over embroidered tweed skirts with the prettiest white broderie anglaise stand-up collared shirts. Bill Gibb's new knitwear with matching scarves and berets is decorated with allover, appliqué or border embroidery [from Schlaepfer]. In sharp contrast to his treatment of embroidery for day are the dramatic Schlaepfer silver chiffon and georgette evening dresses embroidered with sequins.[36]

Swiss textile manufacturers, notably Schlaepfer, invented the process of weaving sequins directly onto fabric. These specialty fabrics, fashionable in disco and party wear in the 1970s and 1980s, were widely sought out by fashion designers. In Gibb's designs the sequined effects are placed so as to highlight the beautiful movement in his flowing evening garments: to emphasize the edge a tiered top (Figure 4.1) or the pillar-like silhouette of a long halter top combined with a long slit skirt (Figure 4.6). It demonstrates another aspect of his skill in the use of fabric design, this time not by 'mixing and matching' but by artfully placing the pattern in relation to the body movements and the cut of the dress.

Kenzo's eclecticism was rooted in his travels, though he also relied on the rich iconography of his beloved books. Kenzo cannot be suspected of using exotic inspirations with the dominant vision of cultural appropriation as it is currently understood. Having established himself permanently in France, he was keenly aware of his constant balancing act between two cultures, feeling neither fiercely Japanese (his origin), nor truly French (his chosen home).[37] His situation as a Japanese émigré in France gave him a unique vantage point with regards to the current discourse on cultural appropriation. He always stated, 'I myself am exotic'.[38] Coming from a nation that had been defeated during the Second World War, eagerly travelling to steep himself in foreign cultures, his personal attitude was one of openness and wonder, ready to embrace novelty and diversity with zest and joyful curiosity, finding beauty everywhere to translate into his designs. Just like Gibb, Kenzo's mix of ethnic references was the result of his quest for a certain aesthetic in offering a counterculture in fashion for his contemporaries, free from bourgeois constraints and the stuffy conservatism of couture. However, his eclecticism

Figure 4.5 *Illustration by Colin Barnes in Issue 30 of Textiles Suisses (1977) of Gibb garment featuring multicoloured embroidery on tartan wool by Jakob Schlaepfer.*

Figure 4.6 *Further illustration by Barnes in Textiles Suisses of a Gibb evening dress featuring silver and sequin embroidery on flame chiffon by Jakob Schlaepfer.*

blurred the authenticity of each culture and levelled out any differences between native traditions that might be situated at opposite points of the globe. His enthusiasm for the multicultural could also be perceived as a form of casualness which reflected the mix-and-match of hippie styling.

Crahay: 'a master of folklore'

Another well-travelled Paris-based designer who mixed ethnic inspirations was Jules-François Crahay, the Belgian artistic director of Nina Ricci (1959 to 1963) and Lanvin (1964 to 1984). As he did not design in his own name he is little known in the canon of couture despite major contributions. A recent exhibition[39] dedicated to his work has highlighted the need to re-evaluate the exoticism of his design output nourished by the many study trips he undertook during his career. On winning the 1977 'Dé d'Or French haute couture award for Lanvin, he was heralded as the undisputed master of folklore – which 'he did not simply copy, like some, from the illustrations of *Geografia*' and other such media catering to the aforementioned tourist gaze: 'His folklore is inventive, stylized, personal. It comes from the East, from Nepal, Asian peasant women, fierce Mongolians and shy Tibetans and, in the evening, he pays tribute to Visconti with bustles that hark back to the sumptuous details in the movie "Ludwig II of Bavaria".'[40] His folkloric inspirations were in keeping with the couture house's heritage of ethnic cuts and ornaments that founder Jeanne Lanvin collected in samplers and applied to her designs.

The analysis of these designers' bodies of work has become more complex of late. Their collections 'harbour numerous contradictions between a profound interest for these cultures and, at the same time, creations which fantasize a methodical "appropriation" of non-Western objects, producing multicultural collections' – spanning thirty years in the case of Crahay's career.[41] The Dé d'Or award celebrated ten years' worth of his 'luxury peasants'. Like Gibb, Crahay was particularly adept at manipulating textures, colours and patterns derived from his ethnic inspirations. Often, the cut and construction of his creations clearly reproduced Eastern shapes such as the sari or the kaftan, the latter also featuring in Gibb's designs alongside his strong focus on neo-historical cuts. As with Kenzo, Crahay's folklore and Eastern influences are both fictional and real, changing yet enduring, resurfacing in every collection, and based on firsthand knowledge subsequently reinterpreted in garments of generous proportions, creating an imaginary folklore all its own which Gibb equally achieved in his oeuvre.

Yves Saint Laurent: *'A picture book is suffice to take my mind to a place or a landscape [. . .]. I feel no need to go there myself. I have dreamed of it so much . . .'*[42]

Yves Saint Laurent used ethnic inspirations with what today is qualified as a colonial gaze. He asserted that he did not need to travel to faraway lands to understand their exotic beauty believing his fertile imaginative powers served him well enough. He told the reporter Yvonne Baby in 1986: 'When reading a book on India with photos, or about Egypt, where I've never been to, my imagination is fired off. [. . . My] unusually boundless imagination takes me to countries where I don't need to travel. My most beautiful trips are motionless, I take them on this sofa you're sitting on, perusing illustrated books [. . .], surrendering to the pleasure of interpretative knowledge'.[43]

The process of his creative inspiration in regards to foreign cultures stems from the long tradition of the West's fantasizing of the Orient. Born in Algeria of French parents, Saint Laurent was brought up in a political and social system that ignores, to this day, the issues at stake in referencing cultures that had suffered under French colonization. He could send out a 'Bambara' collection inspired by generic African crafts in 1967 and his celebrated safari jacket the next year, almost in the same breath. Both were considered exotic although the 1967 garments were inspired by the colonized's dress whereas the 1968 safari outfits referenced the colonizers' uniforms, in a luxury mode oblivious to the inherent contradiction.

His designs perpetuate a fantasized Orient, a Western construct of otherness as exotic and different, subjugated however seductive, yet no mere figment of the imagination: 'The Orient is an integral part of European material civilization and culture, it has helped to define Europe (or the West) as its contrasting image, idea, personality, experience.'[44] Saint Laurent was enthralled with colours, shapes and crafts from foreign places, which he absorbed, digested and reinterpreted in his own idiom. He allowed himself to dream up a fantastical syncretic reconstitution, more especially with regards to the countries he had never visited such as China or India. His translations of cultures he had encountered firsthand were more literal, as in the case of Japan, Spain or Morocco.[45]

Both Crahay and Saint Laurent, as Europeans, continued a long-standing creative process of using folklore and exoticism in their designs. Crahay, like Kenzo and Gibb, came from the 'outskirts' to a fashion capital. His prolific tenures at the head of two leading French fashion houses meant that he was totally conversant with Parisian couture, yet his travels allowed him to open up haute couture to new horizons in a less domineering way than the motionless lens used by a Saint Laurent. The latter processed cultural references and themes in more 'monochromatic' idioms than Gibb, Kenzo or Crahay, applying exactly the same couture methodology to his collections referencing historic periods and painters' oeuvres.

Conclusion: Revivals between inspirations and appropriation

The various ways these designers appropriated ethnic sources and references offers the opportunity to reflect on this particular aspect of creation in design. Today in fashion design schools, taking inspiration from foreign cultures to reinterpret them in dress has become a pressing issue. Students and teachers are much more aware of the political implications of cultural appropriation.

In Western fashion design education, the history of capitalist urban Western fashion is taught, but not the evolution of dress in other parts of the globe. Furthermore, the term 'fashion' is denied to these cultures of dress, which are perceived as unchanging or slow-changing, traditional in a folkloric even disparaging sense. In contrast, the educational requirements are far broader in 'foreign' universities. Audrey Bartis, a body and image sociologist who studied then taught at the Institut Français de la Mode in Paris, recounts her realization of the 'educational divide between Western nations and the rest of the world, and the symbolic harm it signifies. [. . .] I was impressed by the richness of art history references, both Eastern and Western, of two students from major Indian cities. When I pointed this out to one of them, the answer strongly impressed me: "At home, we are compelled to know not only Western culture but also our own culture and, more broadly, all Asian cultures".[46] In Europe, the knowledge of native regional dress is often not taught in fashion courses, but left to the field of anthropology. Nowadays, students are asked to observe and analyse their own background, social and cultural roots, to 'other' themselves instead of exoticizing the Other. This is an important shift but the onus of 'talking about your own cultural roots' is still all too often expected of non-white and non-Western students, indicative of a blind spot in Western society and the long reign of the capitalist haute couture system.

Bill Gibb consistently delved into his own regional and national heritage. Furthermore, his design process was steeped in the unique blend of nature, femininity and historicism popularized by the British tradition of fantasy. Though he fully participated in the vibrant scene of the London fashion revolution, his position as an outsider coming from Scotland set him apart from the ways ethnic sources were integrated in fashion designs; his approach and the outsider Kenzo's are very similar in revisiting their native dress and aesthetic heritage as a basis for their designs. Kenzo's and Crahay's way of appropriating and 'remixing' world folklore combined reality and fantasy. They both travelled extensively and were eager to immerse themselves in different cultures for a firsthand experience. However their multiculturalism in fashion, displayed with ingenuity and enthusiasm, never took into account the people representing these different cultures, who were not integrated in the design process nor in the redistribution of commercial benefits. Kenzo, an immigrant, felt not only different but 'exotic' in his chosen homeland – using this position to define the design DNA of his brand. His own culture, seen from a distance, enabled him to rethink the foundations of Parisian couture, particularly in cut and pattern – much as exotic dress enabled earlier Parisian designers to 'uncorset' tailored dressmaking and silhouettes, introducing different garments with a new interaction between dress and body. Kenzo blended 'cultural appropriation' both ways: he was attracted by the Other, and by way of his own life experience, othered himself, thereby gaining new insights in the possibilities offered by his native culture. This constant balancing act of his is now a pathway that is suggested to design students: start by gaining a deeper understanding of your own culture, its blind spots as well as its richness, before integrating other ethnic inspirations.

This is exactly the course that Gibb's inventive process embraced. He constantly referenced not only the textiles, colours and patterns of northern Scotland's material heritage, but also the palette of the Scottish countryside and the beauty of its natural environment. As Kenzo did, he combined these with unusual elements that boldly highlighted them. In London, when working for Baccarat and then under his own name, his creative idiom translated perfectly into the bohemian styles channelling an idealized vision both of the past and of folkloric dress.[47] This served as an enduring foundation he used in combination with various cultural and historical references he was attracted to further along in the highly original designs produced throughout his brilliant career.

5

An Interview with Kaffe Fassett, Artist

Kaffe Fassett is a world-renowned craftsman having dedicated over five decades to promoting knitting, needlepoint and patchwork. Born in San Francisco in 1937, he moved to London in the mid-1960s and met Bill Gibb soon after. Through their creative collaborations, they transformed British fashion with their mix-and-match bohemian styles. In the following interview with Josephine Steed and Shane Strachan conducted in November 2023, Fassett reflects on Gibb's designs and career and what he would have made of fashion today.

Figure 5.1 *Drawing of Kaffe Fassett included in Gibb's portfolio submission to the Royal College of Art in 1966. AAGM Collections: ABDMS081998.*

Could you tell us a little bit about how you first met Bill and then subsequently began collaborating together?

Well, we met at a nightclub on the King's Road and I asked him what he did and he said that he was a designer. I asked to look at his work and when I saw the drawings, I was just blown away. They were the most beautiful fashion drawings, and I thought his ideas were interesting. They were very much of the time – Ossie Clark and all those people were designing and it seemed kind of in that vogue. We just kept meeting and I was very interested in the fact that he was this young Scottish farm boy who was trying to make it as a designer.

I was introduced to Janey Ironside [Professor of Fashion at the Royal College of Art] at that time, and I found her very interesting. She came and talked to us both and we were both beginning to form our ideas about fashion based on the richness of the material we found at the Victorian & Albert Museum. I was absolutely obsessed with Indian miniatures and Persian miniatures and so I was dragging Billy to look at all this pattern and I was getting him excited about the idea of designing something which would use a lot of different patterns. And Janey said, 'Oh, forget all of that – that is going to be a thing of the past. The future of fashion is that they will pour a serum into a form and that will come out as the outfit, and there won't even be seams, let alone embroidery!' How sad I thought that we were gonna walk around in space suits made of serum. But we still persevered somehow and came up with our creative ideas which turned out to be absolutely on the mark.

It was just such a fruitful time and I think that it was in the air, this whole thing about creating and being turned on by what we were turned on by in those days: going down to flea markets and finding amazing things of the past, and that whole movement with The Beatles where they inspired people to dress in uniforms. You were terribly excited if you found a doorman's uniform with epaulettes or something. So it was kind of dressing up and doing things that were beyond the simple fashion ruling the day – a time when you think of Jackie Kennedy in her little pink coat with her little pink pillbox hat. That was very smart and modern and grown up, and we weren't at all interested in that.

How did your initial ideas come about and how did you progress them?

The way it started – Billy said, 'I'm going to Scotland to find ancient tartans because I'm going to do a collection that reflects my history.' Well, I love history and so did Billy. He took me to this little farmhouse where his grandparent's raised him. His bedroom there was painted like an Egyptian tomb (Figure 5.2). This little farm boy on this kind of desolate Scottish landscape – a very hard-working place – and here was this little fantasy that he was building. So that was very touching to me because, in a way, I was kind of the same. I understood where he was coming from and I also applauded the fact that he had the confidence to create and not be ashamed, because, you can imagine, being a little kid – even a city kid – growing up, your peers, the people around don't believe in creativity or books or anything like that, and so to have the courage to design dresses was quite extraordinary.

Figure 5.2 *Egyptian-inspired drawings which decorated Gibb's childhood bedroom. Courtesy of Patricia Davidson.*

His grandmother was a fabulous woman – she had lots of imagination. I'm sure that she had a huge influence on Billy. He wouldn't have been quite so courageous about being a creative person and having imaginative thoughts if it weren't for this wonderful grandmother. She encouraged that. I remember her singing wonderful folk songs. She had poetry in her soul.

That trip was the absolute pivotal moment. We went across this wonderful Scottish landscape with the beautiful colours of heather and bracken which I just loved. When we got to this mill where the fabric was being produced that Billy was going to use in his wonderful outfits, they also had knitting yarns in these beautiful, subtle colours of that landscape. All I could think was about all the knitting I'd seen in England and America that was just harsh, crude colours – stark white and very contrasting colours; nothing subtle, nothing painterly. And here was this palette of exquisite colours, so I bought twenty colours of the heather and grasses and peat and all the wonderful things of the landscape.

I said to Alice Russell, [part-owner of Alice Paul Boutique in Kensington with Gibb and her sister Annie between 1968–69,] who was in Billy's group, 'Do you know how to knit?' And she did, so I said, 'I've got to do something with these wonderful colours.' And she taught me, and I knitted all the way back to London. Of course, being very shy, I took the first sweater I did straight to Judy Brittain at *Vogue* magazine and said, 'What do you think?' It was a mess, but it was a beautiful mess. She told me to design something for the knitting book that they were just about to bring out that was all about Fair Isle. I learned what it was and then I knitted a Fair Isle waistcoat which went into their knitting book.

When I then went back to Judy with Billy's drawings and said, 'This boy I think is incredibly talented and he wants to do a collection. Would you be interested in featuring it if he did this collection?', she said, 'Yes, if you produce knitting to go with his outfits.' Judy recognized right away that Billy had this amazing talent and she wanted us to work together and became great friends with both of us. She was incredibly important. She was an Irish seer, you know – she would just look into the future. She would look at something and she would just see the possibilities of it. She discovered a lot of craftsmen and craftswomen in those days and brought them to the fore and gave them a platform.

I said, 'Wonderful,' because I'd been saying to Billy, 'Look at all the patterns that are together in these wonderful Indian paintings. There's Paisleys and there's stripes and there's checks and there's flowers and everything else.' So we went and found wonderful prints and then we put them with woven stripes and plaids and things, and then I did a piece of knitting that brought those two worlds together and that was added to the outfit, so it was definitely pattern on pattern.

I had much more ambitious ideas about what I wanted to do with knitting, but had to come to terms with the fact they had to be very simplistic if this knitting was going to be reproduced, so I had only two colours a row and I had a repeat that was within twenty-four stitches. All of these things were imposed on me because the last thing I wanted was to design something which could never be reproduced and therefore couldn't enter his collection.

That was my big struggle and that's where Mildred Boulton comes into the picture. She was a machine knitter and I saw that she could reproduce more complex things, and I just wanted to find out what was practical and what were the limitations. I realized it's better than nothing to have some little stripes of colour and so forth, even though it's very restrained. It was still more interesting to the fashion people than nothing at all, or very plain, one-colour knitting.

How did Bill work as part of his creative team? Did he come up with the original concepts and then ask each of the team to work on different aspects?

There were these wonderful fabric painters and embroiderers and people like that, and he would say, 'I've got an idea for this big, wonderful dress. I want a leopard to be crawling up the side of the dress,' to a painter and she would paint it out – that sort of thing.

But with me, I would come with ideas and say, 'I've just been to Turkey and I've seen wonderful wall paintings done by the old monks back in the old days – that would be a great theme. Let's do that for the knitwear,' and that would kind of inspire him to do certain shapes and so forth, responding to that seed idea. I feel that I would often give him inspirations and, in turn, I found him very exciting, because I wasn't terribly interested in the shape of knitwear, but he was, of course. His structure was his big strength, whereas I was all about decoration and what colours and what patterns would go onto those shapes.

I would say that most of us were just very, very happy to be part of the team and to be part of this great creative movement that was Billy Gibb. He had probably a little more discipline at that time than we did because it was a very loose time – you know, everybody was smoking pot, getting drunk and it was kind of a very loose lifestyle. I remember I very often would be late going to a meeting with him where he was gonna tell me about what we were gonna do in the next collection and one day he just said, 'My time is valuable and I expected you to be here half an hour ago,' and he laid down the law. And boy! I was always on time after that because I thought, 'Okay, if that's important to you. Fine, I'll do it.' I liked it that he was being more responsible and that we weren't just floating in and out like an Andy Warhol film schedule or something. He was under huge pressure and there was always the big sewing room with people sewing and people measuring and models walking up and down, trying things on and so forth.

I remember one of the things that was difficult was that they kept finding very posh places to have showrooms – these incredible little shops that he got set up that had to be furnished and they were very expensive. One was in Bond Street and he went bust shortly after that.

I remember that we often weren't paid. When I wasn't paid for what we did, his backers would say to me, 'Oh, for God sakes! If you're going to play with the big boys, you gotta act like a big boy and take the money when it's there or don't complain.' I mean, just horrible talk, but then we just thought, 'Well, okay – that's the establishment. These are the big money people and of course they're going to act like that. They don't understand us artists.' I was living on a shoestring at the time and I knew how to pull in my horns and live quietly and live without the money for a while.

Do you feel that was a part of the downfall, the fact that the brand grew too quickly?

Yes. It was undisciplined in a way, and it was always a very strange thing of – did you do commercial ready-to-wear, or did you do high fashion? – you know, making special clothes for special people and getting commissioned and all of that. It was people trying to decide who they were and all of the big designers had a lot of problems because it would look like it was taking off and growing very fast, but then the money really wasn't there, and it was very tricky to organize production lines and decide what you did for bread and butter, and where you have the two things going on – very creative, high-thinking kind of outfits, and then maybe little miniskirts and shoe designs or something that kept the money rolling in that was very pedestrian supplying the big shops. It was very difficult to decide who you were and when you were losing your integrity as an artist as a designer.

The impression I got was that the people around him didn't want him to go too commercial, but at the same time, if he didn't, he was gone. When you think of all those other designers, they produced production line pieces so they would go into shops and there was much more stuff going on. I think Billy never became that commercial. He had wonderful ideas that could have; he had a beautiful line that could have carried into beautiful coats and wonderful dresses and things that could have been more commercial, but I think that they were always trying to be much more high fashion.

Today, sustainability is a big concern. Thinking about Gibb's career and how it progressed from the early 1970s into the late 1970s and early 1980s, there was a gradual shift from more natural textiles towards more synthetic fibres. Do you have any reflections on that shift?

I think Billy did use lots of different kinds of fibres. He was interested in all kinds of things like that – what prints he would find and what sort of fibres. He also loved when we travelled through Morocco together, he was fascinated by women in the fields that would be wearing what looked practically like evening dresses – sort of lacy, silvery, sequinned things, and old plastic shoes and things like that. He loved the whole mixture of people working in kind of fancy clothes. So he was interested in playing around with artificial fibres or anything that he could experiment with, but I don't think any of us were thinking about sustainability and all of that stuff at that time.

You've talked a lot about being inspired by other cultures from trips to the V&A and abroad to Morocco, for instance. How do you feel Gibb's work should be viewed today within the context of the debate around cultural appropriation versus appreciation compared with when you were working with Billy?

You know, my own observation of it, living through it, was that we took anything we could as inspiration, you know: Native American, or African, or Indian saris and all of that. You grabbed what you could and you tried to fit into the fashion shapes of the time and of the European . . . what was acceptable to be worn. We would just grab stuff, and it was a joyous game, you know – 'Here's a theme: what can you make of this?' It was kind of like Project Runway where they take the students into a hardware store and say, 'Make a fashion outfit out of something in this hardware store.' That kind of thing. We were just grabbing inspiration where you could, and of course the hippie movement was all about making an outfit out of an old Indian bed spread or an African robe which you added sequins to, or something, and made it into a dress. It was playful with a lot of creativity and a lot of sheer enjoyment of things.

I remember lots of hippie kids were very into Native American culture, you know, with long fringes from leather jackets, beading on things and so forth, because it was beautiful and romantic. And that was the whole thing: it was in the spirit of romance and beauty and fun, rather than being terrified that

Figure 5.3 *Detail from 1975 'Moon and Buddha' knitwear collection. AAGM Collections: ABDMS023893. Photo by Mike Davidson.*

you were stealing the identity of an African or a Native American. You didn't think about those things. And in a way, I'm sort of sad. I remember I had a wonderful teacher when I went to drama school for a while and I remember the teacher saying, 'Everything should be grist to your mill.' As a creative person, you know: grab whatever you can in life and you make something wonderful out of it and you present it to the world to make them happy. That was the whole thrust – to make life better and happier. Drag you out of despair and into the light. So that's the way I look at things.

But I think that I can sort of understand when things get commercialized. I mean, I felt, in a way, the same as those African and Native Americans who got upset at their culture being used, when the fashion houses of the world like Yves Saint Laurent and so forth grabbed our hippie experiments and made them into commercial fashion. Suddenly, here were these little outfits that were just complete little mock costumes of what we were doing but made very rigid because they were mass produced and you could find them in all the street stores. But they came from our finding crazy clothes in charity shops and dressing them up by putting a bit of ribbon or braid or embroidery on things and making them our own and suddenly that was commercialized. I remember thinking, 'God, what the hell is this?' and you'd see people you know wearing a ribbon around their hair or something, and it was suddenly very set, and I remember feeling quite upset about that – that they're taking our ideas and they're making them ugly and they're making them commercial. So I do understand that side of it.

But I feel that what Billy was doing was much more creative than that. Really things had a beautiful flow still. They weren't this kind of set, commercialized thing. He would seek out and find the wonderful and eccentric.

Any final memories of Billy or thoughts you'd like to share?

Travelling with him, it was always fascinating. I remember going through Oklahoma and we went to a little fashion show and they had ice-cube heels. That was the big thing – these little clear plastic ice cubes on the heels of these shoes and he was *fascinated* by that. And then the little poodle skirts – the little balloon skirts and things. Because he looked at the world in a wonderfully creative way. I didn't appreciate it enough at the time. When I think back, it was just delightful, you know. I think as creative people, we all responded to his manifesting something that we could see was beautiful. The way certain artists come along in life and they produce something that makes you realize that life can possibly be better.

Well, what a trip down memory lane. All these things . . . You know, you forget all these attitudes you had and all the stuff that was swirling around. It was an incredibly rich time.

6

Gibb's knitwear in the 1970s: collaboration, innovation and 'slow' fashion

Josephine Steed

Introduction

Gibb's fashion collections included a myriad of textiles where he recognized the value of artisan making and collaborative working which became a hallmark of his practice. Referred to in the 1970s as 'the museum pieces of the future' by writer Helena Matheopoulas,[1] Gibb's love of textiles is apparent throughout his collections where they create a visual and sensory explosion of juxtaposing patterns and textures, such as florals with geometrics and contrasting prints with knits and woven fabrics. Gibb used his innate haptic and sensorial understanding of materials to convey the implicit storytelling within his work where his strong connections to his Scottish roots were attributed with his love of embellished textiles and knitwear. Throughout his relatively short career, Gibb worked in collaboration with many other designers, including knitters (Mildred Boulton and Kaffe Fassett), printers (Sally MacLachlan and Janet Taylor), embroiderers and appliquers (Valerie Yorston and Lillian Delevoryas) and weavers (Richard Womersley and Otterburn Mills); of these, the most notable collaboration was with artist and designer Kaffe Fassett. Fassett's unique knitted designs for Gibb's collections became synonymously linked with the brand's identity where his extraordinarily complicated, multi-coloured knitted designs incorporated his revolutionary hand-knitting techniques. This chapter considers the values that Gibb's knitwear demonstrated which resonated during the 1970s around environmental and sustainable production methods celebrating craft heritage and traditional artisan skills that are now often referred to today as 'slow' design in opposition to mass-production. As the fast fashion mass-manufacture model needs rethinking, these values of 'slow' making visible in some of Gibb's knitwear become more prescient for informing a viable and sustainable future for the fashion industry. This chapter reflects on Gibb's knitwear and how it led to innovations which can be reviewed today through a contemporary lens, potentially offering pathways towards a more relevant model for fashion design in the twenty-first century.

The 1970s – a Golden Age for knitwear

The 1970s, the decade in which Gibb's career was most active and successful is significant due to changes in culture and society which had a lasting impact on textiles and fashion innovation that still resonate today. Here fashion mirrors the society of the time,[2] whether this be as escapism into the world of fantasy and storytelling as found in Gibb's creations, or as a reaction to the political and social unrest of the times as seen in the mid-to-late 1970s by the doyenne of the punk movement, Vivienne Westwood.

Assumptions around knitting associated with domesticity and gender began to change as feminism and queer politics led to a rethinking of fixed stereotypes. As a previously marginalized movement, during the 1970s, feminism challenged the social, cultural and political status quo resulting in legislative changes: the Equal Pay Act (1970) followed by the Sex Discrimination Act in 1975. New thinking through feminist writers that emerged during the 1960s such as Gloria Steinem and Betty Freidan questioned the body, fantasy, desire and identity which manifested into a 'naturalness' in fashion, as women strove for a more authentic and expressive self.

In her seminal book *The Culture of Knitting*, Joanne Turney posits that the 1970s enabled a positive reappraisal of knitting's cultural production where changes in mass manufacturing were taking place, together with an economic shift from production to consumption.[3] Further, like our social and cultural situation today, the 1970s were a time of unprecedented change and political and economic turmoil whilst also being revolutionary, 'sometimes florid, innovatory, risk-taking and occasionally awkward and inconsistent'.[4]

In the early 1970s a new wave of designers in Britain including Fassett and Gibb, and others such as Patricia Roberts, came to the forefront for their creativity in knitting where their innovative designs reflected the free-spirited bohemian lifestyles of the new generation: while the 1960s has been described as a time of dreamers, the 1970s heralded them in as a new generation of creative entrepreneurs focused on turning those dreams into commercial reality. Unique to Britain's fashion at the time, they created a new revival in knitwear, described by fashion writer Suzy Menkes as a 'Knitwear Revolution'.[5] Menkes also highlighted the distinct approaches between designers like Roberts who worked independently as knit-only specialists, and those whose collaborations brought knitwear into fashion collections as seen with Gibb and Fassett.[6]

Figure 6.1 *Hand-knitting sample by Kaffe Fassett for the Autumn/Winter 1976 Byzantine collection with instructions for translating to machine knitting. AAGM Collections: ABDMS067474.*

Set against this background, Gibb's designs reflected this time of freedom, creativity and individuality through his use of flowing fabrics, folklore-inspired embroideries, multi-coloured patchworks of materials and his own Scottish roots using Scottish-inspired weaves and Fair Isle knits. According to Christine Rew in her book to coincide with the Aberdeen Art Gallery's 2003 exhibition, *Bill Gibb: The Golden Boy of British Fashion*, knitwear was where he made his 'most important contribution to British Fashion'.[7]

Collaboration

Without doubt Gibb's knitwear was only made achievable through his partnerships, most notably with his closest collaborator and partner Kaffe Fassett who, together with machine knitter Mildred Boulton, were instrumental in making his knitwear commercially possible. Colour inspiration for his whole collections would often be first developed from knitting samples by Boulton and Fassett. While Fassett innovated through his experimental use of multiple coloured yarns (sometimes up to twenty different colours in one design), texture, and intarsia knit patterns, Boulton was able to then interpret his hand-knitted samples into machine knitted garments. The handwriting by Fassett as shown in Figure 6.1 notes his requests to Boulton where he articulates the collaborative nature through the first suggestion of reversing the pattern — 'think we shall like it' — and requesting the machine sample retains the hand knit qualities: 'Lovely if it could be bumpy and homespun as This sample!'.

Described as a person with a 'generosity of nature', Gibb fully acknowledged the contributions by others as co-creators, recognizing their equal value as central to his design ethos.[8] Fassett and Gibb first began to work together in 1969 after *Vogue* journalist Judith Brittain suggested that they collaborate. This led to an initial collection featured in *The Sunday Times* in December 1969 and both American *Vogue* and British *Vogue* around the same time.[9] Following further collaboration on knitwear elements for earlier collections, including one design that was chosen by *Vogue* editor Beatrix Miller as Dress of the Year 1970 (Figure 3.11), a full knitwear collection inspired by their trip to Morocco was created in 1974 as part of Gibb's Autumn/Winter collection.

Brittain understood that knitwear designers would struggle to sell independently as knitting was not seen as commercially viable on its own. Knitwear at that time was mainly solid colour plain knitting with garment shapes such as the twin set. In the UK, the only few exceptions were heritage knitting patterns from the Scottish regions such as the distinctive two-coloured patterned Sanqhuar in the Scottish Borders and Fair Isle and lace knitting with textural and colour variations from the Northern Isles of Fair Isle and the Shetland Islands.

Fassett first became interested in knitting when he bought a selection of richly coloured yarns inspired by the Highland landscape which he had seen at a woollen mill in Inverness whilst on a trip with Gibb to his Scottish homeland in 1968. A California-born artist, flamboyant, confident and open to trying new creative techniques, Fassett first tried knitting with the aid of a fellow train passenger while travelling back to London and, on his return, he developed designs for *Vogue Knitting*'s Spring/Summer 1969 issue thanks to the support of Brittain; the design was also showcased in American *Vogue* that year. In his subsequent collaborations with Gibb, their different personalities and design strengths complemented one another, and they soon began to work symbiotically together. Gibb completed the look through informal often oversized square shapes, such as a poncho or a kimono shape to accentuate the intricate knitting detail. The garments could be styled separately or as an ensemble, by layering, mixing and matching with other pieces in the collection, with contrasting colours and textures creating unique silhouettes and highly decorative looks.

Fassett describes working with Gibb's intuitive and innovative processes with knit: 'I would give him a knitting design and he would turn it into the most amazing leg of mutton sleeve — things that no-one else did in knitting.'[10]

Figures 6.2 and 6.3 *Caramel and mint patterned knitted jacket made with the synthetic Courtelle and Lurex yarns, 1981. AAGM Collections: ABDMS024230.*

As orders flooded in, production moved to a factory with industrial machines — Harry Green of Gould's in Leicester — which created new challenges but also innovation. Natural yarns were no longer viable technically and were replaced with synthetic yarns (figures 6.2 and 6.3) where they lost the qualities of the woollen hand-knits in order to produce fabric consistency across bulk orders.

Whilst it could be argued that they essentially lost elements of the design concept, Fassett worked hard to retain many of the qualities in the original knitting swatches where as he reminisced in an interview for this chapter:

> I think with Billy, I had to keep being simpler and simpler in getting things that would fit onto a machine. And then when we get onto big industrial machines, they were very, very limited. They said you could do anything you want, and then when I would do something with six colours, they'd say, 'Can't you do it with three?' and just kept cutting me down all the time. So I finally thought of things that I could do, like for one collection we did space dyed yarns so that one of the threads was five different colours being put into this design, but I had to work out how I could . . . still make it look anywhere near as interesting as using twenty-five colours in an outfit when I was doing my own knitting, but I finally figured out a way to do that.[11]

Figures 6.4 and 6.5 *Machine-knit kimono from the 'Moon and Buddha' collection, 1975. AAGM Collections: ABDMS015722.*

Factory knitting production was limited primarily to only producing modified fully-fashioned plain garments or knitted fabric for cut and sew.[12] It was not until the 1980s that technological developments by manufacturers like Stoll and Shima Seiki enabled more creative production using multiple yarns and patterns. Additionally, the small batch production required by designers made finding manufacturers willing to support few and far between. Gibb and Fassett were therefore fortunate to be able to work with Gould's alongside Boulton for more complex knitwear patterns.

For the 1975 'Moon and Buddha' Collection (figures 6.4 and 6.5), Fassett reflects on the design challenges and solutions when working with Gould's for the knitted kimono style jacket:

I remember going up to do the first samples for this collection and we were sitting there with machines rolling and I put the design onto the machine, and I was going to have it as a black background with these big disks of multi-colour. I thought it was going to be very chic and it just came out looking like a funeral. It was just hideous and it was really tacky, so I just suddenly said, 'Try this ochre colour', that was one of the colours that was in this multi-coloured mix. They tried the ochre colour as the background instead of black and it was just magic. It was like old gold! You know – this instant decision and these huge machines rolling and thousands of yards of fabric is coming out and we were able to change it and make it come out beautifully. That led to one of our most important collections. It was really, really wonderful.[13]

During the 1970s, Fassett also worked for Italian fashion house Missoni. Missoni were and are still today (Figure 6.6) renowned for their knitwear where, together with the founders Ottavio and Rosita Missoni's technical knowledge of machine knitting and their distinctive intricate patterned knitwear, they experimented with multiple colour, which would have had an impact on Fassett's collaboration with Gibb as can be seen in his 'Moon and Buddha' collection where there are clearly some similarities where he was able to push the boundaries of design for machine knitting.

Figure 6.6 *Missoni's Spring/Summer 2011 collection at Milan Fashion Week in September 2010. Photo: DPA Picture Alliance Archive / Alamy.*

Gibb's knitwear as 'Slow Fashion'

Hand-knitting can be described as a 'slow craft' where tools are simple — just two needles or 'pins' and a ball of yarn – and its repetitive process of inter-looping stitches to slowly create a fabric. The physical nature of knitting is often referred to as mindful making, where it can be used as a therapeutic activity to alleviate stress promoting well-being.[14] Yet, it can also be highly frustrating where concentration is needed particularly when complex stitches and multiple yarns are being used. Here reading a pattern requires a level of de-coding, understanding abbreviations whilst not dropping stitches. It also can be highly creative and through its slow transformative process from yarn to fabric, an emotional connection can be built with the knitter who is also often the eventual wearer. Through the investment of time, skill and materials the knitting becomes embodied with new meaning beyond its physical final presence and can become a legacy item with emotional attachment. In the 1970s, knitwear collections seen on the catwalks and in fashion magazine drove a new interest in domestic knitting with home knitters keen to replicate the high fashion looks at a fraction of the cost. This led to a revolution in knitting, particularly a craze for hand-knitting, which created a new industry and the launch of several knitwear designers such as Patricia Roberts, Sandy Black, Suzannah Read and Sasha Kagan to name just a few.

Most notably trailblazer Patricia Roberts was applauded as the first British designer to bring hand-knitting to contemporary fashion. She not only produced knitwear but also opened the first shop of its kind in London in 1976 selling her knitwear, pattern books and also her own ranges of luxury yarns. Her books set a new precedent for knitting publications too using fashion photography to promote hand-knitting as highly fashionable. In an interview for the Victoria and Albert Museum (V&A), Roberts describes how Fassett first became aware of her designs and the impact it would have on his own creative knitting, referring back to his first knitting experience on the train from Scotland to London: 'He told me how that seeing a young girl on a train knitting the "Grapes and Cherries" sweater from one of my early books inspired him to design his own knitwear.'[15] Unable to source suitable natural fibre yarns, designers developed collaborations with yarn producers such as Rowan Yarns. Others such as Roberts produced their own yarns, with Patricia Roberts Yarns and Woollybear Yarns, for customers to knit her designs. Silks, mohair, mercerized cotton as well as cashmere, merino and angora yarns all became available in multiple colours specifically to produce designer hand-knits. There were others also, such as Sasha Kagan, a knit and crochet designer who in 1974 created her first hand-knitted commission for Alice Ormsby-Gore (the then girlfriend of Eric Clapton who was also photographed in Gibb designs for British *Vogue* in 1970 and *The Telegraph Magazine* in 1973),[16] establishing her handmade knitwear business and selling her debut collection to Browns in South Molton Street, London.

Contrasting the dominance of fast fashion today, the 1970s saw many with skills in dressmaking, mending and repair, as well as knitting which had been passed down from mothers and grandmothers enabling them to customize, adapt and make their own 'designer' clothes using bought patterns.

Figure 6.7 *Drawing of top and skirt for* The Daily Telegraph *Autumn/Winter 1982 pattern offer. AAGM Collections: ABDMS070419.*

Through the publication of designer knitting patterns, DIY fashion was made possible for those unable to afford a designer piece of knitwear in being able to knit their own. These patterns were made readily available in women's magazines and newspaper supplements where Gibb produced several knitting patterns providing a more inclusive and democratic opportunity for those to own their very own Gibb knitwear. The first of Gibb's knitting patterns was published in 1974 for *The Sunday Times*' 'Look!' column. More soon followed in other publications including *Vogue Knitting* and *The Daily Telegraph*. As Gibb's business faltered in the late 1970s, collaborating with magazines and newspapers with knitting patterns became a valuable income stream in the early to mid-1980s (Figure 6.7).

As Avril Groom who commissioned Bill Gibb for her 'ADD-itions' series in *The Daily Telegraph* comments:

> I had been a big fan since I was at college — I had those original *Vogue* pictures on my wall, so it was a real joy to work with him', she says. 'I can't believe we actually published knitting patterns in the newspaper — usually linked with a company like Rowan Yarns — so that readers could knit themselves an original Bill Gibb.'[17]

As Turney highlights, 'To knit a designer sweater connotes personal investment in that designer or brand, as well as the ideology or "personality" such a designer or brand affords. The ordinary (knitting) becomes extraordinary.'[18] Further, in her book *Folk Fashion, Understanding Homemade Clothes*, Amy Twigger Holroyd refers to the term 'folk', as clothes making by individuals, often amateurs creating clothing not for commercial gain but for their own personal satisfaction, for themselves to wear or as a personal gift for those close to them. Holroyd further argues that the 'slowness of making offers benefits in terms of sustainability because it slows consumption and also builds emotional attachment, which prompts us to keep wearing our homemade items over an extended period'.[19] Gibb's work relates to this ethos as his interest in collaboration with artisan makers to create high quality legacy pieces together with enabling other types of consumers to 'make their own' Gibb has led to treasured and collectable pieces that still exist today. In NJ Stevenson's chapter, 'Souvenirs of style: a web of memory association' for this publication, NJ discusses the curation of the Fashion and Textile Museum 2008 exhibition, 'Billy: Bill Gibb's Moment in Time', where the narrative evolved around the lender's emotional attachment to his clothing, ensuring the continued preservation and wearing of his work prescient with new thinking today around fashion and sustainability.

Conclusion

Gibb's knitwear today continues to be recognized as groundbreaking where his collaborations with Fassett, Boulton and Gould's of Leicester produced innovations in techniques, patterns and garment shapes that helped to pave the way for future generations of designers specializing in knit to push the boundaries of possibility. Today's interest in knitting undoubtedly stems from these pioneering designers in the 1970s who repositioned knitwear as contemporary design, making it fashionable for a new generation of consumers. The availability today of a myriad of coloured and textured yarns and hand-knitting patterns transformed perceptions of knitwear as being plain and old fashioned and made new innovations possible.

Simultaneously, other designers in Europe were transforming machine-manufactured knitwear into high fashion statements. In Italy the Missoni family developed technological innovations that are still today core to their business and brand identity. In France designer Sonia Rykiel also paved the way for fashion knitwear with her iconic, skin hugging finely knitted and colourful garments, which became synonymous with the 1970s, and heralded her as 'the queen of knitwear'.[20]

A revolution in knitting indeed happened during the 1970s which Gibb was very much a part of. In the 1980s many of these British designers became household names producing and publishing designer knitting patterns and all-in-one kits with yarn, needles and materials. Their legacy continues today with trendy businesses, activities and events that have emerged in the twenty-first century such

Figures 6.8 and 6.9 *Black throw with multi-coloured fringing and coat dress with electric-blue trim from the Autumn/Winter 1976 Byzantine knitwear collection. AAGM Collections: ABDMS023987 and ABDMS023986.*

as 'Wool and the Gang' established in 2008 at the forefront of a new hand-knitting craze together with a plethora of knitting cafes and festivals and celebrity knitters.[21] The user-driven website Ravelry, supports inclusivity as a social media platform for amateur and expert knitters across the world with in the region of a million subscribers that share information including patterns and yarns.[22]

In terms of Gibb's own knitwear — some of which is still available today as vintage wear, some over fifty years old — they remain contemporary pieces often worn by celebrities and influencers today, as well as on permanent display and in museum archives. For instance, in 2019, British celebrity Rita Ora wore a Gibb knitwear ensemble from his 1976 Autumn/Winter Byzantine collection (figures 6.8 and 6.9). Their attraction today possibly lies in that they were and continue to be both highly fashionable whilst also being comfortable and wearable. *The Daily Telegraph* writer Ann Chubb remarked how 'only someone who has actually owned a Bill Gibb knit can appreciate the gap they fill in a wardrobe. Their rare blend of comfort and practicality, together with their astonishing, yet subtle mix of colours enable them to be worn from morning to midnight'.[23]

Gibb's final knitting project prior to his untimely death in 1988 focused on a book of vintage Hollywood knitting patterns which could be seen as a return to his childhood passion for glamour, history and costume.[24] The book reproduces iconic Hollywood stars' knitwear for a contemporary audience including designs worn by Judy Garland and Gary Cooper. Throughout the book, his fashion illustrations re-interprets each pattern as a contemporary design, a skill he retained throughout his short career of reflecting backwards and forwards to create a lasting legacy of work that is still of significant relevance today.

British *Vogue*, January 1970

Whatever the Hippies have done,
they have given new freedom to fashion.

Exclusive to Fortnum and Mason,
Bill Gibb's latest collection
is a great rainbow garden –
a patchwork of earthly patterns.

> *On this page,* what happy anarchy:
> a floaty flower-printed blouse
> and intarsia-knitted waistcoat
> above a sweeping skirt of tartan pleats
> in muted shades of blue and green
> bordered by further flower power.

Below, rebel in a check polo neck
and matching shooting jacket
edged with cream and cobalt blue.
Or, *opposite,* shock in a tartan smock
and Fair Isle jumper tied together
by a scarf fringed with rust and beige.

> *Next page*, a magpie assemblage:
> a caramel suede maxi under a coat
> of soft chamois, trumpet-sleeved
> with leather thongs and amber beads
> strung together to decorate
> its tiny-bodiced Mediaeval shape.

Make ready for this new decade
of organised fashion anarchy
in multi-patterned fusions
tailored in glorious confusion.

Poem inspired by:
Ernestine Carter, 'The Mixture as Never Before', *The Sunday Times*, 21 December 1969.
Anonymous, 'Glorious Confusion', British *Vogue*, January 1970.

Figures 0.5 and 0.6 *Dress for Baccarat in 1969 combines patterned prints, checks and florals with leather thongs.* AAGM Collections: ABDMS023985.

Part Two

Gibb's Fashion Legacy

This section opens with the author of *Bill Gibb Fashion and Fantasy* (V&A, 2008), Iain R. Webb, providing new insights into Gibb's impact and legacy on the catwalk show through an exploration of his solo and group shows, including his seminal Autumn/Winter 1972 show at The Oriental Club filmed for the BBC, and the Royal Albert Hall retrospective fashion show in 1977 which brought together a spectacular array of British celebrities from this time. As extravaganzas, Webb posits that Gibb was one of the greatest fashion showmen, paving the way for later designer such as Christian Lacroix, Alexander McQueen and more recently John Galliano couture collection for Maison Margiela to name just a few.

Following her curation of the 2008 exhibition, *Billy: Bill Gibb's Moment in Time*, NJ Stevenson explores how her methodology provided personal perspectives on Gibb's legacy through a 'web of memory association' which also provided a narrative of the fashion industry in the 1970s. She describes designing the exhibition to focus on the embodiment and provenance of his designs, exploring their production, consumption and value at a time when British fashion was not the global industry we see today, bringing new meaning to Gibb's work.

Stevenson's chapter is followed by 'Stories from the Aberdeen Archives, Gallery and Museums' collection', an interview with curator Morna Annandale which provides further examples of how personal stories related to donated Gibb garments bring new light to his design legacy in Scotland and beyond.

Madeleine Marcella-Hood et al.'s chapter explores Gibb's legacy in the age of social media. They discuss how his creative legacy continues through being shared and co-created via online platforms such as Instagram where contemporary issues around environment and authenticity are re-examined, informing and educating new audiences, whilst also interpreting how his original designs are still relevant today.

Karen Cross's chapter, 'From Gibb to Gucci: how folklore fashions comfort in turbulent times' focuses on the physical and psychological aspects of Gibb's designs that were central to his design principles and have relevance today as trends in clothing have changed. Cross discusses their wearability and their adaptability in terms of both comfort and practicality, and also connects Gibb's design interest in folklore and 'romantic eclecticism' with Gucci's 2020 collections where looking to the past and comfort nostalgia is seen as the antithesis of our modern technologically-driven culture. It ends by reflecting on how folkloric practices such as Gibb's encompass a more sustainable ethos.

The Oriental Club, 26 April 1972

From the tip of her well-coiffured head
to the soles of her platform shoes,
Kellie's always ready to jump on a jet
whenever a camera clicks
in some faraway place.

This Highly Individual Face
left The States and ditched her degree
when some guy in Chicago
threw stardust in her eyes, saying,
'You should be a model babe!'

Being black Cherokee,
some designers are scared
of people staring at her skin
instead of the fancy clothes she's in,
but Billy knows better.

As a coat billows behind her,
Kellie glides up the catwalk
in a special treat for autumn-winter:
a crepe dress edged with lace
that she spreads wide like wings.

And next her circular skirt swings,
as her marabou and ostrich hat –
feather boa to match – drips
with velvet ribbons, glass beads
and fabric flowers made of suede.

To finish, she's the minx in lynx,
hand-painted on a white wool dress
with leg o' mutton sleeves – and dangling
from her neck, suede and leather strings
hang toward her python-skinned shoes.

Between shoots and shows,
she's just a Blue Jean Kid
who enjoys needlework
to keep her mojo flowing –
some petit point, some heroin.

But there's no better kick
than audience applause
to make her feel like a goddess.
Especially when she hears them say,
If only I could walk that way.

Figure 0.7 *Multidrawing of coats, tops and knickerbockers; Autumn/Winter 1972. AAGM Collections: ABDMS070169.*

Poem inspired by: Frances Horsburgh, 'It's "Cool" Being a Top Model', *The Herald*, 26 April 1972: 8.

7

The show must go on: was Bill Gibb the greatest showman?

Iain R. Webb

Anna Piaggi, *Vogue Italia*'s late great fashion editor, once enthused that Bill Gibb's fashion shows were the hot ticket in London. She said: 'Bill created such a beautiful atmosphere on the catwalk.'[1] No ticket was hotter than Gibb's spectacular Royal Albert Hall retrospective staged in November 1977, billed as a ten-year celebration. The evening, a charity event in association with World Wildlife Fund and Royal Lifeboat Institution, had a showbiz mood from the get-go, with actors Anthony Valentine and Gerald Harper in leading roles.

Kate Franklin, Gibb's PR and longtime collaborator, contacted the designer's faithful celebrity clientele, including actresses Lesley Ann Down, Eileen Aitkins, Angharad Rees and Una Stubbs, and invited them to model their own Bill Gibb frocks on the catwalk. 'Which was a great mistake,' said Franklin, 'because although it was absolutely wonderful, you couldn't get them off the stage.'[2]

Another model for the night was Lesley Ebbetts, then Fashion Editor at the *Daily Mirror*. 'It was a huge surprise when Billy asked me. I think he'd just opened his Bond Street shop and I was there doing a story about it,' she remembers, 'and this dress came out and Billy said he wanted me to wear it in his show'.[3] Ebbetts immediately dropped the story about the shop and organized a photo shoot featuring her modelling the dress (Figure 7.1) and everything leading up to the night. The dress Ebbetts was to wear was a white silk Qiana jersey evening gown with fluted cuffs, complex pleating down the front and decoration in the form of tiny beading. 'It had a life of its own,' she says. 'It moved so well on the catwalk. I took it back to shop and Billy said you must have it. I still have it.'[4]

The show also featured musical acts including pop singer Linda Lewis, Arlene Phillips' Hot Gossip dance troupe and The Orchestra of the Royal Marines School of Music along with the rather odd addition of punk poet John Otway. A particular highlight for a teenage Hamish Bowles, now *Vogue* magazine's Global Editor at Large, and the Creative Director at Large of *World of Interiors*, was ballet

Figure 7.1 Daily Mirror *fashion editor Lesley Ebbetts in a Qiana jersey dress with shell motif from Gibb's 1973 collection ahead of his 1977 retrospective. Photo: Trinity Mirror / Mirrorpix / Alamy.*

dancer Wayne Sleep's hilarious performance dressed as Olympic gymnast Olga Korbut. 'He channelled her, obviously in drag, flicking his unitard and tossing his perfect pair of pigtails.'⁵

Bowles had long been a fan of the designer and was excited to attend the show. 'As a schoolboy I was possessed by the glamour and invention of his designs,' says Bowles. 'And in the announcements of his tenth anniversary show, there was the promise of untold splendours being unveiled in the splendid setting of the Royal Albert Hall. I did everything that I could to secure a ticket. I was up in the gods, but it gave me a great view. [The show] ended with a cascade of balloons, black, white and yellow for the bees that fluttered across Bill's clothes, in fragile little enamelled buttons or alighted on his shimmering embroideries. Magic.'⁶

Later, in *American Vogue,* October 2005, Bowles would reference Gibb in his review of the Autumn/Winter 2005 Haute Couture shows in Paris: '[Christian] Lacroix's imagination melded shapes and prints evocative of seventies London design gods like Bill Gibb . . . with the lush palette and opulent fabrics of the religious icons of the High Renaissance art.'⁷

Ebbetts remembers how guests such as Bowles sat in boxes or regular seating around the auditorium while celebrities and models, who were a part of the show, sat around the stage-cum-catwalk at little

Figure 7.2 *Cindy White backstage at the Royal Albert Hall in 1977 wearing a lurex dress from Gibb's 1973 collection. Photo: Niall McInerney / Bloomsbury Fashion Photography Archive.*

cabaret-style tables. When not modelling for the designer, Ebbetts attended all Gibb's collections. 'I can't ever remember a dull show,' she says.[8]

British *Vogue* reported that during this retrospective show Gibb also unveiled his Spring/Summer 1978 collection along with his 'first luscious lingerie'.[9] 'I've always wanted to design the sort of peignoirs that women dream about,' Gibb told the *Daily Telegraph*: 'Beautiful lingerie you could wear as evening dresses as well.'[10] *Drapers Record* reported that the show also featured, 'half-naked men draped in bed linen.'[11] This was another new range designed by Gibb that featured broderie anglaise and his trademark bees in lace.

Running at over four-and-a-half hours, it was a show that edged fashion into the arena (quite literally) of entertainment. To put this in perspective, eight years later, 'Fashion Aid', which was the fashion industries response to the LIVE AID fundraising concert for famine relief in Africa, was staged at the same venue. 'Fashion Aid' featured thirty-four designers including international giants such as Issey Miyake, Giorgio Armani, Calvin Klein and Yves Saint Laurent, and over five hundred models.

Throughout his career Gibb took part in many such high-profile group fashion shows including 'Designs in Fashion', staged by the British Overseas Trade Board at the Royal College of Art in 1973.

In 1976 he featured in a 'Best of British' fashion show, presented by Prudence Glynn, then fashion editor of *The Times* newspaper, at Chatsworth House in Derbyshire; the event was televised by ITV. In 1980, Gibb was among the line-up of designers in *A Faerie Tale* at The Park Lane Hotel in aid of The Maria Scleroderma Therapy Trust, befittingly billed as an 'Evening Journey into the Realms of Fantasy and Imagination'. Other lavish charity events included shows for the National Playing Fields Association and Variety Club of Great Britain.

In November 1972, *The Evening Standard* newspaper reported on a 'fashion spectacular' at Les Ambassadeurs Club in Park Lane, which Gibb participated in alongside John Bates (for Jean Varon), Jean Muir and Zandra Rhodes: 'They could have staged it twenty times over and still had standing room only. Such collaborations between rival designers is rare in this country – and unimaginable in Paris. But then, this particular quartet have such formidable, such individual talent that they can afford to be friendly.'[12] In an article in *Over 21* the following February, Gibb noted that the Les Ambassadeurs show was for raising profile with overseas buyers. 'And it showed that four young designers could get along together without bitching,' said Gibb.[13]

Despite the camaraderie and obvious success of such outings, the designer was most happy when staging his own shows. 'He loved to see his clothes on a catwalk,' confirmed Franklin.[14] However, a catwalk show is a big budget production. At that time, Franklin estimated that just producing a collection could cost between £20–30,000 with sizeable show costs on top. 'In England we're not good at finding people to back things like that,' said Franklin, 'which is a shame because Bill was a good showman. I think the best at the time.'[15]

Following the Albert Hall gala show, which Gibb referred to as 'an act of hubris', the designer's business experienced financial collapse.[16] Undeterred by these financial difficulties, the yearning for a catwalk show became the devil on Gibb's back. So, in 1985 he returned to London Fashion Week, unveiling an Autumn/Winter collection called 'Bronze Age'. The designer explained: 'I think the Bronze Age . . . is reflective in the apparel of the young people in the streets, their arbitrary mode of dressing . . . fighting to retain individuality.'[17]

This statement mirrors Gibb's own fight to retain his personal artistic vision while fashion itself had moved on to Power Dressing and Body Con styling. It is telling that Suzy Menkes' selection for Dress of the Year 1985 at Fashion Museum Bath was a black and gold figure-hugging strapless dress by Bruce Oldfield. The following year Colin McDowell nominated Giorgio Armani's neo-masculine, wide-shouldered Italian tailoring.

While Gibb's 'Bronze Age' presentation appeared out of step – the show being deemed 'over-produced' by Bernadine Morris in *The New York Times*[18] – a review in *The Washington Times Magazine* titled 'English Eccentricity Reigns', was more favourable: 'Quality workmanship was evident at a glance in the intricate garments.'[19] The writer also listed an abundance of hair extensions, false gold eyelashes and gold lipstick. Other reviews noted Gibb's fabrications: cork juxtaposed with metallic leather and lamé.

Figure 7.3 *Gibb travelling with Kate Franklin. Courtesy of Iain R. Webb.*

Model Michele Paradise, who appeared in this show cocooned in toga-like garments that wrapped around her body, says: 'I feel very lucky and honoured to have gotten to work with him. He did not so much direct me on the catwalk, but he said: "Be yourself. Be as dramatic as you want to be. Be fabulous!" When you are a model, you are rarely seen as a person. He treated me as a friend, not an object for his creativity, and that stood out. After working for him people were very impressed. It showed how revered and loved he was.'[20]

Paradoxically, it was another ex-St Martin's graduate, John Galliano, who was receiving plaudits for his plundering of the past in a show called 'The Ludic Game', and with just as much fake hair and over-the-top accessorizing. Galliano has admitted to being a big Bill Gibb fan. Certainly, the way in which they both conceived and visualized the total package demonstrated a shared approach to fashion design. Fashion writer Brenda Polan acknowledged: 'For a designer like John Galliano, it was never just the clothes, it's the whole show – the roof tops of Paris, etc. – the *mis-en-scène*, like when we'd sit on little sofas and we'd kind of be part of a 1930's cocktail party. For John it was the whole performance. The whole concept.'[21]

Down the years, Galliano has continued this immersive approach to his shows: his Spring/Summer 2024 couture presentation for Maison Margiela provoked euphoric reviews. The showmanship was totally captivating, from an illusionary film directed by Baz Luhrmann to the choice of location, which one journalist described as 'a rancid Parisian nighttime joint with bare floorboards, cafe tables, dim mirrors, and a bar overflowing with spent drinks.'[22] An opening performance was provided by singer Luc Bruyère, aka Lucky Love, accompanied by a gospel choir while the closing look was modelled by actress Gwendoline Christie.

Gibb's shows were equally multi-layered, often involving other artists. His Autumn/Winter 1974 show opened with singer Brenda Arnau, while a later show presented at the Hyde Park Hotel in March 1977 (Figure 7.4) featured pipers from Glasgow and Inverness, c/o British Caledonian Airways, playing 'A Scottish Soldier (The Green Hills of Tyrol)', previously popularized by singer Andy Stewart.

Throughout his career, Gibb presented collections in glamorous venues around the world including New York, Singapore, Nairobi and Yugoslavia (where the designer was given the key to the city of Trogir). In 1977 he was invited to participate in a Best of British Fashion show at the British Embassy

Figure 7.4 *Autumn/Winter 1977 Ready to Wear show at the Hyde Park Hotel. The dress features embroidery by Swiss company Jakob Schlaepfer. Photo: Tim Jenkins/WWD/Penske Media via Getty Images.*

in Paris. However, while Gibb was constantly travelling, he loathed flying. 'It's one of my phobias,' he told Caroline Baker in *Ritz* newspaper, admitting he took 'a little pill before I go . . . it's yellow.'[23]

Despite this phobia, the designer audaciously staged an in-flight fashion show on the new Air France Airbus. He told a reporter, 'I'm afraid of flying but we were so busy it didn't matter'. The reporter noted how 'Fashion models stalked the aisles.'[24]

One of those models was Cindy White, who says: 'The craziest [show] was . . . the inaugural flight of the Airbus from London to Paris for all the executives and sponsors. That was a tight squeeze, to say the least, and with all the champagne not to mention turbulence there were a few unintended lap dances.'[25]

White fondly remembers the sense of close family that Gibb created, 'which was all down to his natural warmth and sincerity. He was probably the kindest person I encountered especially being a newbie [model] and very nervous. Although, he did drop me in the deep end at the first show I did for him at the old Covent Garden by giving me the finale outfit – a beautiful red feathered jacket. I came out [onto the catwalk] to the March of the Toreadors from Bizet's Carmen. It was a baptism of fire for sure, but with his encouragement and also from the other models who had kindly rehearsed it with me – there were a lot of steps to descend in heels – I somehow managed to pull it off.'[26]

'I remember working alongside other models including Ike, Selena, Hazel, Carina Frost, Gaby Longhi and Annabel Hodin. There would be no more than ten girls at the most in each show, so we always had many changes in those days. It was all about making the best show with often the tiniest budget, but we would all go anywhere anytime for Bill.'[27]

Gibb's seasonal catwalk shows were meticulously planned from models and location to the musical soundtrack. Kaffe Fassett, Gibb's then partner remembers: 'Billy's shows were so exciting . . . there was just a theatricality . . . and you just went home with these images pierced on your brain.'[28]

For Gibb, it was always about putting on a show. Being a designer was far from just a job for him. In 1976 he spoke of his relationship with his backers and how they wanted him to go more commercial and into mass production. His backer offered him his own car, a flat, a raise in salary, everything he wanted. Gibb chose to leave: 'I never want to be anything but my own master as far as design is concerned,' he said.[29]

Gibb's desire to design beautiful clothes and to see those designs on a catwalk or magazine cover showed little regard for commercial potential – a mindset shared with his contemporaries. 'People didn't care about being a brand, being global,' confirms Manolo Blahnik, another Gibb fan. 'We only cared about the shoe or the dress. I remember how wonderful it was, the excitement – going to parties for the dresses. We only worried about doing something fabulous, not thinking about money.'[30]

It is this thread that runs deep through the DNA of British fashion designers and connects Gibb to present-day practitioners, whose only focus is the creative pursuit to push fashion forward, regardless of financial stability. Gibb's enduring relationship with the catwalk show has become a template for

British fashion designers down the decades. To extend the discussion and better understand Gibb's deep-rooted obsession, it is useful to examine the modus operandi and motivation of contemporary fashion designers, specifically two with a shared Scottish heritage: Pam Hogg and Alexander McQueen. Hailing from Paisley near Glasgow, designer Pam Hogg has long been a fixture at London Fashion Week. In recent years her ethos highlights the potent motivation behind staging a show every season despite having no ready-to-wear retail outcome and 'zero financial structure' for the production of her designs. 'It's my platform for expression and a way to allow my ideas to evolve,' she explains. 'I love having a goal to work towards.'[31]

While this reasoning might sound extremely pragmatic and professional, for Hogg the inspiration runs deeper:

> I feel I'd die if I didn't get to show . . . It feels unfinished if it's not in motion. I use the catwalk as my canvas . . . I can stand back and look at a piece for days . . . There is, of course, a point where the deadline won't permit me to work further. It can be frustrating, but it gives me time to reflect and refresh my ideas and I can't wait to get started all over again even though I'm completely broken.[32]

Gibb's sister Patsy recalled how even after a hugely successful show Gibb always thought he could have done better.[33] 'It's the artistic side of things that just about kills me as I work so intensely on every single detail,' says Hogg. 'I just let my ideas flow hoping at some point a financially stable person will recognize the potential.'[34]

Yet those wished-for financial backers are not always the answer. In 1980, Ian Jack wrote a story in *The Sunday Times* titled 'Rags to Riches to Rags', which highlighted the reality. 'The fashion business is notoriously undercapitalized. Its glamour has often attracted backers who see quick returns in the odd combination of publicity and novelty . . . even serious investors are not immune.'[35] Jack goes on to focus on Gibb's own problematic relationship with funding:

> Here the potential designer would do well to study the Bill Gibb story. Over the last ten years Gibb has had two backers, men who made money in pop music, art galleries and property. Both were experimenting with the fashion business and both experiments failed. Everyone agrees Gibb is the most talented creator of sumptuous, if sometimes fanciful clothes . . . his shows in the mid-seventies became extravagant social occasions. Yet . . . today he is starting again.[36]

The late Alexander McQueen is still feted as one of the most celebrated and influential designers of his generation whose legacy continues to inspire. Fiercely proud of his Scottish ancestry – McQueen wore full Highland regalia to accept his CBE in the Queen's 2003 honours list, while his ashes were scattered in Skye – the designer often referenced and made political comment around his heritage, explicitly in shows such as 'Highland Rape' (Autumn/Winter 1995) and 'Witches of Culloden' (Autumn/Winter 2006). Central to McQueen's design ethos were these dramatic, performative shows.

Katy England, McQueen's former right hand, stylist and longtime collaborator, acknowledges that for the designer the show itself was the main event and how his working process confirmed this: 'Once he had the bones of a show idea together, he could then progress with the clothing design,' says England. 'Designing the collection and designing the show ran along, side by side, but of course the scale and possibilities the show space offered a whole other world to what could be achieved with the clothing.'[37]

England also recognizes how McQueen could not really become properly excited about his collection until he could visualize it as a show. She remembers how, 'Lee [McQueen's given name] always wanted an extra wow factor and had a clear vision of what could work beautifully in his show environment and to complement his selling collection. There are so many examples of the incredible pieces made only for a spine-chilling show moment – from Mr. Pearl with his minute waist parading down the runway in 1995 at "The Birds" show, to the razor clam dress created for the 2001 Voss show, to Shalom's white cotton trapeze dress being sprayed by robots in 1999. Each show has many examples, and I believe these really special pieces were the things Lee loved to create the most.'[38]

Even though McQueen's often controversial vision at times presented a harder, more confrontational edge, his designs also reflect Gibb's love of historicism, a realm of escapism accessed by designers during uncertain economic and politically unstable times. In 1985 Gibb told the *Edinburgh Evening News*: 'Reality is so horrific these days that only escapism makes it bearable at times.'[39]

'For sure Lee was a designer who was led by his heart,' continues England. 'He allowed himself to dream and the show and collection was created with his fantasy narrative at the forefront of his mind. He wanted to create shows that would entertain, provoke and at the very least cause some sort of emotional reaction in people . . . The minute the show was done he'd be calling up Sam Gainsbury [McQueen's show producer whose job it was to turn the designer's concepts into a reality] the very next day saying he'd got the idea for the next one.'[40]

It was these same creative tensions that fuelled Gibb. And these same conversations continue in fashion colleges and art schools around the world and are perhaps now even more relevant for young designers as they try to balance the need of the consumer and commerce with their desire to not only function as creative artists, but also address questions of ethics and sustainability.

Gibb shared this uneasy relationship with fashion: 'I . . . live these clothes, day and night . . . But, in the end, when I see them, I really don't like them, I'm too close to them. I think "how indulgent, what does it all mean? I shouldn't be into this exotic trip". But that's just the Scottish puritan upbringing in me!'.[41] Even more tellingly, in an interview with *The Clothes Show*'s Jeff Banks, Gibb revealed, 'I always hated showtime.'[42]

This feeling is familiar on both sides of the catwalk. As a fashion editor there can be times when you will tire of the four-week-four-city fashion circus. The travelling from one side of the world to the other, racing between show venues only to wait for over an hour or more to watch a show that lasts less than ten minutes. However, all this is soon forgotten when a designer transports you into their world

Figure 7.5 *Gibb backstage at the Oriental Club ahead of his April 1972 show. Photo: Evening Standard/Hulton Archive/Getty Images.*

with what is known as 'a fashion moment'. I count myself extremely blessed to have been witness to many such moments. There is one 'moment', which I wish I had experienced.

In my eyes – and perhaps for Bill too – his debut show, staged at the Oriental Club in London's West End, was probably his most exciting and memorable of all (Figure 7.5). Fortuitously, the show, or rather two shows (one in the morning and one in the evening), were filmed by BBC TV for a documentary series called 'All in a Day'. It makes remarkable viewing and gives insight into the peculiar cocktail of one part glamour, two parts chaos that makes for a fashion show. Director Keith Sheather's shooting script reveals:

> 9am. Five models arrive, [Ike, JJ, Kellie, Priscilla and Kay], each girl has her own mirror in the Dressing Room.[43]

Model Kay Tench (then Brooker) remembers how she 'adored working with Bill and loved wearing the outfits. They always felt so good on the body with a feeling of pure luxury and quality. His shows were always fun, and I enjoyed working with Kelly whom I met through Bill, as she would always do his shows too. Kelly was a mix, I think, of Native American and African American so we were kindred spirits at that time.'[44]

9.15am-11.00. Hair Styling done by Christopher at Vidal Sassoon. Each girl does her own make-up under supervision of a make-up girl.

9-11am. Library and Ante-Room: Flowers arranged, Seating checked, Food and drink laid out. Guest list checked. All supervised by Kathleen Franklin.[45]

There is a slot in the schedule for a photo call with Suzy Menkes, then Fashion Editor of *The Evening Standard*. At the end of the documentary Menkes is filmed telephoning through her review to the newspaper copy takers: 'Bill Gibb . . . rocked the fashion world.' [46]

11am. Guests arrive – approximately 75 invited to Morning Show. These will include the following to be picked out for special attention by the cameras: Twiggy, Diana Rigg, Suzy Menkes, Ernestine Carter.[47]

Other journalists, including Beatrix Miller, Grace Coddington, Michael Roberts, Janet Street-Porter and Caroline Baker, were joined by photographers Cecil Beaton, David Bailey and Tony Snowden.

11.15am: SHOW: there are approximately forty garments to be shown in the collection . . . each garment will be modelled for one minute to accompanying music.[48]

The soundtrack for the show included songs from the musical 'Godspell', Gilbert O'Sullivan's 'Alone Again Naturally' and 'Floy Joy' by The Supremes, all hand-picked by Gibb.

At mid-day the script just reads:

REACTION – Bill presented to audience – champagne – buffet.

Gibb later told photographer Mick Rock: 'The people in the audience have always been absolutely tremendous. You always know when it's going right, because you get a surge of warmth coming from them. It's a marvellous thing to feel; that they're there, digging what you're doing.'[49] There is no documentation to confirm if the show actually ran to this schedule although, as anyone who has ever attended or been involved with a fashion show will tell you, this is highly unlikely.

Of that debut show Gibb told *Women's Wear Daily*: 'I want to paint a picture – I'm catering to girls who want individuality.'[50] That sense of uniqueness still resonates, and Gibb's clothes are still seen during showtime, not only influencing the catwalk of designers such as John Galliano, Giles Deacon, Charles Jeffrey, Matty Bovan and Lowena Chopova, but his actual designs being worn by A-list guests on the front row. Supermodel Kate Moss, at Louis Vuitton menswear, January 2015 (Figure 7.6), and musician Roisin Murphy at the Royal College of Art Graduation Gala, June 2009, both favoured the same vintage Susan Collier 'Lovat' print dress from Gibb's Spring/Summer 1974 collection.

Figure 7.6 *Kate Moss arriving at Louis Vuitton Menswear Fall/Winter 2015–16 in the 'Lovat' print dress from Gibb's Spring/Summer 1974 collection and a 'Gibb for Philip Hockley' fox fur and suede coat. Photo: Pierre Suu/GC Images.*

The dress Murphy wore once belonged to actress Meg Wynn Owen, a close friend of Gibb. Murphy acquired the dress via Steven Philip, fashion consultant, collector and founder of Identity London Ltd fashion resource studio. 'My clients are drawn to Bill Gibb's designs as they need very little explanation. His designs are a staple in my studio,' says Philip, who also provided the Bill Gibb for Philip Hockley fur coat worn by Moss. 'There is an extra-specialness to his designs and part of that appeal is also to do with who originally wore them: everyone knows Charlotte Rampling, everyone knows Elizabeth Taylor and Twiggy and Streisand. If those dresses could talk. I am always wondering where she wore that dress?'[51]

He continues: 'In all my years as a collector I have come across few that are near the level of craftsmanship Bill possessed. He concentrated on all the details. It was almost couture. He didn't repeat himself. His clothes were totally different to Ossie's or Biba.'[52]

A few months after his debut show Gibb returned to Scotland to present the collection to his home crowd. *The Aberdeen Press and Journal* and Aberdeen Milk Marketing Board sponsored three live catwalk shows, billed as 'The Fashion Event of the Year', at the Royal Darroch Hotel. 'He's Coming . . .' ran the headline.[53] The newspaper noted there were 500 guests at each show, paying a ticket price of 45 pence for a two-hour long production, which they deemed, 'The fashion that stunned the North.'[54]

'In hindsight,' Gibb's mother told me, 'I think it was too ahead of the time for Aberdeen. I don't think they really understood or appreciated it. It took Aberdeen a while.'[55]

Yet it is from his earliest days, growing up in Aberdeenshire, that it is possible to trace Gibb's overriding desire to 'put on a show'. In an article in *Woman* magazine, headlined, 'We Couldn't Have Wished For A Better Son', the writer noted that, 'While other boys climbed trees Bill Gibb's favourite game was dressing up the other kids in the family and posing them in tableaux'.[56] His sister Janet remembers him taking bedspreads and curtains from the house to dress her and her sisters as noble looking damsels.

It is a narrative that was highlighted in *The London Fashion Guide for Spring 1975*. It commented: 'Costume design was his first love, and when he carried it over into fashion, the result was some of the most incredible creations ever to appear on or off stage. They combined fantastical elements of all periods and styles, invited comparison with Poiret in his heyday, and won him the Vogue award as Designer of the Year ... the climax came with the famous "map dresses" [High Summer and Autumn/Winter 1971 – see Figure 7.7 and Figure 7.8], vaguely Renaissance in period, completely Gibb in style, and the closest thing to the Greatest Show on Earth that a dress will ever be.'[57]

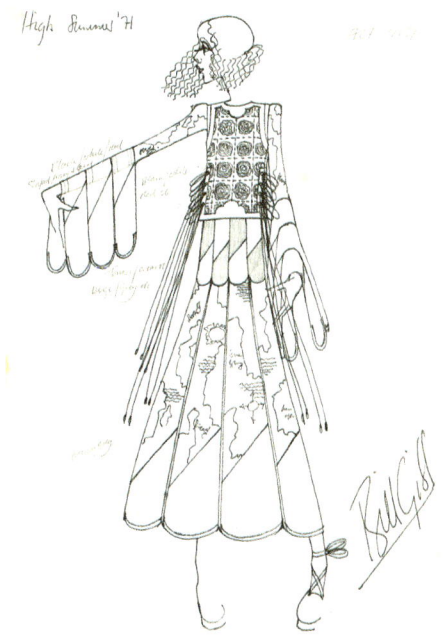

Figure 7.7 *Drawing of top and skirt with map print for High Summer 1971 collection. AAGM Collection: ABDMS067520.*

Figure 7.8 *Detail from 1971 Bill Gibb for Baccarat ensemble: satin printed with red and grey sixteenth-century world map. Courtesy of Kerry Taylor Auctions.*

An editorial in *Vogue* magazine in November 1977 promised that Gibb's Albert Hall show would be 'no ordinary fashion happening';[58] with guest appearances from Fenella Fielding and Twiggy alongside Lewis and Sleep, 'it would take a lot more razzamatazz than that to upstage the outfits themselves,' noted the writer, who went on to highlight, 'the immensely complex designs, the hundreds of ideas that go into every dress.'[59] Another journalist writes, 'Bill Gibb's designs are not so much clothes as lavish productions.'[60]

'He loved that we loved his dresses and appreciated them, and you appreciated by wearing them,' remembers Lesley Ebbetts. 'For Bill the show was the thing, but the showman part was all in the design. He was 100% into the creation. It was all about the creativity.'[61]

In September 1972, Gibb told *Flair* magazine: 'I surround myself with books – Bellini to Bosch to Erté to history of the plant kingdom . . . I like to design clothes with a lot to them, clothes one's continually discovering new things about . . . Gosh, I didn't know that was there!'[62]

'They were really about fantasy, they were fantastic clothes,' says fashion designer Jasper Conran, who was a one-time assistant of Gibb's in the late 1970s. 'They were really, really gorgeous things. Women adored them because those dresses did all the work for you.'[63]

Ever the showman. Perhaps, after all, Gibb didn't need a catwalk or fancy venue, the models, hair, make-up, over-the-top accessories, Wayne Sleep or the Royal Marines orchestra? Perhaps, the reality is that the show was there all the time in the dresses that Bill Gibb designed.

8

Souvenirs of style: a web of memory association

NJ Stevenson

Introduction: arm in arm

In May 2008, I spent several days in New Pitsligo, Aberdeenshire, looking through Bill Gibb's personal effects. My research journey had first started in 2006 at the home of the model Jan de Villeneuve, who I had been introduced to for a previous project. De Villeneuve had pieces from many designers who she had been friends with and worked for during her time modelling in the 1960s and 1970s, but it was her collection of Bill Gibb garments that was so breathtaking in its abundance. I knew of Gibb's work from dramatic images in 1970s *Vogue* editorials, but De Villeneuve's collection, seen in her home, was a complete wardrobe, documented by surrounding family photographs – her enthusiasm for this designer who had produced such a body of work and who she remembered so fondly was inspiring.

Gibb's belongings had been stored in the home of his parents in Scotland since his death in London in 1988 at the age of 44. In stark contrast to the huge piles of knitwear, prints, silks, taffetas, fine wools and embellished garments that I had seen at Jan de Villeneuve's home, there was none of the richness of texture and opulent folds of fabric in Gibb's own belongings. His sister Patsy Davidson had told me that, on visiting her brother in London, she had been astounded at the sparseness of his flat, remarking, 'He didn't have anything – he never had anything.'[1] The material traces of Gibb's life's work were papers, photographs and drawings stored in boxes in a bedroom. On the bookshelf I found a copy of a 1969 edition of Remy Charlip's *Arm in Arm*,[2] and in this American children's book I found the colour and complexity of design that I associated with Gibb's work. The visual poetry is comprised of unexpected combinations that are captivating and delightful. One poem, 'Part Tree Part Cloud Part Sun Part Water Part Mountain',[3] is an illustration of those components joined with a rainbow colour gradient to make a strange object of natural elements, which reminded me of Gibb's signature multi-referential style. Of the possessions the Gibb family lent for the Fashion and Textile Museum 2008 exhibition, *Billy: Bill Gibb's Moment in Time*, it was the subtitle of Charlip's book – *A Collection of Connections, Endless Tales, Reiterations, and Other Echolalia* – which seemed a fitting description of the narrative that emerged through engagement with the exhibition participants and lenders.

Exhibiting a web of connections

I was not the first researcher to visit New Pitsligo. Former Aberdeen Archives, Gallery & Museums Manager, Christine Rew, had spent hours there preparing for Bill Gibb exhibitions at the Aberdeen Art Gallery in 1998 and 2003 and the corresponding publication, *Bill Gibb: The Golden Boy of British Fashion*.[4] Iain R Webb, writer and curator, had also been there not long before me, researching his book, *Bill Gibb: Fashion and Fantasy*,[5] and an exhibition which opened at The Fashion Museum, Bath in 2009, which he curated with dress curator Rosemary Harden.

Each exhibition had been initiated through different factors: Rew was well placed in Aberdeen to celebrate a success story of local talent and worked to acquire a comprehensive Bill Gibb archive for Aberdeen Art Gallery. Webb had been inspired by Gibb in his youth and had been approached by Kate Franklin, Gibb's former business partner to work on the project. The Gibb proposal I developed for the Fashion and Textile Museum had come out of my MA Fashion Curation final major project at London College of Fashion and had resonance with the institution's twentieth-century exhibitions policy and the fact that the museum had been founded by a contemporary of Gibb's, Dame Zandra Rhodes. The timeframe and narrow budget margin of the Fashion and Textile Museum precluded making an exhibition comprised of institution loans, necessitating an alternative approach.[6]

In order to help amass a collection of garments that put together a narrative of Gibb's work, Jan de Villeneuve put me in touch with other people connected to Gibb who she knew also had pieces. A spider's web of friends and colleagues started to come together. The research journey became a quest, often tracing people who had lost touch with each other. Gradually it became clear that Gibb's personality had inspired loyalty and people felt very strongly about remembering this person they all called Billy. Many lenders had a personal connection to Gibb as well as to their garments and other objects – samples, letters, cuttings, sketches, and the enamelled bee brooch that Gibb gave all his friends – were personal mementoes which meant more to them than their material worth. People were continuing to wear their clothes, or had passed them on to their daughters, so not only were they a reminder of the designer and shared times, but thirty years later the garments were still existing in the present. By constructing an exhibition from personal collections, the pieces included also came with personal stories as their owners were concerned with contributing to the recognition of their much-missed friend.

Figure 8.1 *Bill Gibb for Baccarat suede dress made for Liz Taylor in Billy: Bill Gibb's Moment in Time, Fashion and Textile Museum, 2008. Courtesy of NJ Stevenson.*

Memory in museum clothes

Fashion curators often employ a mixed methodology touching on museology, memory studies and fashion curation theory to help them make sense of telling stories with clothing.[7] For the Bill Gibb exhibition at the Fashion and Textile Museum, the research framework was shaped organically as lenders came forward to offer their pieces. Engaging with clothing is one of the most emotive ways to stimulate memories that are stored within them with each layer of wear;[8] Raphael Samuel writes of memory as, 'an active, shaping force', saying it is 'dialectically related to historical thought, rather than being some kind of negative other to it'.[9] The memories of the lenders were activated by engaging with their garments in the context of lending them to the museum as part of a retrospective, seeing them in a different light. In this way, their memories enabled me to contextualize their loaned garments and shaped the narrative of the exhibition. The Gibb pieces that had been kept as part of a private wardrobe were material souvenirs of another time.[10] The function of these souvenirs was to tell Gibb's story in 2008 and, as Gibb was no longer able to tell this himself, the testaments attached to the lent garments brought them to life, adding another layer to my research. However, the nature of piecing together a collection from a web of connections meant that only the stories of those involved were included. Curatorial decisions that shape a retelling of history have been criticized as, 'dictating what should be remembered and what forgotten',[11] but Dennis Nothdruft, Head of Exhibitions at the Fashion and Textile Museum, sees the approach of making private collections public as, 'adding interest', and giving opportunity for an 'alternative narration'.[12] This method of curatorial practice had resulted in a way of showing fashion where the object choices were determined by what people had kept, combining traces of other lives with that of the subject of the exhibition. The 'active shaping force' of memory produced an emerging portrait of a well-loved charismatic man who surrounded himself with a loyal clan of people. Their testaments started to reveal a narrative of how the fashion system worked in London at that time: a closely bound network which often blurred boundaries between life and work, combining creativity, excitement and a sense of drama with an element of chaos.

It was this piecing together of a non-encyclopedic composite collection of personal stories and cherished garments that had been worn on so many different occasions that gave me the idea of the title of the exhibition – *Billy: Bill Gibb's Moment in Time*.

The institutions that did lend to the Fashion and Textile Museum exhibition were the two most connected to Gibb. Gibb's sister Patsy supported Fraserburgh Heritage Centre to lend the wedding dresses Gibb had designed for his sisters and a 1969 Baccarat tan suede printed two-piece. Aberdeen Art Gallery lent three ensembles which were mounted behind glass and included the Ascher tweed dress that Kate Franklin wore at the 1972 inaugural Bill Gibb Ltd show at the Oriental Club. Franklin, by now elderly and keen to have Gibb's memory preserved, was supportive and instrumental in finding pieces. Her dress was contextualized by her appearance in an episode of the BBC documentary series *All in a Day* focused on Gibb, titled 'The Collection',[13] which showed Franklin at work during the 1972 catwalk presentation and which was one of several films playing in the main gallery during the exhibition. The first section of the exhibition was called, 'Vision', illustrating how Gibb combined elements to create unexpected and arresting combinations in one garment.

The main instigators of the connections were Patsy, De Villeneuve, Franklin and knitwear collaborator Kaffe Fassett, as well as a group of people associated with the Fashion and Textile Museum, many of whom knew both Gibb and Zandra Rhodes. So eager were people to help that we were able to amass an exhibition collection of many key pieces from Gibb's career from the wardrobes of private lenders. We took the decision to include extracts from lenders' testaments on the outfit labels rather than using the curator's voice, giving the story authenticity, and giving ownership to the community who had facilitated the exhibition. Jenny Dearden, former wife of Small Faces guitarist Steve Marriot, lent several ensembles including a marbled-leather and crepe two-piece and a Qiana jersey sequinned 'shell' mini dress which had been modelled by Charlotte Rampling (alongside a leopard) in *Harpers & Queen* in February 1973. Part of the caption quoting Dearden read:

It was a much smaller world in those days, where you inevitably all crossed paths at some point. I bought all my things from his studio. The shell dress was originally long but it got muddy at the hem. I remember wearing it in Japan when Steve was playing there and it being admired by Kansai Yamamoto. I think the marbled leather outfit was a one-off, probably a sample.[14]

Provenance of the objects like this added to the narrative. Lenders were not just the wealthy, but others connected to the fashion system: models, technicians, shop staff, industry professionals. Peter Wright, Gibb's assistant pattern cutter, also lent several pieces including a suede 1971 Baccarat dress which had been made for the actress, Elizabeth Taylor. The dress is printed with the same swallow motif used for the Renaissance-inspired gown that Gibb designed for Twiggy to wear to the premiere of Ken Russell's film *The Boy Friend* in 1971. However, according to Peter Wright, Taylor's dress 'was never finished because it didn't suit her'.[15] (Figure 8.1)

The engagement with the lenders avoided a 'greatest hits' approach, revealing – as with Wright's testament – the complex path of commerce. It is known that Gibb was not able to sustain the success of his label. Including information on the provenance of each item of clothing, the exhibition provided a picture of production, consumption and value. As a whole, it pieced together the story of an alternative community of support in a time when the infrastructure of the British Fashion Industry was less corporate.

Interview material revealed how Gibb's circle of friends were able to collect so many of their pieces. Among De Villeneuve's mementoes was an invoice for a blouse that she had bought from Gibb for a fifty per cent discount. She had been friends with Gibb since 1973 when she, 'met Billy doing a show with Thea Porter in Yugoslavia'.[16] Over time, she became concerned at the lack of business acumen: 'I did feel that something should be done. The company was not working commercially'. She explained that,

> In the summer of 1978 I helped Billy with a week-long sample sale, ringing all my friends to come round. I was paid in clothes so managed to expand my wonderful Bill Gibb wardrobe with many special outfits that I still treasure. It was always an inspiration to spend time with Billy, such a lovely man and talented designer.

Sally Pasmore, the partner and studio manager of the photographer John Adriaan, was also a close friend of Franklin and Gibb, and shared similar concerns:

> I got some of my Billy clothes when he went bankrupt for the first time – I rescued them and brought them back to the studio to sell off to try and make them a bit of cash and from then on had a sale every time he went under. I collected a lot of his old stuff from Harvey Nicks that hadn't sold when they wanted to put new stuff in the store. It was really a network of mates. We knew Justin from photographing Twiggy and used Jan a lot to model. There was the most amazing goodwill around Bill and Kate . . . All his friends bought his clothes wholesale; it was the opportunity to buy,

but we were walking adverts – that was Kate's justification for letting us have them at wholesale. I've never worn any other clothes where I've been stopped in the street.[17]

Franklin's career had been in publicity and she also struggled to meet the gap in business knowledge that Gibb lacked from his fashion design education and had no interest in addressing. Pasmore voiced the frustration that she felt at the time:

> Kate was instrumental to the setup. Billy could be quite careless. I think careless is a good word for him. He was totally disinterested in the running of the business. He just didn't find marketing very interesting. He really was just interested in designing. Certainly not selling at Harvey Nicks. He didn't turn up for meetings. You could almost say that he sabotaged things as a way of making a point that he wasn't interested in the business – he was completely unmercenary.[18]

It could be said that putting together the exhibition collection began to mirror the way that lenders relayed to me how Gibb had navigated the fashion industry in the 1970s. Goodwill and loyalty became important factors, reflected in a willingness to assist and a warmth for Gibb's memory.

Figure 8.2 *Custom-made wedding dress made for Irene Andrae at the Fashion and Textile Museum, 2008. Courtesy of NJ Stevenson.*

The process was friendly, creative, chaotic and informal: as people came forward to be involved, the word spread overwhelmingly quickly. The strategy of collecting testament developed naturally – these were stories that interested me and I thought would interest other people. A telephone call to the museum from Barney Wan introduced us to his friend, Irene Andrae. Chinese-born Andrae had been due to marry in London in February 1970 and needed someone to make her a traditional red tunic and long pleated skirt. Wan, then Art Director at *Vogue*, suggested Gibb. The deciding factor for Andrae was that she could afford Gibb as he was relatively little-known at the time. Gibb hand-painted the heavy moss crepe with flowers and incorporated the chequerboard pattern into the design which was characteristic of his early work for Baccarat. Andrae was photographed in the dress for *Vogue* by David Montgomery. Now divorced, she donated the dress to the museum (Figure 8.2).[19]

Wedding dresses were a constant of Gibb's design output (Figure 8.3). Meaningful to their lenders, they often came with personal stories. Gibb's sisters' dresses were his wedding gift to each of them, although they 'weren't given much say in the style'.[20] The daughter of Roald Dahl and Patricia Neal, Tessa, had commissioned a coral-pink taffeta wedding dress from Gibb. They had drunk champagne on the morning of the marriage and he had told her stories to make her laugh as she got dressed to

Figure 8.3 *Section featuring Gibb's sisters' wedding dresses alongside Tessa Dahl's pink taffeta dress. Courtesy of NJ Stevenson.*

calm her nerves; later Gibb had remodelled the dress for a ball.[21] A silk dress for Dahl's friend Charlotte de Klee was hand-blocked with a butterfly print by Janet Taylor in 1985. Gibb's only design brief from Charlotte's mother was that the bridal gown should disguise the fact that Charlotte and her husband Rupert had already started their family.[22]

Tales of exchange

Gibb would clearly have been happy working on a couture basis with private clients, but this would have been hard to sustain within the structure of the British fashion industry in the 1970s. As well as offers of knitwear – one of Gibb's most successful commercial ventures designed in collaboration with Fassett – the most frequently offered pieces to the exhibition were the Qiana jersey pieces, Gibb's interpretation of Hollywood glamour combined with the contemporary slinkiness of disco. These were a mainstay of the Bond Street shop: working late one night with the television on in the background, I turned round to see Joan Collins wearing Gibb's Qiana in *The Stud*.[23] Several of the lenders had worked in the shop and had kept many pieces, but I was rarely offered clothing that had been bought from other luxury stores in London. Ann Barr, who had been Features Editor of *Harpers & Queen* and Women's Editor at *The Observer* offered a tiger print green coat which she had bought in a second-hand shop in Notting Hill. Barr told me a story about crossing the road one day when,

> a man shouted from a car, 'That's a lovely coat.' I said, 'I know, it's by Bill Gibb.' He said, 'I know, I am Bill Gibb.'[24]

The contribution was late, but Dennis Nothdruft and I decided to include it in the display because we felt that the story had resonance with the way that the exhibition had come together.

A further last-minute addition came by way of Olive Campbell who had telephoned offering three mini-dress ensembles from 1968. While still at the Royal College of Art, Gibb had been commissioned to design a collection for the Henri Bendel department store in America. On his return, Gibb left the RCA before completing his scholarship and set up the Alice Paul Boutique with three student friends. The shop was situated next to Biba in Abingdon Road, Kensington and was open for just one year. The labels in the outfits read, 'Alice Paul designed by Elphinstone Gibb' – Elphinstone being Bill's middle name. They had been lent by Olive Campbell for Gibb's tenth anniversary Albert Hall show in 1977 and were still on the Bill Gibb hangers on which they were sent back, with the tags bearing the names of the models who wore them. Campbell had inherited the outfits from her friend, beauty writer Willa Beattie, who had been given them by Annie Russell who had a hairdressing business in World's End and knew Gibb.[25]

Provenance of some of the loans could not have been anticipated. In Aberdeen, I went to the home of Liz MacKinnon to pick up an animal-print pile skirt, black crepe jacket and pale blue moss crepe

Figure 8.4 *Cut out of Clive Boursnell show photography. Courtesy of NJ Stevenson.*

Figure 8.5 *Adel Rootstein mannequin wearing gold lace dress custom-made for Meg Wynn Owen. Courtesy of NJ Stevenson.*

dress from the first Bill Gibb Ltd 1972 collection. These had been bought from a boutique in Inverness owned by Evie Grant, Gibb's aunt.[26]

Display

By the beginning of October, we had thirty-three lenders and many more people who had come forward who had known or worked with Gibb. The proliferation of garments could have presented a problem for the design of the exhibition, but we found that the museum's circumstances inadvertently presented us with a solution. The Fashion and Textile Museum had closed after a shortfall of funds and had recently been sold to Newham College of Further Education. In its first incarnation, the museum had borrowed mannequins from Adel Rootstein, but they had been returned. The sheer volume of clothing, the tiny size of some of the garments and the insistence of some lenders that they were displayed in a way that showed the movement of the clothes, meant that we had to devise an inexpensive hanging system so that we could include more pieces and make them look less static. The open display meant that we could use hangers suspended from the ceiling so that the volume of the garments was demonstrated and denoted finding them in people's wardrobes. The exhibition designer was Stacey Williams who incorporated many visual references to Gibb's work with elements of art deco, the chequerboard, the peach and mirrors of the shop fittings, and we carried that over to the text and brochures. Factual information was written as a fairytale, and we used lines from nursery rhymes and contemporaneous songs of the 1960s and 1970s to evoke the different sections. Music was an important element in the fashion shows, and a playlist of these songs and others played in the gallery.

Williams used illustration to reinforce the storybook feel, interpreting editorial images in a mural on the gallery walls, which also avoided having to pay copyright for photography use that the museum could not afford. However, the photographer Clive Boursnell had photographed Gibb's fashion shows and allowed Williams to use some images to make life-size cut outs, because she wanted to achieve 'a sense of walking into a really fabulous party'.[27] (Figure 8.4)

The Fashion and Textile Museum was the right home for this exhibition. Dennis Nothdruft had worked for Rhodes ever since she had opened the museum, was familiar with the way that her generation of creatives operated and had a naturally flexible approach. The institution did not have a rigid structure of regulations and Nothdruft was open to suggestions and keen to facilitate an exhibition that reflected Gibb's vision. He secured the loan of two original 1970s mannequins from Rootstein, made up to resemble the models from the Oriental Club 1972 show. One of the mannequins was seated on a swing in the centre of the gallery wearing a leather coat from a large collection owned by Ann Chubb, the former *Daily Telegraph* Fashion Editor, which was donated to the museum by her family (Figure 8.6). Williams and I wanted to convey the fantasy, fun and originality of Gibb's work and the mixture of the glamour and the pastoral, and so Williams also made a forest of birch trees in the gallery. The other mannequin was dressed in a gold variation on a design from the Spring/Summer 1976 collection loaned by Meg Wynn Owen an actress who was a close friend of Gibb's. The dress had been made for her as a present and the mannequin's wig was a long red Rapunzel plait falling from the upstairs mezzanine into the gallery below.[28] (Figure 8.5)

The knitwear was on the other side of the mezzanine gallery. Kaffe Fassett had allowed me access to his entire archive. We wanted to show how the knitwear collaboration was borne out of his and Gibb's partnership and we included Bill's sketch of Kaffe, lent by the Gibb family, made on a trip to America in 1967. Each season there was an entire knit wardrobe made up of interchangeable pieces of different patterns and colourways. The exhibition was offered a huge amount of knitwear which kept arriving. In order to demonstrate the myriad combinations of pieces, and to show how people had responded to the exhibition, we made the decision to keep adding to the display throughout the exhibition run.

Figure 8.6 *Image of whole gallery at the Fashion and Textile Museum showing Adel Rootstein mannequin on swing wearing leather outfit. Courtesy of NJ Stevenson.*

Williams placed framed photographs of lenders with Gibb within the murals on the walls to contextualize their pieces and added other ephemera as clues to the story. During my visit, Gibb's mother, Jessie, had made mince and tattie soup for lunch which had been a favourite of Bill's.[29] Patsy typed the recipe for me and we added this to the display. Many pieces in the exhibition incorporated a nostalgia for the homeland with heather shades, pastoral motifs and mixes of plaids and tartans. Gibb's work seemed to draw a fairytale thread between the London fashion world and a remote part of Scotland with its own identity and spirit. Stories from friends verified how Gibb combined those two entities: Twiggy arriving at the farm in a Rolls Royce; the models staying with Gibb's parents for a fashion show in Aberdeen; Kaffe Fassett inspired by the colours of the highlands and learning to knit on the train.

Conclusion: this is not the end

The narrative of *Billy: Bill Gibb's Moment in Time* developed into a London fashion story of the 1970s, but the subtext was how Gibb's warmth inspired a sense of belonging. Using the testament of participants who had known him demonstrated how Gibb formed a club of people of which the membership was the bee brooch.

Much of Pasmore's, De Villeneuve's and Franklin's clothing which incorporated the recognizable bee motif was included in a section in the exhibition entitled 'Friends', which was contextualized with memory, and in Pasmore's case, a contact sheet:

> Billy was one of John [Adriaan]'s favourite people to photograph – he was elegant in his ancient clothes and relaxed with the camera so that John was able to take lovely revealing pictures. Our favourite is the one where Billy is smirking at John in a conspiratorial way wearing an old dress shirt with frayed cuffs. Looking at the set of contacts it brings Billy back to life – reinforcing the memory of the sweet and complex person he was and how we all miss him. I had ten years of lovely clothes and fun and laughing a lot.[30]

The way the exhibition came together mirrored the environment which Gibb came from and which he created around him. Franklin had told me, 'When Billy and I were not together at work he would phone me every hour for one reason or another. Then, around midnight, the telephone would ring and he would say "Kate, one last thing..."'[31] The response, as the news of the exhibition at the Fashion and Textile Museum spread, was a souvenir of the way that people had warmed to Billy during his lifetime – an inspiring deluge of contact.

In the archives at Aberdeen Art Gallery, I had discovered that the Remy Charlip book, *Arm In Arm*, was not just a book that Gibb had enjoyed, but a reference for the costumes that Gibb had designed for Charlip's ballet, 'Mad River', at the London Contemporary Dance Theatre in 1974. I had contacted Charlip but did not receive a reply. A week after the exhibition had opened, an email from Charlip's executor, Erika Bradfield, explained that he had had a stroke, but we were welcome to use illustrations from the book in the exhibition as I had asked. We printed the last poem from the book, a multicoloured spread of hands holding a book entitled, 'This Is Not The End', which recursively repeats to give the impression of infinity.[32] The print went into the last section of the exhibition which we called, 'The Cycle' and had pieces which had been bought second-hand, handed down, were from a film costume archive or used as teaching examples. This explained how Gibb's aesthetic had fallen out of fashion for a time, but had once again become influential – by 2008 his work had become collectable, and had provoked those involved with the exhibition to look at the nature of friendships and inherited memory. As a fashion curator, the legacy of the experience was to inform my future practice. The methodology of engagement and listening which contextualized the pieces lent by Gibb's friends, family and associates also provided a web of memory association, demonstrating how clothing can reveal stories of lives as well as work.

9

An interview with Morna Annandale of Aberdeen Archives, Gallery and Museums

Following NJ Stevenson's reflections on curating loaned Gibb garments alongside personal stories for a temporary exhibition at London's Fashion and Textile Museum, the following interview provides additional insights into the provenance of Gibb garments, but from a museum collection's perspective. In April 2024, Josephine Steed interviewed Morna Annandale, a Curator at Aberdeen Archives, Gallery and Museums who cares for the Decorative Art collections of ceramics, glass, costume, textiles, jewellery and metalwork. You can get further curatorial insights from Morna in Chapter 15.

What does it mean for AAGM to hold so much of Gibb's work?

We are very proud and grateful to care for the largest collection of Gibb's work. It seems fitting since he grew up in nearby Aberdeenshire. It is a fantastic resource for exhibitions, displays, educational visits and researchers.

Do you have any stories that you could share about your acquisitions?

We have several garments where we know who wore them, for example the blue lurex dress (Figure 0.1) was worn by the Duchess of Bedford in the 1970s and we have various garments worn by Bill Gibb's manager and publicist Kate Franklin.

The donor who owned the red wool dress (figures 9.1 and 9.2) taught nursery nursing. She told us the story of how she bought the dress, which was displayed in a 'sale' window in a boutique in The Grassmarket, while taking students from Dundee College on an educational visit to Edinburgh in about 1975. She was keen to get something authentically Scottish to wear at her brother's wedding in

Figures 9.1 and 9.2 *Red wool dress with cream trim from Autumn 1973 collection. AAGM Collections: ABDMS076368.*

London. This Gibb dress with the wheat and bee motif fitted the bill. Her one concern was that the dress might be somewhat warm in London at the height of summer. As it turned out, the day of the wedding was overcast and distinctly cool!

The dress was subsequently worn on many special occasions, conference dinners, retiral celebrations, christenings and at a reception in Holyrood Palace. In July 2006 the donor decided the time had come to part with her treasured dress. Feeling that it would be an appropriate addition to the Bill Gibb Collection in Aberdeen Art Gallery, she offered it as a donation. In her own words she wanted the dress 'to have a good home where it would be well looked after' and felt it was right that it should 'return to the roots of its inspiration in the North East.'

What is your favourite acquisition in the collection?

AAGM recently acquired a suit comprising a tight-fit marbled leather jacket in blue, green, and yellow with an embroidered collar in peach satin, a long skirt in peach satin pleated from a shell shaped

Figures 9.3 and 9.4 *Marbled leather suit jacket and satin skirt (1973) once worn by actress Charlotte Rampling. AAGM Collections: ABDMS095712.1-3.*

panel, and a sleeveless matching top (figures 9.3 and 9.4). It was made in Spring/Summer 1973. This beautiful satin and marbled leather outfit came about after Bill Gibb was asked to provide four examples of his work for a photo shoot for *Harper & Queen Magazine* in 1973, shot by Barry McKinley. Gibb had been asked specifically to create one piece that he believed would be ideal for the actress Charlotte Rampling, who modelled the clothing for the shoot. Gibb is thought to have created the ensemble in one week and is said to have worked nonstop to complete it. On the day of the shoot, he realized that he had nothing to put under the jacket and it is thought he ran up the buttoned satin top in just one hour.

Although the other three outfits featured in the shoot went on to be produced in limited numbers, this satin and marbled leather ensemble is unique. Due to its extreme complexity in design, and high cost, it never went into production.

Are there any dream acquisitions that you would like to see become part of the collection?

I would love to acquire more one-off commissioned garments that have been cherished by the owners and have strong stories about them. In particular, outfits by some of Bill Gibb's loyal and well-known customers like Twiggy and Bianca Jagger. It is an added bonus if we have the corresponding fashion drawing in our Bill Gibb Archive too.

10

Restyled and reimagined: exploring Bill Gibb's digital legacy on Instagram

Madeleine Marcella-Hood, Christina Reid and Peter Reid

Bill Gibb's impact spans a range of audiences, from his hometown of Fraserburgh where his contribution to Scottish textiles and local heritage are celebrated, to global audiences where fashion designers and industry experts admire and remain inspired by his work.[1],[2] His bold and daring designs, which were regarded as progressive for their time, are still described as contemporary today and, in this sense, his contribution to fashion is upheld and protected.[3] Gibb's work is on display in iconic international museums and galleries, including the Metropolitan Museum of Art (MET) in New York, the Victoria and Albert (V&A) Museum in London and local North East Scotland venues, such as Aberdeen Art Gallery and Fraserburgh Heritage Centre.

In the more than thirty years since Gibb's death, the media landscape has changed dramatically. The fashion industry is defined by increasing standards of immediacy,[4] and, as a result, has been much criticized for its detrimental impact on the environment.[5] Although not the focus of this chapter, it is important to recognize this as a significant feature of the broader phenomenon of fashion at the time of writing, which is a pivotal moment for the sector. Visual social media are key platforms for contemporary fashion communication and a significant and evolving field through which to study fashion. Although credited and criticized for their impact, the impact itself is undisputed, particularly in terms of social media having revolutionized and democratized the industry,[6] making fashion more accessible and creating a two-way dialogue between industry insiders and consumers, where the latter are increasingly powerful:

> The thing about Instagram and fashion is that it has absolutely taken down the sense of the velvet rope and has pulled the curtain aside on the entire experience that used to be for a select 100 people

in the world. Now it is there for millions of people to consume (Eva Chen, Director of Fashion Partnerships at Instagram).[7]

Social media have widened access for fashion commentary, criticism and debate. This was initially observable through the advent of bloggers, who attracted much attention from fashion scholars.[8] In the mid-to-late 2000s, when the fashion blogging phenomenon began, these individuals were met with scepticism, but social media influence and content creation have evolved into an accepted and recognized form of labour and an important feature of the contemporary fashion system.[9]

As a result of the shift towards visual content over the written word, and increased commercialization of the platforms they occupy, the role of a 'blogger' has morphed into that of an 'influencer'[10] and since progressed further towards that of a 'content creator'.[11] The shift away from the term 'influencer' recognizes the creative expertise and effort that often goes into producing output for social media platforms and is perhaps also a result of individuals' reluctance to identify oneself as an 'influencer', particularly for those who maintain their platform as a hobby or creative outlet and not for commercial purposes.[12]

Instagram was launched in 2010 as a photo sharing application and very quickly became the media platform of choice for fashion,[13] not just amongst bloggers/content creators, but also more traditional members of the industry such as editors, journalists, stylists, designers, brands and models. Although other platforms exist and continue to emerge, Instagram is still recognized for its significant impact on visual culture and relevance for the fashion industry.[14] This resonates with the thoughts of Iain R. Webb who argues that, during his career as a designer, Gibb created his own visual culture.[15] However, with around 62 per cent of Instagram users aged 34 years and under,[16] the platform is interesting in the context of his legacy, where many users would not have been born during Gibb's lifetime.

An exploration of the #BillGibb hashtag on Instagram in 2024 revealed over 2,000 images had been attributed to the designer. It might reasonably be argued therefore that his legacy is being immortalized, reinvigorated and exposed to new audiences through digital platforms like Instagram.

Digital legacy is a term usually applied to the online data and information left by someone after their death.[17], [18] In the last twenty years this has generally meant the legacy that a person themselves has created through websites, blogs, social platforms and other forms of media. It has become an important facet in connection with inheritance rights both for individuals and online providers, with many providing legacy or inheritance functions.[19] However, an important and significantly different aspect of digital legacy concerns output that is curated or co-created by others; this could relate to people, brands, events, places or circumstances in the past. It is this second interpretation of digital legacy that this chapter focuses on: how a legacy around Bill Gibb's work is created, co-created, re-created and curated in the digital environment, where Instagram is adopted as a field through which to explore the phenomenon.

Figure 10.1 @LauraKitty (Laura McLaws Helms) on Instagram, 2018.

Figure 10.2 @LauraKitty (Laura McLaws Helms) on Instagram, 2016. Photographed by Lisa Candela.

Imagery is powerful and provokes strong, visceral reactions.[20], [21] The way we understand images, the way we react to them and feel about them can reveal important things. Increasingly, as this research suggests, images can also tell us important things about the way we reimagine people, places, objects and/or experiences. Most text and imagery created prior to 2000 was not born digital but, in many cases, have migrated to become a digital asset. Therefore, images and conceptualizations of Gibb's work were not created digitally but have become so both by accident and design, through official and unofficial routes. This enables the near-endless dissemination, repurposing and reinterpretation of imagery surrounding his work. It is added to by co-creators, who can take their own images and add them to the online canon connected with Bill Gibb to reinvent digital exhibitions and collections of his work.

Branding as a theoretical concept has increasingly attracted academic interest and much of the literature in this field focuses on luxury fashion.[22] The literature recognizes that brands are dynamic entities, which are co-constructed with a range of audiences, where recognition is attributed to stakeholders who actively facilitate the co-creation of identity and meaning.[23] This phenomenon is fuelled by the rapid growth of social media where, again, visual platforms are recognized at the forefront and where 'community members', in this case those connected with Bill Gibb, can disseminate attributes such as product information, brand knowledge, expectations, evaluation, usage and experience.[24],[25] Co-creators represent a variety of audiences and can be viewed as collaborative partners, reinforcing and evolving Gibb's contemporary identity and in doing so generating cultural, symbolic and affective value.[26] In this manner, co-creation is seen to arise from strong emotional relationships with a brand, product or, as is also relevant in this case, an individual.[27]

Although branding is not the focus of this chapter and Gibb's legacy is observed more as an individual and creative force than as a business, it is important to acknowledge branding as a lens through which the theory of co-creation has emerged. Branding is a significant aspect of contemporary fashion design and communication.[28] It could certainly be argued that twentieth-century designers like Gibb have helped define modern ideas around luxury fashion branding through artistic originality and consistency.

In order to explore Gibb's digital legacy on Instagram, a qualitative analysis of the hashtag #BillGibb was carried out, to which 2,075 posts had been attributed at the time of writing (May 2024). The research was exploratory in nature and so, rather than confining the investigation to one theory of visual analysis, a more open thematic approach was taken. Three broad themes were uncovered that help illustrate how Gibb's legacy is conveyed on the platform: 1) the reproduction of iconic Bill Gibb imagery; 2) the promotion of vintage garments and retail; and 3) the contemporary reimagination of his designs. This chapter will explore these themes in more depth, with reference made to some of the individuals who are contributing to and co-creating his legacy.

Iconic imagery

An icon is a symbolic representation of something or someone and, in this context, an iconic image is one that is recognizable and has been reproduced across a variety of media.[29] Fashion scholars have long debated the attributes of a fashion icon, definitions of which have been updated over the years to reflect shifting celebrity culture. There is some agreement that in order to be iconic in fashion an individual, artefact, or in this case an image, must translate shared meaning to the viewer, e.g. a visual impact that conveys a particular period in time in terms of style and appearance, and an influence that is culturally as well as aesthetically significant.[30],[31]

This theme applies mostly to the sharing of historic Bill Gibb photoshoots and extends to photographs of the designer himself. A number of these posts feature other icons; for example, Twiggy appears a number of times in the set, shared by different users and most commonly in a photoshoot by Justin de Villeneuve, wearing a 1971 Bill Gibb design. These images are interesting in the context of digital legacy because they add to the narrative surrounding not only Bill Gibb, but also Twiggy. Together they connote a spirit of that time and, in this way, contribute to a shared sense of fashion history.

Iconic images of this sort were shared by a range of users, all of whom might be termed fashion enthusiasts. These individuals describe themselves in a variety of ways, including 'twentieth-century fashion specialist', 'fashion observer' and 'time traveller'. In the captions that accompany these images, words like 'obsessed' are used to emphasize their passion. The images are often described in detail, for example referencing the date, publication and photographer. In doing so, the image is credited to its rightful producer(s), addressing any potential issues of ownership and copyright. These narratives educate and inform other Instagram users, as potential new audiences, on the work and significance of Bill Gibb as a designer, and in doing so extend his legacy.

Gibb's relevance to contemporary fashion is highlighted explicitly in many of these narratives, for example one user observes 'this could be a current shot' when describing an iconic photograph, taken by Clive Arrowsmith for *British Vogue* in 1972. In this image, the model wears a Gibb design and poses side on, causing the snood component of the garment to appear like medieval armour. The leather and armour-like top half of the dress contrasts strongly with softer elements, such as the floral-embroidery detail, the fullness of the skirt and the delicate placement of the model's hand. To researchers and Bill Gibb fans, this image is even more recognizable as it features on the cover of Webb's book *Bill Gibb: Fashion and Fantasy*.[32] Indeed, the book itself appears more than once within the image set and is iconic in and of itself.

Through the reproduction of iconic imagery, it could be argued that Instagram users are co-curating Gibb's digital legacy in a similar manner to which physical venues portray his work. In doing so, they preserve and strengthen arguments about his past significance and impact but, by placing this in the context of the present, the legacy is updated and expanded to new audiences.

Vintage fashion and retail

Vintage retailers and collectors as a group are the biggest users of the #BillGibb hashtag who mostly use this to promote and sell garments. In these examples, a garment tends to be shown in one of three ways: as part of a flat-lay composition (Figure 10.3); pictured on a mannequin (Figure 10.4); or styled on a model (figures 10.5 to 10.8). Often, the garment is photographed in a variety of ways and shown as part of an image carousel or collage, where the viewer can see the garment as a whole and more detailed shots are included to highlight quality, craftsmanship and authenticity. These images provide the functional purpose of supplying buyers with additional pre-purchase information but also work

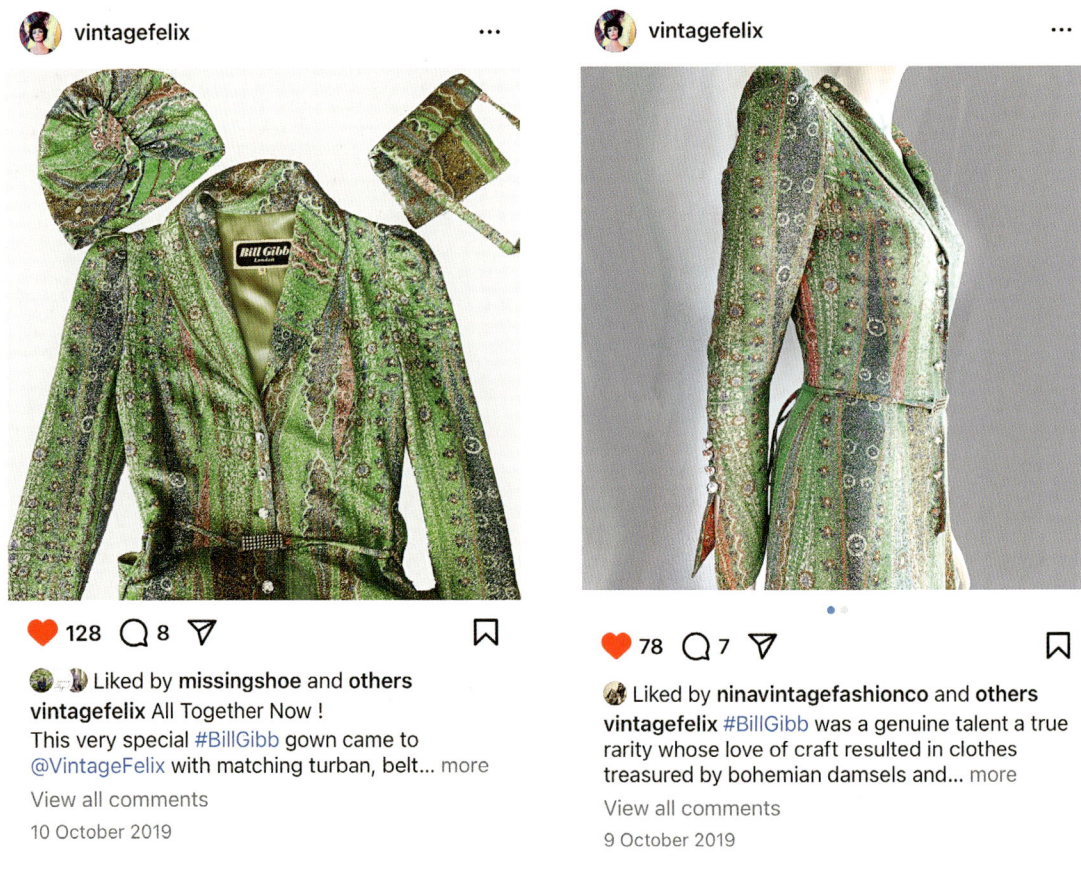

Figures 10.3 and 10.4 *@VintageFelix (Felix Gaona) on Instagram, 2019.*

well to convey Gibb's own attention to detail and imaginative aspects of his designs, for example buttons and embroidery. In most cases, the label is shown to convey that the garment is a genuine Bill Gibb.

'Flat-lay' style photographs are a dominant feature of Instagram as a platform. The origins and definition of 'knolling', which is the art of arranging objects and photographing them in a flat-lay style, such as is illustrated in Figure 10.3, emerged in 1987 and has been popularized further as a contemporary fashion photography technique through Instagram.[33], [34] This demonstrates some of the ways in which Instagram is contributing towards aesthetic culture more generally and how visual aspects of Gibb's legacy are evolved through modern creative techniques. The bathroom 'selfie' (Figure 10.1) is another example of a photography style that was brought to the fore through Instagram.[35]

Vintage retail is recognized as a significant growth area that has great value as a solution to problems surrounding fashion and the environment.[36] Designers like Gibb predate many of the contemporary

Figures 10.5 and 10.6 *@Karen_VintageBoutique (Karen Stott) on Instagram, 2024.*

issues faced by the sector today as well as vintage fashion as an industry in and of itself. Designers and their work therefore take on new emphasis and meaning as conversations around sustainable fashion progress. There are implications here for the legacy of fashion designers more broadly in terms of recognition and impact beyond their immediate career where, as the appeal and value – both material and psychological – of vintage increases, so too might the significance of fashion design as an art form.

Restyled and reimagined

The final theme to be discussed is the reimagination of Gibb's designs through new creative content, where his garments and designs form a key component of these conceptualizations. These are interesting because they not only showcase Gibb's original designs but, in their styling and composition,

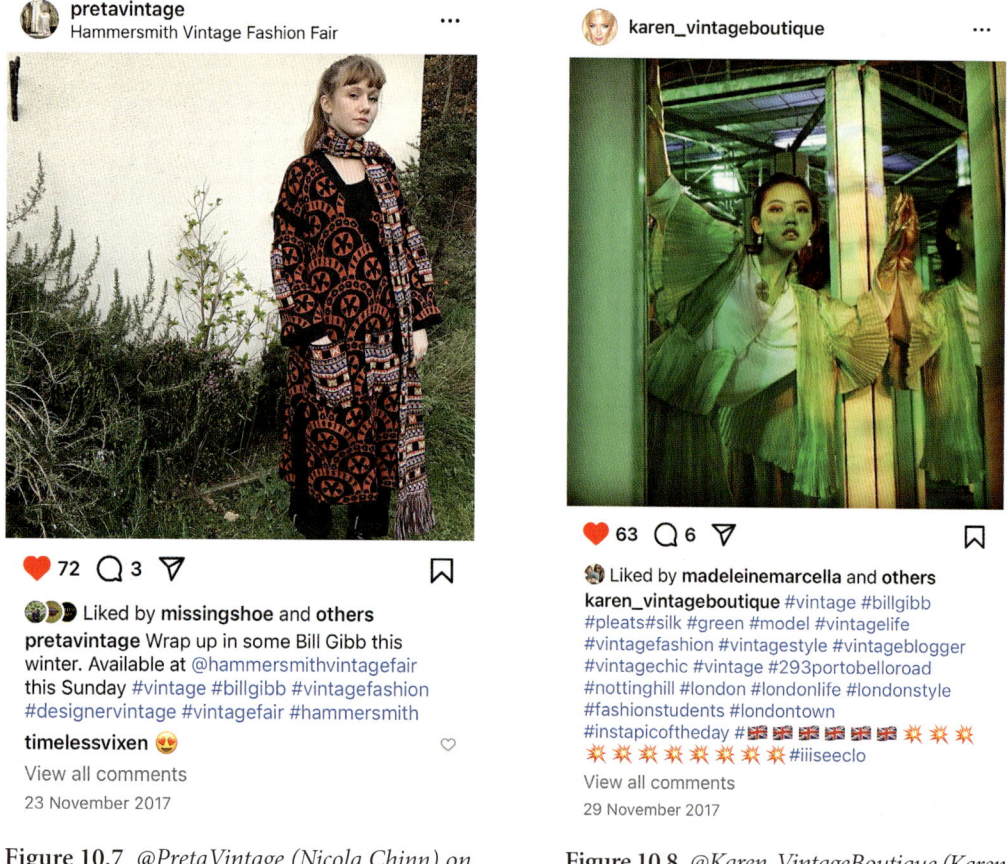

Figure 10.7 @PretaVintage (Nicola Chinn) on Instagram, 2017.

Figure 10.8 @Karen_VintageBoutique (Karen Stott) on Instagram, 2017.

they provide insights into how these are interpreted and imagined today. It is worth noting that, at times, where an image was not known to the researchers, the distinction between historic and current imagery was not always obvious. This further emphasizes the contemporary or perhaps simply timeless nature of Gibb's designs and the mood these elicit to the wearer and the viewer.

The restyled images feature mostly dresses, but there were also jackets, tops, skirts, suits and knitwear in the set. Sometimes these images are styled against a dramatic and/or natural landscape background where the setting appears to form an important and intentional aspect of the image composition (Figure 10.9). Othertimes, these are set against a plain and non-descript background, for example a wall, where the garment and its wearer are at the forefront of the image. Some of these images are shared by vintage retailers and others by individuals who use Instagram as more of a creative outlet through which to explore and showcase fashion and personal style. Words used in captions describing the restyled garments include 'heavenly' and 'dramatic'. One individual asked her

Figure 10.9 *@Vintage_Egyptologist (Colleen Darnell) on Instagram, 2021. Photographed by Mennatullah Hossam.*

followers, 'Can we all just agree that this Bill Gibb would make the most exquisite wedding dress?' Many of the Instagram users who contribute to the hashtag, whether retailers or enthusiasts, do so recurrently, suggesting a greater commitment towards documenting, preserving and co-creating Gibb's legacy – a feature of co-creation that is recognized elsewhere.[37], [38]

Some of those who have contributed to the hashtag more than once were pictured wearing the same garment in different locations and situations and sometimes spanning across years (e.g. @LauraKitty in figures 10.1 and 10.2), suggesting a genuine attachment to the garment and the designer. Indeed, in the process of carrying out this research and collecting the imagery for this chapter, contributors were enthusiastic in their responses, often taking the time to send additional imagery and share their thoughts. In a world where influencer culture on platforms like Instagram and fashion criticism more generally is criticized for being constructed and controlled by corporate motivations,[39] this is refreshing.

Social media is often criticized for aiding if not leading the idea that clothing is disposable and can only be worn and photographed once.[40] With this in mind, users of the #BillGibb hashtag exemplify a

Figure 10.10 and 10.11 *@TimelessVixen (Lauren Lepire) on Instagram 2023. Modelled by Lauren Lepire. Photographed by Douglas Walker.*

progressive and potentially impactful community who place a high value on fashion and clothing and are promoting this to others. Given Gibb himself was regarded as forward thinking, it seems apt that those championing his legacy most vociferously are similarly aligned in this attitude.

An interesting theme in the styling of many of the images was the inclusion of outdoor, natural elements (figures 10.2, 10.10 and 10.11). These work well to convey some of Gibb's more romantic designs and again, in today's world, keep the viewer grounded by highlighting the physical and uninterrupted environment. For those of us based in North East Scotland, these also remind us of Gibb's own rural upbringing and heritage.

Conclusion

This work has stemmed from an interest in the aspects of Bill Gibb's work and life that have emerged through Instagram and the people that are co-creating his legacy on the platform. The findings reveal a digital legacy that is in keeping with the wider fashion and cultural contribution for which he is recognized. This research contributes to our understanding of how a legacy can be preserved and conveyed today, extended to new audiences and made more accessible by those who are co-creating this actively in the online space. Gibb's influence and contribution to 1970s and 1980s fashion is recognized strongly in the digital reproduction of iconic images of his work, mostly in the form of old photographs, which, due to the lengthy descriptions that accompany these, are informative in educating new audiences. His impact is extended to the present, where contemporary issues surrounding the environment and authenticity turn our attention to solutions like vintage retail. Finally, there is a clear desire amongst the most creative users of the hashtag to imitate and honour the style, look and feel of Gibb's original designs and the imagery surrounding these, whilst simultaneously reimagining these in the present day.

11

From Gibb to Gucci: how folklore fashions comfort in turbulent times

Karen Cross

The comfort of fashion

Comfort is an ongoing trend in fashion and lifestyle products,[1] inherent in the ongoing casualization of dress in contemporary Western society and exacerbated by the Covid-19 pandemic and stay-at-home lockdown dressing.[2]

Comfort in clothing can be physical, physiological or psychological. Physical comfort relates to garment fit (e.g. loose or tight), weight (such as heavy fabrics), tactile qualities (smooth, soft, scratchy) and performance (e.g. wicking). Physiological comfort, described as resting or quiet comfort,[3] is concerned with the thermal regulation of the body. Psychological comfort is related to the wearer's values, roles and social being, and the psychological comfort gained from clothing is identified as under-researched in literature.[4] Rew confirms the physical comfort of Gibb's designs, stating: 'Many of his earlier dresses featured giant dolman sleeves, cinched into tight long cuffs; they came straight from the waist and wide square armholes, making the dress unrestricting, effortlessly comfortable and incredibly elegant'.[5] The effortless comfort of Gibb's loose dress styles can, of course, relate to physical comfort, however the psychological comfort gained from being free to move, bend and breathe through daily tasks cannot be underestimated, given how restrictive women's garments have been throughout history.[6]

A 1981 article in the *Daily Telegraph* declared: 'Only someone who has actually owned a Bill Gibb knit can appreciate the gap they fill in a wardrobe. Their rare blend of comfort and practicality, together with their highly creative patterns and their astonishing, yet subtle mix of colours enable them to be

Figure 11.1 *Cream Qiana jersey top and skirt, 1973. AAGM Collections: ABDMS093638.*

Figure 11.2 *Dolman sleeve silk dress, 1973. AAGM Collections: ABDMS071568.*

worn from morning to midnight.'[7] This corresponds with a contemporary desire for cross-over clothing; where women increasingly juggle different roles every day, requiring styles that can be worn to multiple places, situations and events.[8] These provide an element of psychological comfort, or confidence, being one less thing the wearer needs to worry about in their busy and complex life. They also represent a sustainable way of dressing, reducing waste in wardrobes full of clothes that are seldom worn.[9]

Gibb himself hinted at the psychological comfort of his clothes, stating: 'I design with a discriminating woman in mind, probably a career woman with great style and confidence, a woman on the move and in the know, with a vibrant personality to carry the clothes off.'[10] Confidence is a key element of psychological comfort, linked to well-being, a much-discussed topic in current times.[11] The concept of hedonic well-being relates to feeling good through looking good.[12] In a 1974 *Vogue* article, British actress Meg Wynn Owen conveys the sense of hedonic well-being she gained from wearing Gibb's clothing, stating: '. . . they make me feel so good when I want to get dressed up . . . they are so special'.[13]

In addition to hedonic well-being, one can experience eudaimonic well-being – psychological comfort gained from clothes that have meaning.[14] This aligns with a slow design ethos,[15] a carefully considered, holistic approach which leads to an increase in the bond between object and owner; items of clothing that are practical, but that also have emotional and nostalgic connections,[16] that become treasured items of clothing rather than disposable.

The comfort of folklore

The concept of eudaimonic well-being and emotional connection to clothing can be linked to folklore in fashion. Folklore fell out of fashion in terms of academic study early in the twentieth century.[17] Its revival, due in part to English folklore scholars Bennet and Smith in the 1960s and 1970s, coincides with Bill Gibb's work. This revival saw the term 'folklore look' emerge around that time,[18] with youth movements in the late 1960s and throughout the 1970s driving a trend of romantic historicism that focused on crafts and techniques from the past and folk acknowledged as a recurring fashion theme thereafter.[19] Li Edelkoort, one of the world's foremost trend forecasters,[20] emphasized the importance of folkloric influence as an antidote to homogenous and copycat designs driven by artificial intelligence algorithms.[21] In an increasingly digitized and human-less age, the human touch imbues meaning and authenticity to products and brands.[22] Edelkoort describes folkloric design as 'real' and a 'unifier, emblematic of hope', linking it with the reinvention of societies and identities across time.[23] At a time when the very concept of society is struggling, when individual identities are challenged[24] and the fashion industry is under scrutiny for fast, disposable fashion and its role in over-consumption,[25] interest in folkloric design brings renewed currency to clothing styles that embrace meaning, a sense of humanness, history, belonging and longevity. Indeed, folk costume has been defined as a language tool, functioning to communicate attitudes within a community and identifying people with place.[26] Edelkoort champions the future of folklore as a convergence of shared cultural expression, rather than disconnect and division.[27] This contemporary focus on folklore channels the power of nostalgia, a 'sentiment of loss and displacement' and 'longing for a home that no longer exists or has never existed',[28] often involving idealization of the past[29] and a desire for sociohistoric continuity.[30] The relationship between nostalgia and ethnic style encourages creativity, stimulating introspection and powerful emotions.[31] It is said that nostalgia drives the popularity of folkloric imagery, folklore being a way of maintaining whimsy to escape an increasingly cynical and toxic climate.[32] In these uncertain times,[33] nostalgia is somehow 'uncannily contemporary',[34] never going out of fashion. It perceives times that were simpler and safer compared with endemic change at an ever-increasing pace.[35] Fashion psychologist Karen Pine posits that people internalize the characters associated

Table 11.1 *Key signifiers of the folkloric look*

Simple shapes, epitomized by the peasant blouse	Trims of fringes, fur, lace, cutwork and embroidery
Full, dirndl skirts and ruffled or tiered "gypsy" style skirts	Romanticism, evidenced by heart and floral motifs
Corselet-style bodices	Heavy wool fabrics
Short, decorated jackets	Exoticism
Caftans, capes, scarves and shawls, often with decorative borders	Nationalism, evidenced through use of colour and pattern
Boots	Red and black colours, representing blood and earth and evidencing pre-Christian religious practice
Patterned belts and sashes	

with folkloric clothing, leading to the suggestion that: 'In times of change, folklore figures, with their magical, mythical powers, become ones to emulate.'[36]

There is broad agreement in literature on the key signifiers of the folkloric look (see Table 11.1), all of which are evident in much of Gibb's work.[37] Indeed, the European Fashion Heritage Association describe Gibb as one of the best representatives of 'romantic eclecticism',[38] citing his use of past handcrafts and techniques and historically-inspired dresses.

Edelkoort's 2018 categorization of folk looks included the 'Universal Tunic', the 'Square Shape' (e.g. ponchos), the 'Covering Cloth', the 'Farmer's Blouse', the 'Swirling Skirt', 'Legends of Labour' (e.g. workwear, especially in blue), 'Additional Aprons' (echoing labour clothes), darkly coloured delicate lace mourning dresses, 'Folk Flowers', 'Animalistic Adornments', 'Intricate Embroideries', the 'Embellished Mode', regional ribbons and border adornments details.[39] It is worth noting that many folkloric looks are inherently physiologically comfortable (i.e. warm), through the use of wool, fur, layered dressing and scarves and shawls, which can be seen throughout Gibb's collections. Indeed, Gibb asserted that: 'women require layers for daytime'.[40]

From Gibb to Gucci – the comfort of nostalgia (Russian/Cossack)

The 1970s saw ethnic and peasant styles of clothing coalesce into a fashionable folklore look of the time.[41] Gibb's 1974 collection explored Russian Cossack themes. It featured a series of 'gypsy' dresses, 'romantic, full length, with an element of fantasy',[42] echoing folk costume and ethnic dress and using

Figure 11.3 *Gucci Fall/Winter 2008/09, Milan Fashion Week. Photo by Venturelli/WireImage via Getty.*

Figure 11.4 *Drawing of fur coats by Bill Gibb, 1974. AAGM Collections: ABDMS067059.*

furnishing-style fabrics and brocades, topped with embellished fur jackets and coats (see Figure 11.4). Russophilia remained in fashion for several seasons, with Yves Saint Laurent designing his 1976–77 Russian collection, channelling a couture peasant look.[43] Thirty years later, Gucci's Fall 2008 collection (Figure 11.3) was described as a: 'raid on the Russian Cossack folklore department of the hippie wardrobe – the kind of printy, shaggy, peasanty things London groupies picked up at Portobello market in the early seventies . . . rife with references to hussars and the folk textiles of Turkmenistan and Uzbekistan'.[44] The tropes of folklore are easily evident: embellished bodices, fur, tassels, and decorative border designs.

From Gibb to Gucci – the comfort of nostalgia (Gitana/Romani)

Continuing the nostalgia theme, the styles shown in figures 11.5 and 11.6 encompass folkloric fashion signifiers, including the embellished corselet bodice and the layered, ruffled Gitana style skirt, while the black lace trims champion the Maja (female dandy) styles of Andalusian Spain. More than forty years apart, these two examples show striking similarities.

In figures 11.3 to 11.6, the comfort of nostalgia reflects 'temporal connotation', a 'longing for the past', which is idealized.[45] In his 1979 book *Yearning for Yesterday,* American sociologist Fred Davis describes nostalgia as 'a reaction to disruptive and anxiety-producing events', which 'acts to restore a sense of continuity' by looking longingly backwards at comforting images of 'the way things were'.[46]

Davis echoes Bauman's concept of Liquid Modernity,[47] noting that: 'constant change, at all levels and in all realms of social life, seems to be endemic to modern civilisation',[48] perhaps leading to a need for nostalgia as an outlet or safety valve. The more rapid the changes are in society, the more intense the longing for the 'slower rhythms of the past, for social cohesion and tradition'.[49] And that is what these Russian Cossack or Romani Gypsy themes represent – the social cohesion of those specific, visually identifiable cultures as a contrast to an ever-changing, more multicultural world, where identity can be challenging, confusing and disputed.

Figure 11.5 *Drawing of layered lace dress by Bill Gibb, 1977. AAGM Collections: ABDMS067593.*

Figure 11.6 *Gucci Fall/Winter 2020, Milan Fashion Week. Photo by WWD/Penske Media via Getty Images.*

Although 'Fashion has a long history of borrowing from other "exotic" or "primitive" cultures to create new looks',[50] today, the use of folkloric style comes with the risk of accusation of cultural appropriation,[51] with many brands making headlines for all the wrong reasons and making the comfort of nostalgia perhaps a risky proposition. Cultural appropriation is described as someone from a dominant culture taking a cultural element from a minority culture without attribution, compensation or consent.[52] The fashion industry's appetite for folkloric or ethnic styles, an 'attraction for Otherness'[53] is a recurring historical and ongoing contemporary phenomenon, prevalent in both Gibb and Michele-era Gucci designs. Their use of traditional cultural expressions (TCEs)[54] include motifs, patterns, clothing styles and accessories. While the work of both brands can certainly be described as 'independent intellectual creations',[55] in discourse surrounding cultural appropriation there is a tension between creative freedom valued by Euro-American cultures and sense of duty and ethics in re-creating cultural heritage for commercial gain. Gibb and the Gucci designs explored within this chapter are arguably from different eras, and in the time between the folklore-inspired work of each, some countries, cultures and organizations have enacted laws, principles and trademark registrations to protect native culture from appropriation by fashion brands.[56] The development of digital media and its extensive adoption by fashion brands has served both to visualize where copying and appropriation have taken place and to provide a platform for redress which has led to reputational damage for some fashion brands, including Gucci. For example, Gucci's use of a Sikh turban in the Autumn/Winter 2018 collection was criticized as a form of design cultural appropriation,[57] and its 2019 wool balaclava, called out via social media platform Twitter (now X) for its resemblance to blackface imagery, caused cultural offence and accusations of racism, leading to personal apologies from Michele and costly interventions from the brand.[58] Nevertheless, decorative, embroidered and embellished elements of folkloric style were key to both Gibb and Gucci's maximalist aesthetic, with Gibb described as 'a born-again maximalist', who 'broke boundaries and destroyed inhibitions about what could be worn with what'.[59] Similarly, Alessandro Michele's first collection for Italian luxury brand Gucci, was notable for its 'maximalist confidence'.[60] An article on *Vogue Runway* stated: 'He's [Michele] made maximalists of former minimalists and turned the world on to vintage of all eras, cacophonic colour and print'.[61] It is that cacophony of colour and clash of print and pattern that epitomizes both designers. Fashion researcher Jennifer Craik describes this as a form of fashion bricolage,[62] created from a variety of patterns and styles from different cultures, and mixing high fashion and everyday clothes.

From Gibb to Gucci – the comfort of casual (Bohemian layers)

The flared, full skirt shapes shown in figures 11.7 and 11.8 evoke a folklore look and the mix of florals with geometric provides a bohemian clash. Gucci's checked jacket has a woollen, workwear look,

Figure 11.7 *Multidrawing of dresses, tops and skirts, 1972. AAGM Collections: ABDMS067453.*

Figure 11.8 *Gucci Fall/Winter 2020, Milan Fashion Week. Photo by WWD/Penske Media via Getty Images.*

rendered more folk by the frogging-style fasteners and fur border, while Gibb's drawings explore swirling skirts paired with folk tunic tops and voluminous, peasant-style sleeves. Gibb's turban-style headwear and Gucci's snakeskin bag both lend a touch of exoticism to the mix; another folkloric signifier.[63] These styles suggest the physiological comfort of warmth, another signifier of folkloric style, through layering, headwear, and the lofty, primitive textures of knit, wool and fur.

Continuing the casual theme, the looks shown in figures 11.9 and 11.10 pre-empted the Covid pandemic lockdown dressing, representing luxe loungewear. Gucci's Spring 2020 Ready-to-Wear collection's patterned pantsuit is cut in an easy, oversized silhouette with wide sleeves and a nod to 1970s' style when paired with the oversized sunglasses. It is perhaps more structured than Gibb's 1970s knitted pantsuit ensemble, especially with the patent trims and accessories, however both outfits facilitate the comfort of unrestricted movement, in keeping with folkloric garment shapes. They also make use of simplified folkloric motifs inspired by nature and feature contrasting borders at the sleeve ends. Note also the use of black and red (traditional folkloric colours of blood and earth) in the accessories to Gucci's outfit.

 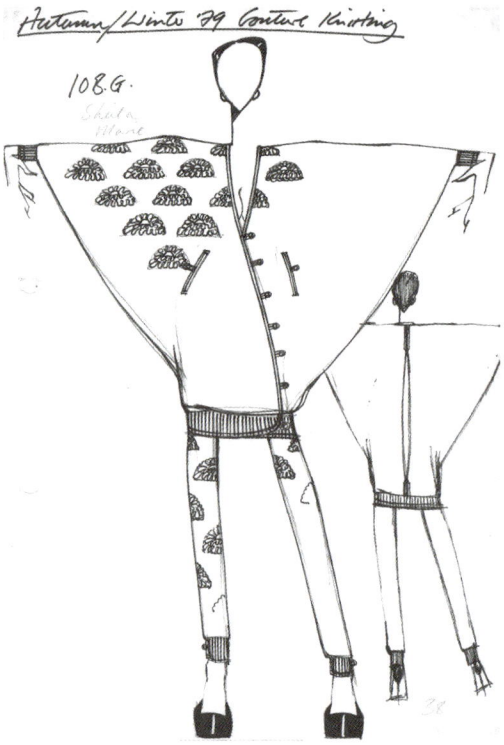

Figure 11.9 *Gucci Spring/Summer 2020, Milan Fashion Week. Photo by WWD/Penske Media via Getty Images.*

Figure 11.10 *Drawing of cardigan and leggings for Couture Knitting collection by Bill Gibb, 1979. AAGM Collections: ABDMS070558.*

Loungewear has been a significant trend in Western contemporary fashion.[64] Traditionally associated with home and relaxation, the continued focus on comfortable dress is linked to the wider well-being trend and is changing norms, with greater acceptance of these styles in public settings and increased casualization in workplace dress codes.[65] If Gibb was perhaps pre-corporate female dressing, it could be said that Michele-era Gucci represented post-corporate female dress. These unrestricting tunic shapes are not just physically comfortable, they provide an element of psychological comfort by skimming the body, offering an element of camouflage.

From Gibb to Gucci – the comfort of camouflage (Universal tunic)

Body image, size, modesty and immodesty continue to dominate dress discourse.[66] Women's dissatisfaction with their bodies, objectification[67] and the fashion industry's influence on the thin-

Figure 11.11 *Gucci Fall/Winter 2018, Milan Fashion Week. Photo by Davide Maestri/WWD/Penske Media via Getty Images.*

Figure 11.12 *Byzantine coat dress by Bill Gibb, Autumn/Winter 1976. AAGM Collections: ABDMS023986.*

ideal[68] are well documented and further debated in both popular and social media. The Universal tunic folkloric shape epitomizes the psychological comfort of camouflage and embraces the cultural construct of modest dress, which has seen some popularity in recent times.[69] It is seen in Figure 11.12, in Gibb's Russian Sarafan-style long overdress (resembling a throw) or poncho, and Gucci's Fall 2018 RTW collection outfit (Figure 11.11), described as 'bolted together from the clothing of many cultures' and featuring 'modest, covered-up folk costume' style dresses.[70] These examples epitomize Edelkoort's description of the tunic as a universal piece of clothing, developed simultaneously in various locations across the globe. Edelkoort sees the Universal tunic as a means to think 'universally instead of nationally'[71] and focus on connection at a time when unity is lacking.

In figures 11.13 and 11.14, the cape shapes skim over the female form, providing the psychological comfort of camouflage. These pleated ensembles channel a folklore look, with their flowing shapes, and feminine ruffle detailing. Gucci's long cape-dress is worn over red gloves and black leather leggings

Figure 11.13 *Gucci Spring/Summer 2020, Milan Fashion Week. Photo by WWD/Penske Media via Getty Images.*

Figure 11.14 *Drawing of pleated jacket and dress by Bill Gibb, 1976. AAGM Collections: ABDMS035647.*

reminiscent of Cossack-style boots. Although feminine, it is structured and contemporary. Gibb's look here is more casual and bohemian, more ruffled and feminine with the pleated jacket worn over a matching dress. Nevertheless, the similarity is striking, with both offering the comfort of unrestricted movement and body cover. These shapes were identified as important in Edelkoort's predictions for the Spring/Summer 2020 season, where she described the 'Square Shape' of poncho styles and the concept of the 'Covering Cloth',[72] hinting at a more camouflaged, conservative dress style where the body is no longer the focus.

From Gibb to Gucci – turbulent times (challenges facing fashion)

Clothes are material in two ways; made of material (or cloth), but also objects, part of material culture. In his book, *The Comfort of Things*, Miller posits that 'people sediment possessions, lay them down as foundations . . . having banked their possessions in the vaults of internal memory, they cash them in at times of need, at times of loss'.[73]

This chapter emphasizes the enduring psychological comfort afforded by folkloric fashion styles, so prevalent in Bill Gibb's work. However, it also serves as a starting point for the exploration of contemporary challenges facing the fashion industry. There is comfort in nostalgia, yet in an era of cancel culture, the tension between cultural appreciation and cultural appropriation sees fashion subject to dispute.[74] Edelkoort's lauding of the Universal tunic, notion of simultaneous similarity and call for unity seems to have gone unheard.[75]

The time of the thin-ideal,[76] body-con dressing and objectification[77] has waned towards a more inclusive period of body positivity[78] and a trend for more modest dress.[79] Even so, the cultural constructs of immodesty and modesty[80] and scrutiny of size continue to divide, driven by social media commentary and judgement. Gibb's modest designs afford cover without overtones of dowdiness, epitomizing the psychological comfort of camouflage as an antidote to ongoing body surveillance.

In an algorithm-driven age of 'speed and greed',[81] the level of detail, design, creativity and craftsmanship in Bill Gibb's work is at odds with mass-produced simple styles, disposable fast fashion and the casual dress norms exacerbated by the Covid pandemic lockdowns and work-at-home culture. Yet, a desire to preserve heritage and prevailing need for nostalgia persists. Folkloric fashion represents slow, sustainable design, providing the opportunity for wearers to gain eudaimonic well-being,[82] or psychological comfort, from clothes imbued with history, meaning and ability to make the wearer feel special. The skills involved in these decorative, embroidered and embellished, fringed and tasselled styles represent clothing and textile heritage across time, worthy of saving and deserving of authentic, respectful and inclusive representation. The ability of folklore to transcend short-term trends presents a sustainable design ethos at a time when fashion is under worldwide pressure to move towards practices that are more balanced, less harmful, and less consumptive. In Bill Gibb's words: 'Clothes have to go on living for a very long time; clothes must be worth keeping'.[83]

Kinsman Morrison Art Gallery, Maddox Street, 30 April 1974

Figure 0.8 *Black and gold knitted jacket and top with pleated gold metallic skirt for Autumn/Winter 1974. AAGM Collections: ABDMS015707 and ABDMS015708.*

Congratulations bovver-booted Bill Gibb
for filling an art gallery full of too many people –
including two Beatles' wives and Bianca Jagger –
and keeping them happy for over an hour.

A leg encased in a striped sock and a boot
now stamps his posters, invitations
and the opening of the show. To follow,
Brenda Arnau set the mood for this collection
by miming to 'Step in the Right Direction'
while covered-up in this season's look:
a polo sweater and kimono-sleeved jacket
in lavender, turquoise, black and bordeaux,
– a knitted tapestry effect by Kaffe Fassett –
all echoed in a skirt in Otterburn tweed,
with even the shoes continuing the theme.

The Don Quixote of the layered look
then piled up sweaters and Dr Zhivago furs,
and cardigans in burgundy and aubergine,
before revealing grand evening dresses
in smoke grey Qiana and the softest of velvets.

To finish, he allied his vast crinoline dress
of two seasons past with his net mantillas of last
in a Miss Havisham look that made Mrs Jagger gasp.

A triumph over commonplace present-day gloom
there was no room to stamp a bovver boot, otherwise
Gibb's final ovation would have surely boomed.

Poem inspired by:

Anonymous, 'Londoner's Diary: a Lot of Bovver', *Evening Standard*, 1 May 1974.

Michael Roberts 'Look!', *The Sunday Times*, 1 May 1974.

Part Three

Reinterpreting Gibb Today

The third section begins with fashion journalist Jeena Sharma reframing Bill Gibb's work through the lens of cultural appropriation given his re-interpretation of designs from a variety of marginalized cultures has gone on to be a rich creative source of inspiration for subsequent fashion designers. Sharma explores this topic in relation to contemporary designers before reflecting back on Gibb's intentions, processes and designs. An interview with Indian musician Asha Puthli, who Gibb designed for in the 1970s, provides reflections on whether Gibb's interest in cultures beyond his own could be considered appreciation or appropriation. This topic is also touched upon by several contributors including Fischer in Part 1 and by Cross in Part 2.

Lynn Wilson's chapter concentrates on the design legacy of Gibb through the lens of sustainable fashion design, construction, fibre and textile selection, and the challenge of creating enduring designs that consumers will care for and circulate. Wilson considers Gibb's pioneering approaches to design and innovation at a time when slower methods of production and consumption were the mainstay and considers how they may contribute to future design as we move towards rethinking about the relationship between fashion and the environment.

British fashion designer Giles Deacon provides the final interview where he talks about first becoming aware of Gibb as a student at St Martins, researching his work, and how he became inspired by Gibb's naturalistic approach to fashion through his Scottish heritage which led to Deacon validating his own research inspiration from his Lake District background. Deacon also argues that Gibb was a 'trailblazer' in his creative collaborations and how his work can still be considered extraordinary to this day.

Following Deacon's reflections on being inspired by Gibb while a fashion student, Shane Strachan and Josephine Steed's chapter discusses the potential benefits of studying Gibb's creative practices within contemporary fashion education through an Aberdeen-based case study: *The Bill Gibb Line*, a student project at Robert Gordon University's Gray's School of Art. They discuss and compare the value of digital resources versus physical archival resources including viewing Gibb's archive collection close up within the collections held by Aberdeen Archives, Gallery and Museums. An exploration of the students' responses to Gibb's work and their subsequent design outputs is shared before being followed by examples of Gibb-inspired postgraduate student projects beyond Aberdeen.

Strachan explores the creative crossovers between fashion and poetry through the research and writing process for his spoken word project *The Bill Gibb Line*, from which multiple poems appear throughout this book. As well as exploring his personal interests in Gibb as a fellow creative from the same town of Fraserburgh, Strachan reflects on his own creative writing process in parallel with Gibb's design methods discussing synergies and inspiration between the disciplines.

12

Bill Gibb through the lens of cultural appropriation

Jeena Sharma

Introduction

Cultural appropriation has acquired the form of a buzzword, weaponized by some to point out the extremities of cancel culture, admired by others to hold everyone accountable for their errors.[1] Widely regarded as a practice where a dominant culture borrows elements and ideas from marginalized cultures without any credit to said culture and often without consent, in fashion, this definition acquires a distinct focus. As noted in the 2023 book, *Fashion Communication in the Digital Age*, the modern fashion discourse as we know it has been largely founded on Eurocentric perspectives and styles of clothing that often do not account for clothing styles outside of the West.[2] It hardly comes as a surprise that a product outside of Western culture is often misguidedly referenced as 'ethnic' or 'exotic' and paints a steady image of how fashion designers of prominence have come to understand and ultimately integrate effects from Eastern European or Asian cultures into their designs. Stemming from a colonialist framework, in this realm, motifs and themes often sacred and of huge religious or cultural relevance to a community, are thrust into dominant Western silhouettes commodifying the motif and stripping away any of its original socio-cultural meaning. In essence, it then becomes nothing more than a capitalist prop promoting stereotypes where the underrepresented culture is neither acknowledged nor consulted, rendering it powerless.

As this understanding of how cultural appropriation within fashion functions has gained further prevalence in the age of social media, no designer, big or small, is exempt from being criticized for it. From Dolce & Gabbana to Chanel and Stella McCartney,[3] many major designers have at some point – and often rightfully so – received criticism for carelessly lifting aspects of other cultures across the world and incorporating them into their collections without a clear acknowledgement or appreciation of the context they are taking from.

While the practice remains pervasive, adapting elements from other cultures is not remotely new in fashion. Historically, some of the most celebrated names in the industry from Paul Poiret to Christian Dior at some point during their career, intentionally or unintentionally, appropriated a culture while attempting to create a more culturally diverse design. A notable example is the 1930s American designer Sally Milgrim, best known for crafting the dress Eleanor Roosevelt wore to her husband's first inaugural ball.[4] Milgrim was famously enchanted by China: the glamour of fabrics such as silk and Chinese motifs of clouds, mountains and medallions in rich colours are clear in some of her surviving work. Ironically, this was at the height of widespread racism against Asian Americans in the United States. Admirers of her work could attempt to excuse this as the ignorance of the past, but when renowned designers such as John Galliano showcased his 'A Voyage on the Diorient Express or the Story of the Princess Pocahontas' collection in 1998 with models donning Native American attire with blankets and dresses embellished with fringes, beading and Ghost Dance symbols that were typically present within the Navajo community, it becomes harder to write it off as mere ignorance.[5,6]

Interestingly, Galliano has famously cited the very subject of this book, Bill Gibb, as one of his all-time inspirations: 'British designers are storytellers, dreamers, and I think this was really the essence of Bill Gibb'.[7] But while Galliano – once ousted from the industry for his racist and anti-Semitic remarks and positions – has been criticized for his previous collections which ridiculed Native American culture to a degree, his predecessors such as Gibb who also borrowed references from a variety of cultures, are rarely examined through the lens of cultural appropriation.

It begs the question that although the runways of some of the greatest designers served as a platform for extravagant storytelling with lavish costumes, showpieces, sets, music and bold themes, is it truly worth all the commendation if we know today that elements of some of those stories were carelessly appropriated? This of course does not mean that foreign cultures are off limits for artists and designers, but rather that they need to emphasize a sense of admiration and pay respect to their sources, especially as the modern world comes to grasp the realities of the impact of postcolonialism on international art and design.

Bill Gibb's engagement with other cultures

When it comes to Gibb, it is not just that he admired prints and patterns inspired by other cultures; it is that it became very much a hallmark of his designs and his identity. While his work largely paid homage to his Scottish roots, other historical and culturally derived references also remained dominant so much so that they became a distinct marker of his designs as he grew in popularity and began to be embraced by celebrities such as Twiggy, Elizabeth Taylor and Bianca Jagger.

Figures 12.1 and 12.2 *Sketches of Middle Eastern and Indian design from Gibb's submission portfolio to the Royal College of Art. AAGM Collections: ABDMS081998.*

By his own account given to *The Guardian*'s Brenda Polan, he spent his childhood 'scribbling in the back of his books – historical figures, costumes'.[8] At Fraserburgh Academy in the Scottish town where Gibb grew up, the head of art at the school grew cognizant of Gibb's historical interests after perusing through his notebook filled with sketches of medieval costumes and Renaissance art, ultimately encouraging him to pursue art and fashion at St Martins. As Marie McLoughlin covered in her earlier chapter, at St Martin's, Muriel Pemberton, then Head of Dress at the renowned art institute, further emboldened the young creative to visit the Victoria & Albert Museum in London which led him to grow even more inquisitive about the global cultures he would eventually incorporate into his designs. Although his work certainly evolved overtime, his interest in history, particularly in the Renaissance period were recurrent themes, while sketches of outfits from India, European folk culture, Japan, and Iran (once Persia) were also prominent alongside detailed notes that demonstrated his curiosity about those cultures.

It is clear that American artist and designer Kaffe Fassett – Gibb's then partner who additionally moonlighted as his design collaborator throughout the 1960s and 1970s – also had a great influence on Gibb's complex mix-and-match designs that in due course became his trademark, solidifying his legacy as a magpie collector of global references.[9]

Throughout his tenure at Baccarat where he was as a freelance designer for three years, his job came with a license to experiment. Fassett remained a collaborator at this time and was tasked with designing knitwear that complimented Gibb's work. To accomplish their goals, Fassett through his own admission 'dragged' Gibb to the V&A. Together they immersed themselves in Indian and Persian artwork and paintings (Figure 12.4) that served as the catalyst for his array of knits, pleated skirts and print blouses.

Gibb's 'gypsy dresses' were soon a hallmark across his collections, which, designed for a string of his early clientele, comprised of a blend of opulent textures, rich patterns and fabrics, becoming known as a classic Gibb design. The inspirations behind these long, textured and romantic dresses were American hippie culture and European and Near-Eastern folk costumes.

Further, when it became time to launch his own independent venture, Bill Gibb Limited, which he kickstarted with Kate Franklin in 1972, he picked the then iconic Oriental Club to showcase a flamboyant collection, loaded with snakeskin beaded streamers, chestnut leather suits and hand-printed silks created in collaboration with local craft makers. There were also a series of opulent outfits featuring exotic feathers, and Japanese-inspired two pieces, snapped up by celebrities of the time.

We can see through his creative journey that the fascination he had with other ethnicities and cultures was not nascent or 'a trend' he hopped on as multiculturalism started becoming the norm in the UK but was in fact a constant feature throughout his work from early childhood (Figure 5.2) into his studies (Figure 12.3) and early collections.

His designs immediately caught the attention of everyone from magazine editors to buyers and celebrities. Yet, during his rise to fashion stardom, celebrities such as Bianca Jagger who were wearing his creations did not lament his use of foreign cultural references, and nor did his harshest critics which is perhaps unsurprising in an era devoid of the critical lens of social media and far more blurred cultural boundaries.

Still, if reviewed today, it could be argued that his heavy incorporation of Eastern cultures treads a very thin line between cultural appreciation and appropriation. But the nuances of what really constitutes cultural appropriation are far too complex to be limited by the popular and aforementioned definition of the term which is when a powerful culture borrows components from a marginalized one to use for their own purposes but with no context or credit to the original culture. Although this is an accurate summation in my view, further expansion is required.

Figure 12.3 *Sketches of Persian motifs from Gibb's submission portfolio to the Royal College of Art. AAGM Collections: ABDMS081998.*

Appropriation versus appreciation

One way to make the distinction between appropriation and appreciation clearer was proposed by Susan Scafidi, the founder of the Fashion Law Institute and author of *Who Owns Culture: Appropriation and Authenticity in American Law*. In a 2017 piece I wrote for the *South China Morning Post*, when interviewed, Scafidi told me about the handy rule of The Three 'S's – source, significance and similarity – that she identified to make the task simpler.[10] Here, she looks at the frequent 'sources' that were part of a designer's work, along with the degree of oppression or disadvantage the 'source' community has had historically. We must also look at whether the concept or product used by the designer holds substantial 'significance' to the source culture and if it was, turned into a blatant copy or altered to a great degree by the creator. Is it a 'slavish' copy as Scafidi calls it?

Let's take an example to test her theory – Galliano's aforementioned 'A Voyage on the Diorient Express' – which, as theatrical and dramatic as his shows were known to be, also featured symbols from the Native American community. Here, Scafidi's formula is fairly simple to apply. For starters, we will examine the references' source: Native Americans or Indigenous Americans, that are largely native to parts of 48 states (including Alaska) across the United States of America. The communities now inhabiting various reservations within the US have also been known for their unique set of clothing, food, fashions, customs and arts often used for inspiration within pop culture and fashion. But while Native Americans undoubtedly have a rich culture, they also faced genocide, extreme violence, marginalization and discrimination at the hands of several generations of European settlers that first came to America following Christopher Columbus.

Now we look at significance of the cultural references. While Galliano's collection came peppered with renditions of the Navajo-inspired headdresses, blankets, fringe work and beadwork, the Ghost Dance symbol was recurring and notable. Interestingly, Ghost Dance is a marker of grave religious importance to the community and symbolic of the old customs and reunited spirits that were brought back to fight the American West settlers that massacred generations of Native Americans – a knowledge that seemingly appears to be absent from the collection or the designer's mind.

As for the similarity part of Scafidi's approach, there is little to demonstrate Galliano collaborated and worked with Native American artists or designers to create his ensembles. There was also no acknowledgement of the source culture and their contribution to his creations. Instead, fans might recall models in sixteenth-century European costumes that were meant to symbolize the 'civilized' lot standing next to the 'savage', a.k.a. the ones in the Native American headgear and Navajo-inspired blankets.

While the idea here was to blend the two cultures by demonstrating a contrast between the two, over time, it has been re-analysed and criticized for exoticizing Non-European cultures, which to Galliano, was common practice at this time, among other designers and even department store styling that frequently put up displays that accentuated their fascination with colonialist ideas of Orientalism.[11] Therefore, it is somewhat safe to classify this as a likely case of misappropriation of Native American culture and elements that should have been celebrated, but were merely used as props to enhance the theatrics of the show with no recognition or financial benefit to their community.

There are also more recent and clear-cut examples such as that of the Canadian brand Dsquared which, in 2015, thoughtlessly decided to call its Autumn/Winter collection 'Dsquaw' – a derogatory term for Native American women – since it featured stereotypical aboriginal outfits. The designers apologized after significant backlash, but claimed their 'intentions' were in good faith. And while intention is a key component in making the distinction between appropriation and appreciation, it can still be demeaning to a marginalized culture if the designer does not honour the integrity of a given concept or idea or does not explain the rationale behind it.

In contrast, there is the more recent example by musician and creative director at Louis Vuitton, Pharrell Williams.[12] For his sophomore Fall/Winter 2024 menswear collection at Paris Fashion Week, the designer reimagined the cowboy aesthetic with models donning silk yoked shirts, chore jackets with cowboy prints and suits with cacti motifs echoing the ranch wear archetype and the western theme (Figure 12.4). Besides his recreation of the western aesthetic, he also included several Black models wearing Native American designs created in collaboration with Native American artists. This included blankets featuring parfleche motifs and bags with hand-painted desert flowers.

Speaking with press backstage, Williams argued that the conventional cowboy portrayal is generally limited and often whitewashed. Meanwhile, he wanted to pay homage to the Native American culture and 'appreciate' it rather than 'appropriate'. Here, Williams's intent is clearly to honour the Native American culture demonstrated through his attempt to dismantle stereotypes associated with the culture and his collaboration with Native American artists to create an array of the designs as part of the collection. Per Scafidi's formula, we can safely regard this as an example of appreciation in fashion.

Figure 12.4 *Pharrell Williams with models wearing his Fall/Winter 2024 menswear collection for Louis Vuitton at Paris Fashion Week. Photo: Francois Durand/Getty Images.*

Looking at Bill Gibb designs through a contemporary lens

Much in line with Williams' intents, Gibb never hid the fact that he was drawing inspiration from other cultures and even named certain collections after local folk traditions or styles. Some of the most notable examples of this are his collections dedicated to his own Scottish heritage entitled 'Highland Fling' and 'Celtic Romance' that both debuted in the mid-1970s and featured heritage tartan fabrics, kilts, and ruffled blouses that romanticized interpretations of traditional Highland dress and culture.

Beyond the UK, he also had a respectable clientele market overseas most notably Iran (previously Persia) in the Middle East. In fact, according to Gibb's own account, noted in a 1976 article in *The Guardian,* the Middle Eastern market comprised of '50 percent' of his label's sales, which Gibb dubbed as 'crucial'. The region's penchant for Gibb's artistry was only further magnified by the fact that Iran remained one of his longest serving sources of inspiration. Take for instance the 'Paisley print', considered an appropriated design in the UK, for the buta motif is believed to have originated from Kashmir, India, but with earlier origins in Persia where it was called the boteh.[13] Gibb was ostensibly a big admirer of the motif as it repeatedly appeared across a range of his surviving work, notably in his Tana evening dress, one of which is held in the V&A's collections, originally worn by singer Sandie Shaw (Figure 12.5).

Figure 12.5 *Detail from Gibb's 'Tana' dress worn by Sandie Shaw in 1972. Photo by Ruth Clark, courtesy of V&A Dundee.*

The designer was likely aware of the pattern's roots: as Aberdeen-based writer Shane Strachan notes in his piece for V&A Dundee that throughout the 1970s and 1980s, Gibb even received commissions from the likes of Farah Diba Pahlavi, the Shahbanu of Iran, albeit at a time when his business was failing on his home turf.[14] Pahlavi, who also became known as the 'Jackie Kennedy of the Middle East' with both her political influence and her Westernized style, was smitten by Gibb's garments some of which may have featured the boteh motif – ironic given the origin of the shape was in fact originally from Iran.

It is also important to note that while Gibb frequently used the mango teardrop or Paisley pattern in his later work, he also explored these motifs as far back as his student years given their appearance in his submission portfolio for the postgraduate at the Royal College of Art (Figure 12.3). Meanwhile, in postcolonial Britain, Paisley – an otherwise intricate hand-woven pattern crafted in India – had been reduced to a cheap factory-made rendition during the nineteenth century in the Scottish town of Paisley and beyond in an attempt to cash in on the popularity of the design together with the town's name.

Veteran Indian musician Asha Puthli (Figure 12.6) – who Gibb famously designed for throughout the 1970s – remembers his fascination with the Paisley print as she looks back at her storage full of extravagant skirts and dresses featuring the motif. The singer can also be seen wearing several of his creations during her performances at the time and on album covers but does not categorize his intrigue with Indian dress or prints as 'appropriation' in any sense.[15] On the contrary, over a lengthy phone conversation, Puthli fondly recalls her friendship and years working with Gibb. She calls him a 'designer's designer – a true genius' and someone who was exceedingly 'meticulous' with every detail of the design while also a remarkable friend who was caring, generous and open minded:

> Perfection in every button he chose, the cream-coloured silk lining which touched my skin as I wore his beautiful gowns, like the soft hand of a friend. His clothes taught me the meaning of real couture. His understanding of fabrics, of colour, his curiosity for history and other cultures and weaving them into his patterns and designs. His creativity went beyond being a fashion designer, with his clothes he was a painter, a poet, a historian.

Puthli further remembers Gibb as someone who found inspiration based on the 'personality of the wearer'. While gazing at a dress presented to the singer by the designer decades ago, she dubs him as a 'total original' who undoubtedly was influenced by other cultures much like 'most geniuses' but embraced and valued that inspiration. To Puthli, there was not a single hint of cultural appropriation within Gibb's work but simply admiration:

> Influence is one thing – you can be influenced by everything we've seen. But that doesn't mean it's appropriation. That's totally wrong. To me, maybe fused with his own original concept. I'm looking at it right now. It's unbelievable, the quilted jacket with every little detail, even the iridescent buttons match, iridescent but it was a genius; pure genius.

Figure 12.6 *Disco singer Asha Puthli wearing one of her Gibb dresses in Germany in 1976. Photo: Schweigmann/United Archives via Getty Images.*

You could say that it is one of the aspects that differentiated Gibb from his contemporaries at the time. While many brands and designers were still copy-pasting references from Eastern cultures to boost their sales, Gibb was conscious of their value and their beauty, adapting and blending them with other heritage historical fabrics to create distinct designs. In part, this consciousness can also be credited to his student years spent visiting museums, admiring historical artefacts and symbols from across the globe, which eventually made their way into his work. In fact, one needn't look beyond Gibb's first major collection showcased at the Oriental Club in the spring of 1972 where he used the best-quality fabrics and collaborated with artists and craft makers to create his dramatic, hand-printed silks, beadings, stamped leather and embellishments to understand just how much he valued true craftsmanship.

Throughout his Spring/Summer 1977 collection, for instance, the kimono silhouette was used extensively (Figure 12.7). To create the elegant range of dresses, jackets and blouses featured in the collection, Gibb drew on traditional Japanese garments and motifs such as wide sleeves, obi-inspired belts, and asymmetrical closures. The pieces were then further enhanced by using hand-painted

Figure 12.7 *Printed silk kimono (1977) on display as part of* Kimono *exhibition at V&A Dundee in 2024. The print was designed by Janet Taylor for Bill Gibb to commemorate the Silver Jubilee of Queen Elizabeth II. Photo by Ruth Clark, courtesy of V&A Dundee.*

embroidery on rich fabrics such as silk, satin and chiffon that reinstated his admiration for Japanese aesthetics.

It, however, cannot be said for certain that his work never crossed the line into the misappropriation territory even if perhaps unintentionally. He certainly was considerably scrutinized and perhaps even unfairly condemned for the smallest hints in his lack of judgement. This is demonstrated most notably in the most scathing critique the designer received for his 1977 Autumn/Winter collection inspired by his own Scottish heritage. In a review for *The Sunday Times* in November 1977, writer Michael Roberts criticized Gibb for what he seemed to have ascertained as a misappropriation of his own culture:

With the fervour of a Scottish Frankenstein, [Bill Gibb] cobbled together Bonnie Prince Charlie's lace jabot and velvet doublet with Rob Roy's kilt and tartan throwover. He then topped it off with Harry Lauder's tam-o-shanter and Flora McDonald's shawl, and – some sort of Macbeth witchery? – hung it all about with bits of dead animal. The whole thing then staggered down the catwalk to the lament of a Scottish piper. And lo, the Loch Ness Monster.[16]

But despite perceived lapses in his judgement, it did not compare to the fallacies of many celebrated designers today whose heights of fame he never reached during his short career. This was most discernibly evidenced in his business failures in the late 1970s and 1980s where while his vision for a romantic, extravagance and fantasy stayed strong, it could not compete with the rising gusts of winds in fashion that favoured a punk look and power dressing. He did not have the knack for commercial success nor a business acumen, the need of the hour during the economic recession in 1980s Britain.

As profits dwindled, however, Gibb, who once abhorred cheap manufacturing, was forced to pander to the mass market in 1979, arguably in a last-ditch attempt. In the throes of debt, the designer partnered up with India Imports, to put together a collection of nine items including coats, skirts and pants all designed by Gibb and made in India within a span of ten days. He told *The Telegraph*:

> I wasn't sure how I was going to adapt to the Indian project. But when I saw the results from the original designs I was amazed at how they had interpreted everything so faithfully, particularly the prints and the colourings. Now I can't wait to go to India myself to work on the next collection in more detail. India inspired me this time – the prints for instance are based on a stylised Indian tree design – so now I know that the potential is endless.[17]

Writer Ann Chubb who documented the production called it a collection that 'captures the essence of his individuality at a price we can all afford'. Priced between £35–£95, this marked one of Gibb's first dips into the franchising and licensing sphere, most of which had meagre financial success. It goes to show that even Gibb, whose desire for maintaining a sense of identity and craftmanship over quick profit was a strong part of his brand, could falter.

Certainly, if examined through the modern lens of appropriation, he would be held to fairer standards and perhaps even questioned for his misguided creative decisions at this point, as one should be. But despite his slip ups and blunders at the tail end of his career, for the most part his legacy is solidified as a man of integrity who often favoured expensive, high-quality fabrics and traditional, slow labour techniques to do right by the many collages of cultures he created through his work.

For most of his life, it is clear Gibb was an artist over anything else and not swayed by the trappings of materialism or wealth whether it was back when he was the most notable designer in the UK or towards the end. A decade before his untimely demise in 1988, thousands of admirers of his work came together in 1977 to watch his ten-year retrospective at the Royal Albert Hall to witness the one thing he immortalized for generations of designers after him for better or worse: a continual quest for glamour, beauty and romanticism undeterred by the barriers of cultural borders.

13

Addressing climate change through Bill Gibb's design legacy

Lynn Wilson

Introduction: Bill Gibb's legacy and the wicked problem of climate change and fashion

It is estimated that the global fashion industry contributes up to '8% of global carbon emissions' across the supply chain from farmed and mined raw materials, apparel construction, chemical coatings and treatments, logistics and consumer behaviour.[1] There is an urgent need to reduce fashion production and consumption and keep in use what we already have. To explore this wicked problem, we look to Bill Gibb as a pioneering crafts person – *Vogue* Designer of the Year, 1970 – who grew up on a farm and created enduring designs that are an antidote to today's '*take, make, dispose*' fashion cycles.[2] The year 1970 also saw the launch of the first Earth Day on the 22nd of April, founded by Senator Gaylord Nelson,[3] to raise awareness of environmental challenges caused by the era, we now know as the Anthropocene.[4] Gibb knew and loved nature, reflected through the omnipresence of his signature unique bumblebee motif (Figure 13.1), a constant throughout Gibb's knit and print designs, created for him by his friend and collaborator, Kaffe Fassett.[5] He retained a lifelong passion for collecting objects inspired by bees, many of them gifted by friends and clients (Figure 13.2).

The future sustainability of Earth is closely associated with the ecosystem of bees, highlighted in the UK by the National Honey Monitoring Scheme (NHMS), a government-funded organization that monitors the decline of the bee population. NHMS have identified multiple reasons for the decline of the bee population: increased agriculture and farming (including natural fibre crops such as cotton and animal farmed fibres such as wool), increase in chemical pesticide distribution in farming (to ensure a constant supply of materials), reduction in flora and fauna landscapes caused by major infrastructure developments (e.g. cities for commerce, industrial factories and retail spaces), and finally, new diseases and climate change caused by all the identified challenges.[6]

Figure 13.1 *Detail of bee buttons on black dress sleeve from 1972 collection. AAGM Collections: ABDMS015726.*

Figure 13.2 *Bee tin once owned by Bill Gibb. AAGM Collections: ABDMS082315.*

Gibb was a designer of his time, when consumers and industry were not fully aware of the environmental impacts of fashion, but Gibb's love of design, attention to detail and material selection means there is a lot we can learn from his approach in order to apply lessons for a sustainable fashion future. This chapter explores three elements of the fashion designs of Bill Gibb, through the contemporary lens of sustainable fashion design: zero waste fashion design, sustainable fibre selection, and the emotionally enduring quality of his designs. An additional section addresses Gibb's fashion legacy through the lens of a Circular Economy Wardrobe, a consumer fashion system that promotes access over ownership, maintenance and repair, and reuse at end of useful consumer life.[7]

Zero waste fashion design: the kimono

Garment pattern-cutting methods traditionally place garment shapes on top of material and cut into it creating 15–25 per cent waste.[8] The pattern cutting and construction of the traditional Japanese

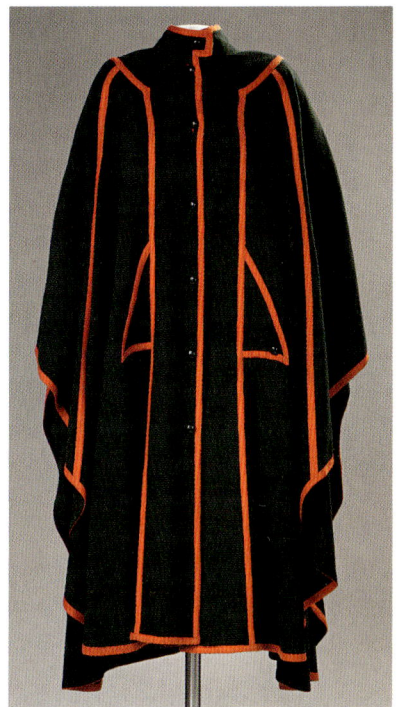 

Figures 13.3 and 13.4 *Green woollen cape with orange trim for the Autumn/Winter 1977–78 Scottish Collection. AAGM Collections: ABDMS076724.*

kimono, often favoured by Gibb and his contemporary Zandra Rhodes, is considered a zero waste pattern design.[9] This section explores Gibb's use of the kimono silhouette in knit and sewn garment construction and discusses new technologies and designers inspired by the kimono working to reduce waste in the fashion industry.

Throughout Gibb's body of work, the kimono is a consistent influence in the box shapes and simple line of garments (figures 13.3 and 13.4), that are then camouflaged and brought to life through luxurious fabrics, embellishments and creative construction of collars, hemlines and sleeves. The yukata, a basic kimono shape traditionally used for everyday wear, and bath houses in Japan, is most like that used by Gibb and other designers appropriating the kimono.[10]

In figures 13.5 and 13.6, a silk chiffon kimono-inspired wrap by Gibb, has a signature bee detail with hand-sewn sequins on the centre of the back panel. The Japanese kimono is constructed from lengths of silk fabric, usually around 12–13 metres, but can require up to 21 metres for an elaborate costume.[11] The design and construction of the kimono enables it to be a zero waste garment suitable for enduring garments that are adaptable to body changes, providing comfort and accessibility for wearer proprioceptive

Figures 13.5 and 13.6 *Cream, green and pink silk kimono-shape wrap with rose print including bee surrounded by hand-sewn sequins. AAGM Collections: ABDMS015711.*

movement. It is not known if Gibb was motivated to reduce textile waste, or garment construction costs, but he said, 'I get interested in all aspects of design and for me "less" sometimes means "more".'[12]

John Galliano, although hugely influenced by Gibb, stretched the boundaries of kimono and cultural appropriation, evident in his mini-mono designs as part of his 1994 ground-breaking 'Japonisme' collection.[13] Whilst Galliano has brought theatre to couture using a kimono silhouette, there is a movement of fashion design researchers committed to the pursuit of zero waste design inspired by the principles of kimono.[14] Their mission is to accelerate the sustainability of the fashion industry through providing free open-source patterns, publishing pattern books and leading higher education research and teaching in zero waste pattern design, inspiring a new generation of fashion designers.[15] Ahead of his time, Gibb offered everyone a chic, free zero waste pattern as part of a feature, 'Just A Little Something I Ran Up Myself', for *Cosmopolitan* magazine in 1978 after they invited him and seven other designers, including Zandra Rhodes, to design a dress pattern for consumers to make themselves.[16] Gibb created an outfit that required

> four straight pieces of jersey and need only be as expensive as the fabric you choose. Cut four 120 × 90cm oblongs of fabric … Overlock the edges and run a ribbon drawstring through the short end of each piece. Two oblongs gathered up and tied on each shoulder make the back and front of the dress.[17]

This example using four identical pieces echoes the rectangular panels of a kimono pattern.

Kimono silhouette in Gibb knitwear

Rew (1994) and Webb (2008) agree that Gibb's greatest contribution to British fashion is his knitwear, which is described in the main as being 'variations on a basic square'.[18] This is most evident in a drawing of a knitted kimono coat (Figure 13.7) produced by Deacon Knitwear and presented at the Courtaulds Show, 1981. A basic square was applied to the design of cardigan jackets and garments associated with a basic block shape – tabards, blanket wraps and ponchos. The versatility in Gibb's design and shape was summed up by Ann Chubb: 'only someone who has actually owned a Bill Gibb knit can appreciate the gap they fill in a wardrobe.'[19]

Today there are three types of commercial knitting manufacturing: fully fashioned, cut and sew, and Wholegarment®.[20] Fully fashioned bespoke garments were knitted by Mildred Boulton for Gibb which enables maximum creativity and minimum waste yarn. Larger productions of jacquard knits were cut and sewn, undertaken by Harry Green of Gould's in Leicester.[21] Luxury brand Chanel is most famous for cut and sewn knitwear to achieve the tailored shape of a Chanel knitted jacket, manufactured by Barrie Knitwear, Scotland, which is now owned by Chanel.[22] Japanese knitting machine company, Shima Seiki, created Wholegarment® knitting machine technology in 1990 which enables an entire garment to be knitted in a single seam-free shape, achieving a complete zero waste process.[23] Other knitting machine companies, such as Stoll, have their own versions, but the fashion industry has been slow to adapt to new technologies that are less resource intensive. Overall, the global knitting industry is challenged by the lack of a skilled workforce as young people reject factory jobs for better paid IT-related work. Gibb's knitwear was predominantly manufactured in the UK, prior to financial difficulties, but if Gibb needed a manufacturer today, he would possibly face UK onshore production dilemmas and need to source manufacturers in Eastern Europe or China. Scottish companies such as Glenmuir ceased manufacturing in the late 1990s when their major client, Marks and Spencer, transferred to overseas manufacturers to cut supplier costs. Today, micro vertical companies where a business takes full ownership of all stages of design, production and their supply chain are increasing in the UK. Loopy Ewe is an example where the designer Katie Allen, left the design world of London,

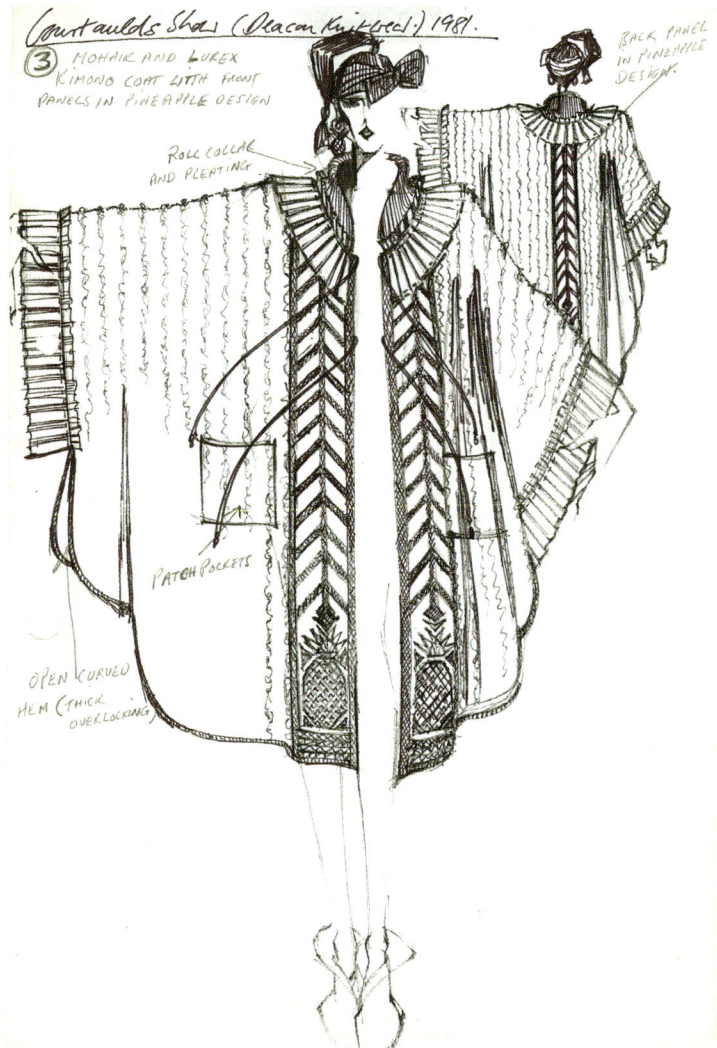

Figure 13.7 *Drawing of 1981 kimono coat in collaboration with Deacon Knitwear for a fashion show for the manufacturer Courtaulds. AAGM Collections: ABDMS070369.*

and now describes herself as a Shepherd, designer and maker, owning her own small farm of 200 sheep to ensure control and transparency of her whole supply chain. As a farmer's son, perhaps Gibb would have endorsed this contemporary model.

Fibre and textile selection

Gibb believed that the 'feel of a fabric is terribly important' and was committed to innovation at every stage of his design process.[24] In his early to mid-career, his fibre and textile selections were driven by creative choices, conducive to a luxury fashion market. In the main, Gibb used natural and synthetic fibres of the day which included luxury chiffons, silk and wool, but also acrylic yarns, lurex and metallic sequins and beading. Leather was also a prominent material in all Gibb collections. It should be noted however that, later in his career, Gibb struggled with the commercialization of his work and eventually succumbed to cheaper international manufacturing (including hand-printed block prints in India in the late 1970s), in order to make affordable fashion for a wider market; these struggles are reflective of the compromises designers still have to make in today's economic market.[25]

This section critiques two prominent luxury materials used by Gibb: silk and leather. Advances in fibre and textile technology that supports the reduction of the environmental and ethical implications of these materials are explored, at the same time challenging the implications for quality and garment longevity.

Silk

Natural animal, insect and plant-based fibres (leather, cotton, wool, silk) were prominent in Gibb collections (figures 13.3, 13.5 and 13.8). Ironically often the bee motif was printed and painted on silk from silkworms, both plant pollinators.

Originating from China, silk is one of the oldest fibres used to produce clothing, due to its strength, versatility and health properties as a natural fibre;[26] it was a staple of Gibb designs. Rolls of silk textiles would have been imported to the UK from China during Gibb's time. Today, it is a controversial industry considered unethical by animal campaigners due to mass mulberry silkworm farming where the worm never completes a full lifecycle transitioning into a moth. Luxury fashion brands such as Stella McCartney, who follow vegan principles have attempted to use 'Peace Silk' which allows the worm to emerge from the cocoon to complete a full lifecycle in the wild but this process does not achieve the quality they require found in farmed mulberry silk.[27] Stella McCartney are now collaborating with Bolt Threads, a fibre technology innovation company at the forefront of alternative bio silk production creating synthetic 'spider silk' which are synthetic 'brewed protein' fibres that can also be made into fleece, denim and fur, displayed in the Museum of Modern Art in New York in 2017.[28]

Hermès, have been the global leader in luxury silk scarves since 1937 and retain their relationship with traditional silk, which are vegetable dyed and screen printed with up to 48 colours, manufactured in a bespoke factory in France and retailing in the region of £450 for a 90 x 90cm square.[29]

Faux and real leather

Leather was a dominant material in Bill Gibb collections of the 1970s, most notably Autumn/Winter 1972 where silver bees designed by Sally MacLachlan were printed onto intricate leather outfits with details such as peplum-cut hems and leg-o'-mutton sleeves (Figure 13.8). Since 1980, the animal rights organization PETA have campaigned against the use of all animal-related products in fashion and recommend faux leather alternatives.[30] Faux leather is manufactured from crude-oil based processes.[31] It is estimated that up to 65 per cent of all apparel worn is made from a crude-oil based fibre (acrylic, polyester, nylon, Lycra), because it is cheap and fast to produce.[32] This is a major part of why the fashion industry is a contributor to carbon emissions caused by overproduction and consumption. In addition, it is the major source of microfibres, polluting oceans and entering the food chain.[33]

Stella McCartney is committed to pioneering faux leather alternatives used in the iconic 'Fallabella' shoulder bag, and shoes emulating the feel of leather, without the cost of animal slaughter which has a high carbon footprint due to farming and land management. Although, the alternative argument is that leather is a by-product of the meat industry and is therefore serving a purpose. Acknowledging that faux leather is a carbon intensive crude-oil based material, that sheds microfibres harmful to the oceans and our food supply chain, Stella McCartney, has invested in 'Vegea' a plant-based, leather alternative.[34]

The long-term durability of alternative materials such as faux leather and synthetic bio-silks is still unknown as new materials develop, but the longevity of the use of leather and silk has ensured that

Figure 13.8 *Bee print deigned by Sally MacLachlan printed on black leather skirt suit from 1972 collection. AAGM Collections: ABDMS071550.*

Gibb-designed garments are still being collected, resold and worn today. Designers working in new materials need to research and consider their robustness and purpose alongside the ethics of any material if environmental and social garment sustainability is to be achieved.

Emotionally durable fashion design

Gibb had no interest in material possessions. His most cherished items were a 'chemist chest' a 'porcelain head' and his 'collection of bees', referring to the objects with a bee motif, that he had collected, or been given.[35] In contrast, Gibb said, 'Clothes have to go on living for a very long time, they must be worth keeping,'[36] illustrating his commitment to creating fashion that Jonathan Chapman calls, 'emotionally durable design'.[37] Webb explains Gibb created a narrative with his clothing designs, summed up by Galliano: 'British designers are storytellers … I think this was really the essence of the romance behind Bill Gibb.'[38] Chapman believes that with the rapid acceleration of digital and virtual worlds, traditional methods of storytelling through consumer object interaction is in decline.[39] Up close to the Gibb collection in Aberdeen Art Gallery archives feels like a masterclass in design, tailoring and style so skilfully crafted and contemporary that a consumer of a suitable size and fit could be easily styled for any occasion today.

The enduring quality and admiration for Gibb's work, is evident in the chapters of this book, the availability of collections in museum archives and private collections,[40] and the price of vintage Gibb on specialist fashion resale platforms.[41] To achieve this legacy, the philosophy of enduring design was built in from the beginning of each collection through meticulous attention to detail at the design stage, selection of fibres and textiles, and close collaboration with manufacturers and craftspeople.[42] Nadege Vanhee, the Creative Director of Hermès, says she strives to create 'a dialogue between the fabric and the techniques of tailoring and embellishment', a philosophy that echoes the work of Gibb, through which he created a coherent narrative across every element of a design.[43]

Today, designers such as Amy Powney, Creative Director of luxury fashion label Mother of Pearl, follow a similar Gibb work ethic when it comes to designing luxury fashion. Powney builds in the narrative of her collections not only through design, but through traceability in the supply chain and use of low carbon fibres. Like Gibb, Powney has been awarded accolades from the British Fashion Council and *Vogue*. Aligned with increasing awareness in the twenty-first century of the interconnected future of the planet and fashion, Powney has been celebrated for her commitment to sustainable design and manufacturing principles that endure against the tide of fast fashion, winning £100,000 in 2017 which she used to further embed sustainability principles in her work. A film, *Fashion Reimagined*, was commissioned by the British Fashion Council which follows her journey and struggles to develop a sustainable supply chain within a luxury brand.[44] Instead of bees, Powney's motifs are large bulbous pearls integrated into the seams of garments, creating sculptural wearable forms like Gibb, influenced by romantic costumes 'of the past'.[45]

Circular fashion consumption

Gibb's belief that clothes must be kept in use aligns to the contemporary concept of a Circular Economy Wardrobe (CEW), a consumer model of keeping clothing in circulation for as long as possible, addressing acquisition, use and passing on of clothing at end of useful life.[46] Figure 13.9 illustrates the CEW concept, which begins with consumer models of access over ownership. Clothing rental is evolving as a popular temporary-clothing access model[47] alongside fashion libraries where clothing can be checked in and out, like library books.[48] This helps to increase access to quality clothing and reduce the need for volumes of cheap fast cycles of clothing. Committed collectors such as Gibb's fellow Scotsman, Steven Philip, rents, hires and even resells Gibb as part of his extensive fashion collection in Brighton – a testimony to the original skilled craftsmanship and durability of each garment.[49]

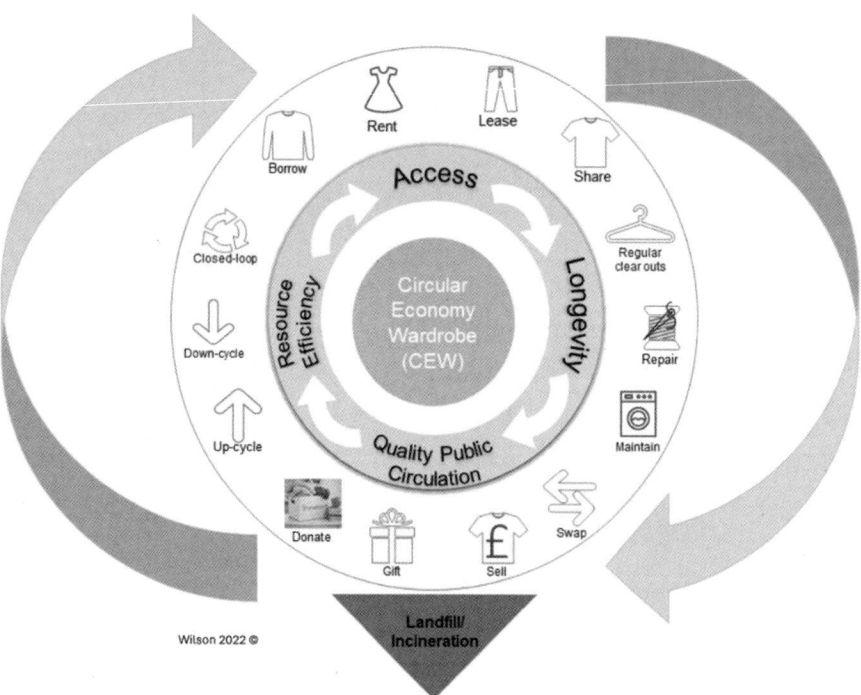

Figure 13.9 *Circular Economy Wardrobe diagram from Lynn Wilson, '"Private sufficiency, public luxury": an exploration of consumer clothing circularity' in Marylyn Carrigan et al. (eds),* Research Handbook on Ethical Consumption *(Edward Elgar Publishing, 2023): 312–26.*

To ensure clothing can be kept in use, consumers are required to have knowledge about how to care for clothing, such as washing instructions for different fibre types, something not often taught in schools. The delicate silk garments with embellishments of a Gibb garment will require gentle hand washing or chemical-free dry cleaning. Owners of Gibb knitwear and museum collections are up against an accelerating moth epidemic caused by climate change and the fact that consumers spend up to 90 per cent of their time indoors, continuously shedding bacteria attractive to household pests such as dust mites and moths.[50] It is recognized that consumers have limited repair skills, and need support and education programmes to ensure they are equipped to repair garments.[51]

In contrast, research also recommends legislating for the provision of higher quality garments, and incentivized repair schemes following the lead of countries such as France who have legislated against cheap clothing.[52] At the end of a garment's useful life, donating to charity shops has been consumer preference since 1947,[53] but fashion resale, through digital platforms such as eBay and Vinted are increasingly popular, with occasional Gibb pieces sold for relatively high resale fees. Some Gibb garments may be beyond repair, but given the passion and commitment of Gibb collectors, it is more likely that they will be repurposed to make new products.

Conclusion

This chapter has explored the design legacy of Bill Gibb, through the lens of sustainable fashion design, construction, fibre and textile selection, and the challenge of creating enduring designs that consumers will care for and circulate. The chapter acknowledges the context of the now vintage 1970s and 1980s that Gibb was active within, and his pioneering approach to all areas of fashion innovation. Being able to reflect on the historic collections of pioneering designers, to be up close and examine their work, and critically analyse their contribution to fashion, is essential to looking forward. It is a futile exercise without acknowledgement of the dominance clothing production and consumption has had on the global climate crisis. Even Gibb, under business pressure, succumbed to working with emerging nations cheaper production options.[54] He was a fast thinker, slow designer, craftsman, maverick and above all, a sensitive human with a love of nature and the bumblebee in particular, who never forgot his place in the world and alignment with nature. This is a lesson for all current and future designers, to secure the pollination of our future.

14

An interview with Giles Deacon, Fashion Designer

Giles Deacon is a London-based couture designer and illustrator mixing fashion, fine art, theatre and grand scale glamour, known for his expertly crafted pieces using bespoke designed fabrics, prints and intricate embellishments. He is a 1992 graduate of St Martin's School of Art where Bill Gibb studied in the 1960s. For his work, Giles received the British Designer of the Year Award in 2006. Shane Strachan and Josephine Steed conducted the following interview with Giles in June 2024.

When did you first become aware of Bill Gibb?

I was very lucky that I knew a friend of my mother who actually owned a Bill Gibb piece in the seventies which was very beautiful – one of the leather printed pieces with the chrysanthemum flowers on (Figure 14.1). I obviously wasn't a fashion follower as such at that age, but I did remember that piece and it only dawned on me years later that that's what it was. So that was a sort of subconscious introduction to Gibb in some way.

But it was really when I was at St Martin's that I first came across his work, researching in the library in St Martin's School of Art as it was then, on Charing Cross Road, and there were some wonderfully basic black-and-white photocopy booklets of fashion shows from the seventies and eighties. One of them had copies of photographs of a show that he did at the Oriental Club in 1972, which was one of his really seminal collections. It really transfixed me, and I then did quite a lot of research on him.

I was intrigued by his upbringing in rural Scotland. This was something that really spoke to me because I was brought up in the Lake District – that sense of the naturalistic referencing done in very elevated, clever ways is something that I've kind of embodied and done my own world of. It was a great starting point for me to see how worlds of high fashion could exist that were complimentary but very different to a Parisian aesthetic and that was something that really intrigued me – Gibb's work was very much *not* Parisian, but that was incredibly exciting; the volume and incredible cuts and use of heavy crepes and bee embroideries and handmade buttons and beautiful bindings and ribbons. It just

Figure 14.1 *Chestnut leather suit with silver chrysanthemum print by Sally MacLachlan and chrysanthemum buttons, 1972. AAGM Collection: ABDMS015704.*

had a great storytelling to it as well – you were very intrigued by what these characters were and what they were doing and everyone always seemed to embody such life and energy. I think that it was all of the combination of those things, all executed to a manner which looked extraordinary to me.

Transport a few years forward and, probably about 1998 or 1999, I'd become friends with Steven Phillip who ran Rellik [now Steven Philip Design Consultancy + Studio]. He'd just started that and

Steven's a huge Bill Gibb fan – from Dundee himself – and he's acquired some of the most extraordinary pieces, so I was very lucky to see them and see how they were all constructed and what the techniques were. Steven has all of the brilliant designs like the grey leather skirt dress and the great big batwing knitwear and they're in beautiful condition as well. I was lucky enough to have a really good examine of them – inside out, laying out layers – and there's really clever work on some of those pieces. From a creative and clearly from a personal perspective, drama was something he very much knew how to play with. You can see that in the cut of his clothes – they're very dramatic pieces and they're very strong visually and technically, and materials-wise they're very bold choices.

They're extraordinary pieces that just had this agelessness to them – they're sent from the future, but medieval, but the seventies. I always loved the fact that they are kind of everything about fashion, but also not, which is what really appeals to me about the best design: it's not just for now. They live in this entity and just sort of *be* these wonderful things that you're intrigued by, that just always look wonderful.

Do you feel there's a relationship between any of Gibb's work and your own?

Absolutely. I mean, not a precise one – I obviously don't copy them, but absolutely from a volume perspective and the way that we both use imagery from a very personal natural world. At St Martin's, I did a whole project based on drystone walls in the Lake District and Herdwick sheep and a whole host of things like that. That absolutely helped inform me and push me on to go with that development and research. So I think in a simple way, it very much gave me validation for my own background research in that way we were all taught at St Martin's: to make it as personal and specific as possible. What's the thing that's you and yours? That's the thing that's going to hopefully encourage people to come enjoy your work, that you're not doing anything generic. You're making it very personal. So, if you are making a layered dress from chiffon that's based on drystone walls, then that's great – go and do it. You know, I love Paris and I worked and lived there and it's a fabulous place, but I think to have that other aspect of narrative is really super to have, especially a British historic perspective.

When it comes to those images of the 1972 collection with the owl prints and so on, I think that one of the things that I've always adored with those images is I love the crowd and I love that people are smoking and how close everybody was. We use that in shows of ours in some of the halls in the city of London where you've got these beautiful panelled rooms and we purposefully bring all of the chairs and front row and make it really narrow to bring that sense of closeness so the clothes are pushing past people and that was all down to imagining what those shows of Bill's would have been like to get that sense of movement. You can almost get that sense of how rooms would have been scented – you can imagine them having like a heavy tuberose smell to them and just being really evocative. I think that's the feeling I get from all of those. I was super inspired by that and tried to bring that sense of feeling to lots of shows over the years.

And we can't not talk about the fashion show on the airplane either which is one of my favourites. I just love the fact that he did a fashion show on a flight from London to Paris. I thought it was such a fabulous thing to do. That would have been a sight to have seen, I'm sure.

Some of what you have said on the ideal wearer of your designs echoes much of what Gibb said about his dresses being for confident, self-assured women, and not just for young people, but women of all ages.

Absolutely. I mean, I've always been about that. I've never been about just dressing a certain age group or demographic. We've always presented as broad an age group as possible where we can and with the resources and people and everything else that can enable that. That kind of broad church, so to speak, is something that's really important. That's where you get life and interesting characters – people who've lived and bring a different energy when they're wearing things. The idea of a homogenized presentation where everybody has the same look and the same age and the same background is something that just doesn't interest me and it never has done. I can see how that diversity would have appealed to Bill very much.

I think within our artistic culture, we have those very strong women as well. From Bess of Hardwick to Daphne du Maurier through to Zaha Hadid to all sorts of artists and writers like Vita Sackville-West. I mean, the list you could build is a very special, very specific list, but they all have a common sense of artistic eccentricity, accessibility and ability, which is really timeless. Long may that last.

What do you think fashion students and designers today can learn from Gibb and his design process?

I think what we can all take away from looking at people like him and his practice is that he clearly had a very precise idea of what it was that he wanted to show and how to show it from a technical and aesthetic perspective and he clearly put the work in and really explored the techniques, the construction and the making. He could do it. He could cut, he could visualize, and the ideas were there: they were thorough, they were developed, they were thought through. You don't happen across that kind of technique of printing on leather just by accident – you have to really explore it. I think that a sense of bold, creative freedom, but with a very precise technical skill is something that all designers should be able to have within their creative portfolio.

I also think he was very much a trailblazer when it came to collaboration. As an independent designer and from a business perspective, it's a way to enable you to achieve certain things and it's a very good way of working. Creative collaboration opens new worlds and it brings new visibility. It also enables you to creatively grow and expand your vision, your outlook, your thoughts and the people you speak to. It's all a good dialogue to have as a creative.

Do you have any final thoughts or memories you would like to share about Gibb?

I obviously never got to meet Gibb. The nearest I got was when I met [Savile Row tailor] Tommy Nutter as they were very good friends. He told me some quite interesting stories about Gibb and his time and some of the collections that were not so great and that didn't work out for him, but it was really interesting to get this overview of his world and his practice and how he went about it.

I just think he's such a wonderful designer for all of those reasons that I've outlined. He still has this endlessly inspiring vision that still speaks to people on so many levels. I think it's testament to the originality and the honesty and just sheer magic of what he did, and I think his work stands alone very much in its own vocabulary of high aesthetic and high discipline, but it's also really beautifully considered. The pieces are extraordinary still to this day.

15

Exploring Gibb's design process within fashion education

Shane Strachan and Josephine Steed

Introduction

Fashion is always reflecting back to look forward in a perpetual iterative cycle of reinvention. As such, understanding the creative processes of past influential designers is a vital educational tool within the global fashion education system. Throughout history, fashion designers have challenged the status quo by tapping into the zeitgeist of a particular era; by carrying out research on a designer, students gain not only a deep insight into their unique creative identity but also the social, political and environmental concerns of the time in which they practiced.[1] As inspiration, the fashion student can then synthesize the research to inform their own creative process through reinterpretations that drive a new understanding of the value of a designer's legacy today. In the context of Bill Gibb's legacy, he is often described as a designer ahead of his time where his creative practices reflect contemporary topics today within design education including craft skills, heritage, cultural appreciation versus appropriation, sustainability, collaboration and innovation.

Gibb himself had a strong interest in fostering the emerging talents of fashion students across his career such as those of embroiderer and textile designer Sue Kemp who was still in the midst of her postgraduate studies when she joined his independent label on its founding in 1972.[2] Ahead of his ten-year retrospective show at the Royal Albert Hall, Gibb showcased a winter collection in Aberdeen's Cowdray Hall on Friday 21 October 1977 to a 300-strong audience in conjunction with the Friends of Aberdeen Art Gallery; the following morning's *Press and Journal* described excitement surrounding this homecoming show at the peak of his career and how it provided local fashion students with work experience on the night: 'The fashion show lasted 30 minutes and judging by audience response it could have lasted as long again. […] A team of six students from Gray's School of Art helped behind the scenes as dressers for the models.'[3] It is therefore fitting that Aberdeen Archives, Gallery and Museums (AAGM), of which the Cowdray Hall forms part, is now home to the largest collection of Gibb's work representing all aspects of his design process from initial sketches to final garments, an internationally significant archive which has been used as a research and educational tool since the mid-1990s for Secondary, Further and Higher Education level students.[4, 5]

To demonstrate the potential benefits of studying Gibb's creative practices today within contemporary fashion education, this chapter reflects on a 2018 student project at Robert Gordon University's Gray's School of Art (delivered in partnership with Look Again Aberdeen,[6] RGU Art & Heritage Collections and AAGM) which formed part of the development of creative writer Shane Strachan's spoken word podcast, film and exhibition, *The Bill Gibb Line*, from which the poems in this book recounting Gibb's career and collections are taken. The work by Strachan and the students went on to be exhibited in Look Again's Project Space in Aberdeen in the summer of 2019 before being re-exhibited on a larger scale alongside Gibb garments in Aberdeen Art Gallery from February 2020 to May 2021. How the Fashion and Textile Design students at Gray's were inspired by Gibb's designs and illustrious career for their own contemporary projects will henceforth be explored alongside key

Figure 15.1 *Shane Strachan performing at* The Bill Gibb Line *exhibition. Photo by Grant Anderson for Look Again.*

issues that arose during their project development including how digital-age students research a pre-Internet designer, and the limitations on accessing precious and fragile archival garments; these aspects are accommodated with insights from Morna Annandale, one of two Curators at AAGM caring for the Decorative Arts collection. The chapter will also explore other Gibb-related student projects from across the UK and potential avenues for further innovative research related to his work.

Case study: *The Bill Gibb Line*

In 2018, a selection of Bill Gibb sketches and pattern cuttings for his final 1985 and 1986 collections were discovered in an office cupboard in Gray's School of Art. They had been donated to the school by his family some years before as a possible educational tool, but staff changes and office moves had led to the series of brown envelopes being buried away in among other files and folders, increasingly threatened with being lost for good. That such significant documentation of one of Britain's biggest fashion designers of the twentieth century could so easily disappear highlights the precarity of our creative heritage, particularly our fashion heritage, as does a winter storm of 2021 which led to the roof of Fraserburgh Heritage Centre being blown off where a display of Gibb's work was significantly damaged.

Serendipitously, not long after these 1985–86 sketches and pattern cuttings finally found their way into Robert Gordon University's Art & Heritage Collections, Strachan had approached Gray's Fashion and Textile Design department (F&TD) in order to potentially exchange knowledge and collaborate with staff and students as part of his research process for a new Gibb-focused project partially funded by the Scottish Book Trust's Robert Louis Stevenson Fellowship. From these initial interactions, the F&TD department at Gray's decided that the third-year undergraduate Industry Project would involve the students creating new garments inspired by Gibb's work and design process with the following project brief:

> Design a collection (menswear, womenswear or a textile product) that is inspired/influenced or evokes the design aesthetic of Bill Gibb's work. Push the boundaries, innovate, re-appropriate and contemporize the Bill Gibb aesthetic. You will use the Bill Gibb's archive as a starting point in order to create a concept that will also represent you as a designer. Investigate fabrication through manipulation, knit, print, colour, placements to name a few; immerse yourself within your concept to produce a strong body of primary research whilst also gathering relevant secondary and contextual research. The brief is asking you 'the designer' what kind of collection you would produce for a Bill-Gibb-inspired Capsule Collection.

As part of this process, students studying on the Fashion Pathway were expected to:

- research Bill Gibb and visually demonstrate an understanding of his design aesthetic and the history, culture, icons, muses, etc., that inspired Gibb and capture him as a person and a designer; conduct primary, secondary and contextual research for their chosen concept
- produce initial paper-based design developments, refined garment design developments digitally and/or by hand, and A3 concept and colour boards, and fabric sampling
- produce a contemporary fashion collection comprising six complete looks as defined sketches which communicated their design clearly, alongside toiles and documentation of the design development
- produce a minimum of two final garments alongside master patterns and pattern pieces
- produce a photo shoot of the final garments, as well as specification drawings on Adobe Illustrator specifying topstitching, fabric placement, buttons, lining, etc.

In September 2018, Strachan delivered a talk to the third-year students which introduced them to Gibb by outlining his background and Northeast Scottish connections, as well as his key collections and collaborators. During this talk, he asked if any of the students had ever heard of Gibb before this Industry Project. Only two students in the class raised their hands, one of them being from Gibb's hometown of Fraserburgh. While disappointing, it meant that nearly all the students were beginning their research process on Gibb with no prior knowledge or preconceptions of his work.

Figure 15.2 *Gray's F&TD Students explore the Bill Gibb archive at AAGM's Aberdeen Treasure Hub. Photo by Shane Strachan.*

Researching Gibb: digital versus physical

What quickly became apparent during the students' research period is that many of them were frustrated by the low number of high-quality images of Gibb's work online compared with the contemporary designers they had often turned to for inspiration in their first two years of study. There appeared to be a heavy, if not sole, reliance on the internet as a research tool and a lack of engagement with, or even awareness of, publications about Gibb's work available in the university library and the city's Central Library. It is clear from student feedback that this has been exacerbated by the Covid pandemic, with students even more keen on digital over physical books, and far fewer students accessing physical resources which becomes an issue with Gibb given previous publications on him are not only now out of print, but are also not available online as e-books. Furthermore, the use of online resources such as Pinterest and TikTok controlled by algorithms and Artificial Intelligence (AI) direct students to mediated imagery and video generated content that impacts on their individual research methods.[7]

At the time the project was running, Aberdeen Art Gallery was also in the midst of a four-year refurbishment and did not reopen until November 2019 where it now has a permanent display of at least one of Gibb's works at all times. However, the students were fortunate to be able to take a study trip to view items from AAGM's extensive Gibb archive at their Treasure Hub store in the Northfield area of the city. As well as a selection of Gibb's personal collection of bee ornaments and trinkets, staff displayed several garments on mannequins to show how they hang on the body, and the students were able to view his original design sketches displayed safely in clear polyester sleeves inside ring binders. This was something of a breakthrough moment for many of these students who had become accustomed to designing using digital tools from the outset, encouraging several of them to (re-)engage with drawing as part of their personal design process. In an interview with Zandra Rhodes for this book, she highlighted how stark the differences in skillsets are between F&TD students across the UK now compared with her and Gibb's time as students stating 'there was no such thing as a computer, you know. Everything was painted by hand. Hand skills and drawing were very important.'[8] Therefore, students studying the works of designers from previous decades before their own lifetimes can lead to new hands-on research pathways and skillsets being developed when opportunities to visit physical archives such as the Treasure Hub are made possible. For many of the students this was their first experience of being able to engage so closely with the physical archive, surveying professional design sketches firsthand and interacting with the curators who could handle and manipulate the garments so that embellishments and folds could be seen more clearly. Curator Morna Annandale explains how other institutions have benefited from similar in-person research visits such as Further Education students at North East Scotland College (NESCol):

Lecturer Leanne Brown told me that she thinks getting the chance to look through Gibb's work was beneficial for her students and helped them to be more confident to develop their own style, especially in fashion illustration in respect to detail, fine lines and shape.[9]

However, it is not always possible or straightforward to make such research trips happen due to staffing, funding and/or transport, especially for Higher Education Institutions further afield from a physical archive like the University of the Highlands and Islands (UHI) in Scotland for instance. Furthermore, while Aberdeen Art Gallery is easier to access year-round than the Treasure Hub, Aberdeen as a city is more peripheral and remote than many other UK cities in terms of its location and transport links, and for those who can make it to the gallery, space is limited with only one or two garments on display at one time unless a further temporary Gibb-related exhibition is being held. This is partly due to the extra care that has to be taken with public display and access of textiles, which are threatened by other factors than the likes of painting or sculpture as Annandale explains:

> Costume collections are easily damaged, particularly thin fabrics like silk and chiffon. Textile conservation can be time consuming and expensive so we do our best to avoid putting our costume at risk. It is best to have costume on display periodically in temporary exhibitions rather than in permanent exhibitions. This protects costume from overexposure to the light which can damage fabric.

Limitations on accessing physical archives like these, especially during Covid-related lockdowns throughout 2020 and 2021, has led to a solution being found in the digital realm – AAGM have vastly increased the digitization of their Gibb costume collections over the last few years, adding to an earlier digitization project of the thousands of Gibb design sketches that they hold. The majority of these images are accessible any time for free through their eMuseum collections site with further digitization ongoing. If this archive was as extensive and accessible as it is today back in 2018, many of the students' original issues around seeing images of a wide range of Gibb's designs in detail would likely have been resolved, and it is encouraging to think that students in other institutions further afield now have easier access to this material. However, it would be hard to argue that having the opportunity to see the archive in person with curators, with stories to tell of the collection and the ability to show the garment in 360° whilst opening fastenings to reveal the lining of the garment and any labels sewn inside – could ever be fully replaced by a digitization. Furthermore, students also gained insight into the conservation requirements of archival garments through the wearing of protective gloves to prevent contamination and the atmospheric conditions requirements for storing.

Student responses

Beyond the initial research phase, the F&TD students at Gray's then spent several weeks developing their own designs from initial concept to final garments, all inspired by Gibb's designs, themes and/or cultural context in different ways. Strachan joined them at different points to hear about the development of their pieces in order to learn more about the fashion design process and to also help him decide which garments he would wear in *The Bill Gibb Line* spoken word film in which the new student designers were each matched with a poem celebrating a different Gibb collection.

Originally, Strachan had intended to only perform five poems in the film, but Charlotte Rose Scoular's design (Figure 15.3) made it hard not to include a sixth poem (on p. 190) he had been working on focused on Gibb's Spring/Summer 1977 collection which features kimonos, lacey underwear and black-lined garments. Scoular was one of the students particularly excited and inspired by Gibb's drawings in the Treasure Hub and she was keen to incorporate her own illustrations onto her garments, as well as mixing historical references from across time by being inspired by both Rococo undergarments and modern-day wetsuits and beachwear.

Figure 15.3 *Shane Strachan wearing Charlotte Rose Scoular's design. Photo by Grant Anderson for Look Again.*

Isle-of-Lewis-born Catherine Macdonald used her own Scottish heritage and the natural environment in her work as Gibb often did. She took inspiration from Scottish landscape, particularly cliffs and rock formations found along the coast, which she translated into various pleating techniques (Figure 15.4). This focus on pleats matched well with the first poem in the film (on p. 8), which mentions both pleats and tartan – Scottish influences which recur in much of Gibb's work.

A poem inspired by Gibb's Autumn/Winter 1974 collection (on p. 142) has multiple references to Gibb's layering of pattern-on-pattern, as well as the piling up of various textures in his garments. Thanks to the suggestion of the third-year tutor Keith Gray, two different students' work was paired together to create this look (Figure 15.5). The orange shirt was designed by Sarah Walker who was greatly inspired by Gibb's mixing of patterns, while the rest of the outfit was designed by Samantha Macdonald who utilized Aberdeen's architecture as inspiration for the monochromatic pattern in her work.

Walker's shirt was partly inspired by West African textile design which prompted necessary discussions in seminars around cultural appropriation versus appreciation,[10] and reflections on how

Figure 15.4 *Megan Davies wearing Catherine Macdonald. Photo by Fergus O'Connor (Robert Gordon University).*

Figure 15.5 *Shane Strachan wearing Sarah Walker and Samantha Macdonald. Photo by Graeme Roger.*

designers worked in the 1970s versus today. Similarly, knowing of Gibb's large client base in the Middle East, Catriona Battensby was inspired by Middle Eastern menswear for a more minimalist garment which features a subtle geometric print on the base (Figure 15.7). This echoed Gibb having to strip back on extravagance and embellishment in his work after his first financial crisis in 1978, and so was paired with the poem (on p. 197) reflecting on Gibb's Spring/Summer 1979 collection.

Some of the students took a more general contextual approach, such as Kirstie Noble who was inspired by the shape of crowds at famous 1970s music festivals like Woodstock. This led to her producing a pair of trousers which echoed the voluminous silhouettes of 1970s designers like Rhodes and Ossie Clark, with hand-painted dyes in bright colours (Figure 15.6). For the matching poem in *The Bill Gibb Line* (on p. 87–88), these trousers were paired with a jumper designed by Kimberley Monaghan who was inspired by Gibb and Kaffe Fassett's innovations in knitwear to experiment with new and innovative techniques herself. She utilized a laser cutter to cut holes in a recycled garment, through which a woollen knit pokes through at specific intervals; she also incorporated crocheted sleeves using cut-and-sew techniques (Figure 15.6). This sustainable fashion approach was much discussed in the seminars with a large focus on how materials could be upcycled or avoid being wasted, which is increasingly seen in degree shows at Gray's and beyond.

Following the original exhibition of Strachan's poems and the students' work in summer 2019 in Look Again's exhibition space, *The Bill Gibb Line* was redisplayed in Aberdeen Art Gallery in February 2020 alongside original Gibb garments and drawings from the archive for what was meant to be a three-month long exhibition. This was majorly disrupted by the Covid pandemic, which led to the work being displayed on-and-off until May 2021 to a far more limited audience. Since this time however, the film and student work has been collected by RGU Art & Heritage Collections, adding to the Gibb-related material rediscovered in 2018 and regularly displayed for new students on campus since.

Beyond Aberdeen

Since *The Bill Gibb Line* project, students in other institutions outside of Aberdeen and Scotland have been demonstrating how Gibb can be a near inexhaustible source of inspiration for the aspiring designer. For example, throughout the development of her final project for her MA in Fashion and Lifestyle Brand Studies at the University of Central Lancashire in 2021, Fiona Godfrey was inspired by Gibb's approach to branding and identity through the celebration of his Scottish heritage and use of symbols from nature, as well as his collaborations with craftspeople:

Figure 15.6 *Shane Strachan wearing Kimberley Monaghan and Kirstie Noble. Photo by Graeme Roger.*

Figure 15.7 *Finlay Rintoul wearing Catriona Battensby. Photo by Fergus O'Connor (Robert Gordon University).*

Gibb's business model became a valued and welcome blueprint for everything I envisioned for my own brand; working with expert artisans to recognise my designs and forming a close creative community, much the same as Gibb crafted his carefully chosen team. As part of a modern sustainable business model, collaboration with others whilst valuing and recognising their contribution is of the utmost importance, and in my opinion was one of Gibb's greatest strengths – community breeds creativity.[11]

At the London College of Fashion, Lucie Shilton's project for her MA Pattern and Garment Technology in 2024 utilized digital garment simulation through emerging technologies (CLO3D and Blender) to develop X-ray-like digital replicas of two 1970s garments by Gibb from the Central Saint Martins' Museum and Study Collection in order to make visible and reinterpret the pattern-cutting

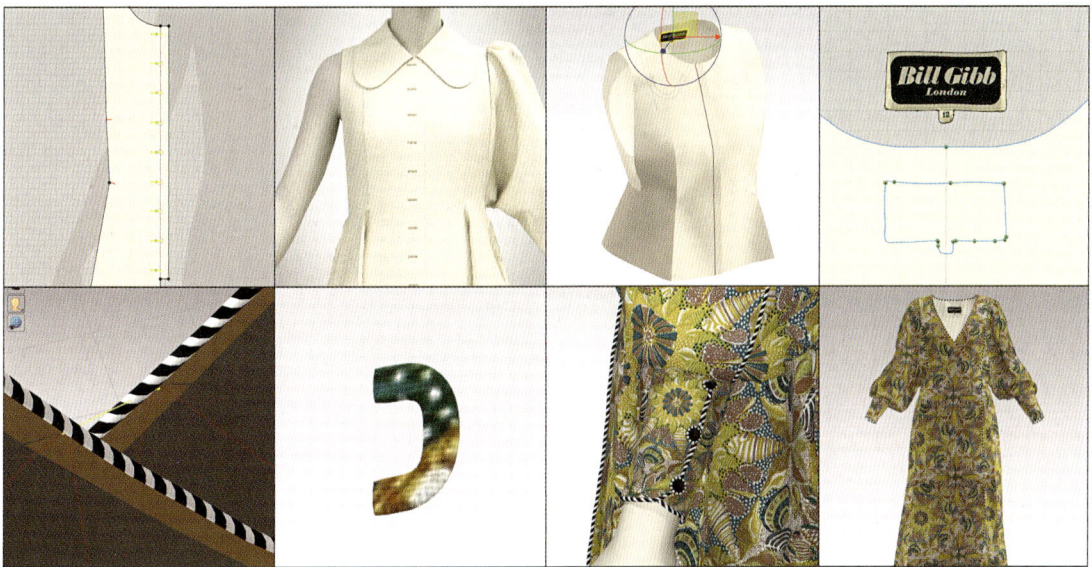

Figure 15.8 *Simulation development of a 1970s Bill Gibb yellow, orange and blue shell print wrap dress from Central Saint Martins' Museum and Study Collection. Courtesy of Lucie Shilton.*

approach used.[12] In an interview, Shilton explained the various stages required to create these digital replicas, as well as a real-life textile replica using digital pattern-cutting tools:

> My research process began with the analysis stage. I worked with the artefacts in an archival setting to gather data and develop an in-depth understanding of the pattern-cutting and construction processes. This stage involved detailed notetaking, close-up photography, technical drawings, and extracting key measurements.
>
> The second stage focused on reinterpreting the garment patterns. I developed these patterns through a combination of manual draping methods and digital pattern-cutting using Gerber and Lectra software. A physical prototype was created and fitted to a live model, testing the garment's functionality and silhouette alongside archival photographs.
>
> In the third stage, I transferred the digital patterns into CLO3D, digitally stitching the pieces to create a 3D simulation. The final outcomes were rendered in full colour and a variation was rendered in a transparent textile which further highlights the connection of pattern pieces. Finally, Blender software was used to develop a 3D-to-2D animation, emphasising the relationship between the individual pattern pieces and the completed form.[13]

This innovative technology provides new insights into the pattern-cutting techniques of the original garments which goes far beyond the limitations of the physical archive and standard 2D digitizations while making this knowledge globally accessible to new and contemporary

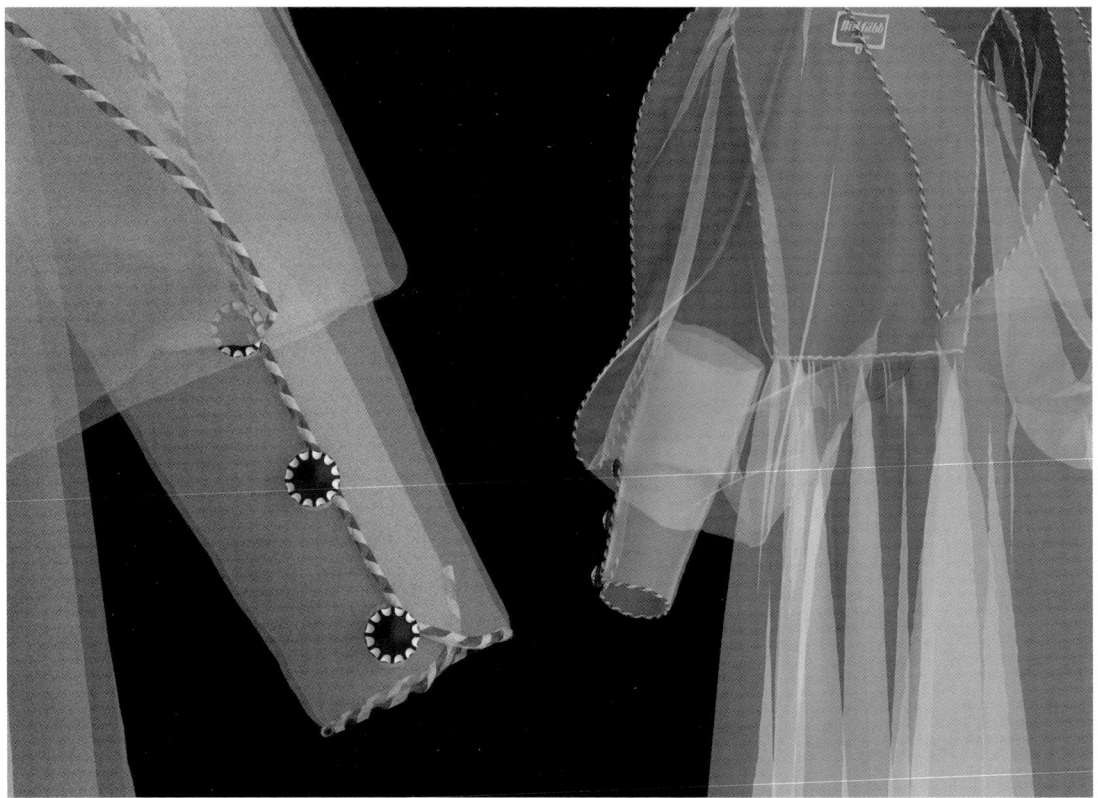

Figure 15.9 *Blender software rendering of 1970s Bill Gibb coat dress with enamel bee buttons from Central Saint Martins' Museum and Study Collection. Courtesy of Lucie Shilton.*

audiences including fashion designers and researchers working in remote locations. The project also demonstrated the potential of these emerging technologies for use in museum settings for enrichment and storytelling.

Conclusion

In summary, the Bill Gibb-focused student industry project at Gray's School of Art was built on an interdisciplinary approach between fashion design, creative writing and museum studies. The outcomes of the project were multi-faceted: an exhibition, performances and film including external input both from Shane Strachan and from staff at AAGM. The project also demonstrated the importance for students to gain an understanding of physical archives that can complement and enrich their other methods of research including digital. Following the success of *The Bill Gibb Line* and the ways in which the project generated a follow-on symposium and this publication, there is clear potential for further interdisciplinary projects which take inspiration from Gibb's life and oeuvre, particularly given the creative collaborations, theatrical showmanship and strong storytelling aspects of his timeless collections and fashion shows.

While significant issues with researching a pre-Internet designer became apparent during the project, the many educational benefits of encouraging students to engage with physical archives over digital resources cannot be understated. Yet, for those with limited or no access to a physical archive, archival digitization and emerging technologies like those utilized by Lucie Shilton are increasingly providing innovative ways for students and researchers to access key knowledge and new insights into bygone designers like Bill Gibb, ultimately extending their reach and legacy in ways that were not previously possible.

16

The Bill Gibb Line: creative crossovers in fashion and poetry

Shane Strachan

As a creative writer and performer hailing from Bill Gibb's hometown of Fraserburgh, I have long been inspired by his farm boy to fashion designer success story. I attended Lochpots Primary School on the same land where Gibb grew up on his grandparents' farm; here I developed creative dreams of my own far removed from the fishing industry most of my family worked in, so hearing of Gibb's story through older family members that had met him, as well as a display in Fraserburgh Heritage Centre, made becoming a professional writer seem more possible. Once I began publishing my work, I increasingly became attracted to the idea of finding a creative way to tell Gibb's story to new audiences. This desire culminated in my 2018–20 poetry project *The Bill Gibb Line*, through which I came to appreciate the skill, artistry and collaborative nature of the fashion industry. It also unveiled the parallels between creating a garment and writing a poem: the collaging of contrasting ideas, the importance of shape and line, the use of narrative and storytelling, and the aesthetics and power of visual imagery, whether seen on the runway or read on the page.

* * *

At first, I had not set out to do a poetry project. Back in 2014, I published a short story inspired by Twiggy and Justin de Villeneuve's visit to Gibb's parents' farm near New Pitsligo in 1972, an event which appealed to me in the coming together of two contrasting worlds – a global supermodel and her flashy photographer boyfriend visiting a family farm deep in rural Aberdeenshire.[1] Following this, I received a Robert Louis Stevenson (RLS) Fellowship from the Scottish Book Trust in 2018 to spend a month at the Hotel Chevillon residency centre in Grez-sur-Loing, France, to work on a longer project connected to Gibb's work. Initially I had envisioned that this would be a prose project along the lines of a biographical novel and so I set about interviewing his family and collaborators and spent several days reading through all the press cuttings and other archival material at Aberdeen Archives, Gallery and Museums' Treasure Hub where precious items are stored and cared for when not on public display. Reading through the reviews of Gibb's work, from his first show in 1967 in a pub at the top of Earls Court Road to his last major show just a few minutes away at Olympia London in 1985, I was struck by the inherent poeticism of fashion language, how it brought together rich, expressive vocabulary from across the world often with onomatopoeic effects. The writerly skill of fashion journalists like Suzy Menkes and Michael Roberts brought the drama and glamour of Gibb's runway shows to life in my mind's eye, and so I wanted to emulate this effect for my readers and realized that poetry would be the form that best captured and heightened this experience.

To create these 'fashion show' poems as I came to know them, I eventually settled on collaging together different snippets of verbatim material from the various fashion reviews and Gibb interviews of the time, repurposing the texts into traditional and new poetic forms that would best express the look and feel of each collection. I see this as being in line with Gibb's own postmodernist collage approach through which he mixed and matched lines and embellishments from a variety of historical and ethnic dress traditions, while incorporating textiles by multiple designers like Janet Taylor and Kaffe Fassett, harmoniously brought together in new and unexpected ways. As the French filmmaker Jean-Luc Godard aptly said, 'It's not where you take things from. It's where you take them to'.[2] The emergence of this approach as Gibb's signature design style is evident in the poem (on p. 83) which describes his breakthrough collection at the end of 1969 as a 'patchwork of earthly patterns', a 'magpie assemblage' of 'multi-patterned fusions / tailored in glorious confusion'.

However, as a writer, I am not working with colourful fabrics in three-dimensional space, but merely the words that represent them. I therefore had to utilize layout, shape and line as much as I could within the limitations of text on a page and this meant exploiting the graphic space on the page for effect. A clear example of this in *The Bill Gibb Line* can be seen in the following poem:

British Vogue, August – December 1971

Travel the world in an ancient map
printed on champagne satin, billowing
above a sea of gold and silver stripes.

In the Baghdad Room of Topkapi Palace,
wake in baggy harem pants and a golden top
with immense sleeves and gilded peacocks.

In a leather-star and medallion-printed smock,
walk in the steps of Cecil Beaton's Bolivian aunt
alpaca'd and bowler-hatted on Lake Titicaca.

With no telephone distractions on Praslin,
finish your trip in a black lancola karate wrap
unwinding on white Seychellois sands.

You'll find it all in Bill Gibb's finest
and final Baccarat collection
back home at Harrods of London.

Figure 16.1 *Detail from multidrawing of 1971 designs including the 'map dress' described at start of poem. AAGM Collections: ABDMS067450. The print is featured in Figure 7.8.*

The layout of the poem mimics the billowing curves of the map-print satin dress described in the first stanza with the subsequent stanzas each taking inspiration from a different international fashion shoot found in British *Vogue* between August and December 1971 to convey the sense of Gibb's clothes transporting their wearers to far off places, before we boomerang back to a Harrods' showroom. As well as being inspired by the visual imagery of these fashion shoots, I also reordered and reworded much of the original text from the editorials, strengthening the rhythm and adding some partial rhyme. Compare the original verbatim with the above poem:

> In the Baghdad Room of Topkapi, full of the ghosts of harem women, black and gold decorations to wear, baggy drawstring trousers, silks, velvets, netted and worked with gilded peacocks for a rich top with immense sleeves gathered in twice.[3]

> Here, cream alpaca smock laced from leather star over skirt; printed with medallions and blanket strip borders.[4]

Along with the lineation and enjambments (i.e. the continuation of a sentence onto the next line without punctuation), the refashioning of the original wording heightens the repetition of the plosive sounds 'b' and 'p', like in 'the Baghdad Room of Topkapi Palace, / wake in baggy harem pants and a golden top', as well as the chiming of line-endings in 'top', 'peacocks' and 'smock'. Beyond an attempt at an aesthetic harmoniousness through sound, in keeping the line length and number of syllables fairly consistent throughout, I aimed to reflect the orderly and pleasing shape and line of Gibb's garments.

All of these elements – collage, line and sound – are taken a step further in formal terms in a poem inspired by Gibb's 1977 Spring/Summer collection which exemplifies Gibb's trademark fantasy fusion at the height of his creative powers:[5]

Bruton Place, Mayfair, 28th October 1976

In the fashion world
  Gibb has gone Oriental
    with striped kimonos
      starkly framed in the finest
        black satin and Indian silk.

  For the trendy bride
    there's a daring wedding dress,
reminiscent of
Victorian underwear
in white broderie anglaise –

Granny won't like it,
  but those old underpinnings
    of her yesteryear
      have been freed from the boudoir
        as tomorrow's outer gear.

  This year's collection
    seems intent on promoting
sensuality:
the necklines have been lowered
and the sides of skirts are split.

And when the skirts whirl
  and slit to reveal the voile
    and lace underneath,
      you get a delicious peep
        at the world's dearest panties.

  We live in tough times
    with our country tottering
  towards bankruptcy,
  but our clothes won't stop being
the ritziest in Europe.

Figure 16.2 *Drawing of pleated kimono from the Spring/Summer 1977 collection. AAGM Collections: ABDMS035670.*

To reflect this collection's mixing of historical British fashion elements with kimono-like shapes and lines from Japanese design I landed upon the tanka, a traditional Japanese poetic form. In its English language variety, the tanka has a strict syllable pattern that is initially similar to the haiku form of three lines comprising five syllables, then seven syllables, then five syllables; it is then extended by an additional two seven-syllable lines. This pattern is clear in the stanza below, the separate syllables emphasized by hyphenation:

Gran-ny won't like it,
   but those old und-er-pinn-ings
      of her yest-er-year
         have been freed from the boud-oir
           as to-morr-ow's out-er gear.

Once again, this involved manipulating and sculpting the original verbatim material anew; in the same way Gibb would drape fabric on a mannequin in different arrangements until he had the pleating or line he wanted, I similarly played around with the words on the page to get an undulating form, rather than sticking to the traditional layout of a tanka poem as one continuous line. I also made subtle changes to the order and word choice in places to gain some rhymes as well as to fit the strict syllable pattern, as is clear when the above stanza is compared with the original verbatim: 'The whole look is reminiscent of Victorian underpinnings. Granny might not like it, but yesterday's underwear has emerged from the boudoir to become tomorrow's outerwear.' While the 1971 poem utilized plosive sounds, there is far more sibilance ('s' and 'sh' sounds) and fricatives (sounds like 'f', 'v' and 'th') in this poem to mimic the sensual textures and line of this collection's garments, the way the voile, silk and satin swishes and sways down the runway. The zig-zagging indentation down the lefthand side could, however, mimic the instability of the times, politically and economically, described in the poem's final stanza with the country 'tottering towards bankruptcy'.

It is important to note at this point that, while verbatim material can be an excellent way to create an authentic sounding voice in creative works, it is clearly problematic when it reflects outdated perspectives and language. This brings up the tension for the writer working with verbatim – Latin for 'word for word' – in terms of deciding to stay true to the original wording in order to hold up a mirror to the past for modern-day readers to see the reality of this time, warts and all, or adjusting the language to be more reflective of modern views and terminology. My choice for these poems was to swap out strongly offensive terms, especially those relating to race, but to retain some aspects of the stark colonial lens recurrent in many reviews of Gibb's work, which is evident in his first ever collection being described as 'exotic' in the first poem (p. 8), the evocation of travel in exoticized terms in the 1971 *Vogue* editorial poem (p. 188) and the 1977 collection being described as going 'Oriental' (p. 190) – a clear exoticization and othering of Asian culture as Edward Said outlined in *Orientalism*.[6] Even if Gibb himself may have not intended for his work to be viewed in this way, I think it is important to highlight how his clothes were evaluated and promoted in newspapers and magazines at this time rather than sanitize and sidestep it, and hope that the speakers of these specific poems clearly belong to the past with readers critically evaluating them in the same way they would a yellowed, fray-edged newspaper clipping.

While the main aim of each poem was to evoke the feel and look of a specific collection, I was also conscious of trying to make connections with Gibb's own story that accumulatively trace the trajectory of his career in relation to the wider context of the time. This was important to me as I wanted to introduce and win over new audiences to Gibb's work who may otherwise have known little of him or nothing at all, and so the poems are generally accessible and quite literal, rather than delving too much into the realm of metaphor which can at times led to an enigmatic, riddle-like quality. The latter is often the case with the beautiful poems in Valerie Wallace's *House of McQueen*, several of which are also partly composed through a collaging of verbatim material, but with far more demands on the reader to 'decode' them. For instance, each sonnet in Wallace's 'Bespoke' sequence takes on the vocabularies of a different muse or patron of Alexander McQueen, collaged from interviews and social media posts, such as the first sonnet from Naomi Campbell's words:

> Who was I – asking with women and concepts
> The whole butterfly night of the world and why
> A wing in a mirror could interpret
> It, and the body's grief and courage. My
> Life begins with every question I face,
> In each wild shape my surgery finds
> When I call out my name with my touch.
> I know the deep privacy of the possibly lost.
> Am I meant to be tempted as I am,
> Unwrap intimacy, take its top off,
> Go deeper, to nerve and blood and calm.
> Everything feels wild. Nothing feels young.
> I have found beauty, pulled back the cover,
> And in my time was some kind of wonder.[7]

Wallace can take more risks with accessibility given modern-day readers are more likely to know of Alexander McQueen and his muses' stories and come to the collection armed with this knowledge. In leaning more towards narrative poetry in *The Bill Gibb Line*, I sacrificed the potential to really experiment with metaphor and meaning in this way, but I believe this is necessary to reach the widest audience possible.

While the majority of the poems before the 1977 Spring/Summer tanka poem trace Gibb's ascendency – often with final stanzas that threaten to become a little repetitive in their adulation – the following poem focuses less on the clothes and more on the man, giving insight into the anxieties he felt during his ten-year retrospective show at the Royal Albert Hall, one of the biggest fashion shows ever held at the time just before his business faced a series of major financial crises: in 1982, he told Brenda Polan of *The Guardian* that the show 'still haunts [his] dreams and wakes him in a cold sweat […] It was, he believes, pure hubris'.[8]

The Royal Albert Hall, 18th November 1977

This ellipse was lit with electric
for The Shah of Persia.
Its walls have rung with the shrieks
of Wagner's prima donnas.
When the Suffragettes met
they occupied every seat,
and Olivier got his act together
over in the West Theatre.

Now this: my retrospective.
Seven thousand in the audience.

Let the show begin, let them see
that these are not dresses,
but time broken and reassembled
into timelessness.

These are not models – they are
hippies dancing in marbled smocks,
nineteen-thirties movie stars gliding
in orange batwing midis, villainesses
strutting in cream dresses trimmed
with salamander skin, empresses
slinking in kimonos made of leather
draped in raccoon tails, flowers and feathers.
All of them all at once: a patchwork
of other worlds buckled, buttoned,
stitched and sewn together.

Twiggy sings a country song
in a fringed leather frock.
Hannah Gordon is a Highland girl
in a frilly tartan smock.
Cleo Laine is Cleopatra
in a gilded peacock top.

But when Wayne Sleep leaps
across the stage invaded by Greek Gods
wrapped in Bill Gibb bed linen,
I unravel at the seams like a burst stitch –
my palms sweat, I feel sick.
I have flown too high like Icarus.

The lights brighten, the music dims
and thousands leave me alone in this
vast ellipse of emptiness.

Figure 16.3 *Singer and songwriter Linda Lewis backstage at Gibb's 1977 retrospective. Photo: Niall McInerney / Bloomsbury Fashion Photography Archive.*

Figure 16.4 *Model wearing knitwear from Gibb's 1977 A/W Scottish Collection at the Royal Albert Hall. Photo: Niall McInerney / Bloomsbury Fashion Photography Archive.*

Through the use of the first-person 'I', the voice of this poem most explicitly belongs to a specific person by inhabiting the viewpoint of Gibb himself. It is not as clear who the speakers of the preceding poems are if simply viewed on the page, especially since they are all written in Standard English orthography. However, when I perform them, I take on a distinctive accent which is often reflective of the particular class and geographical background of real and imagined fashion reviewers, models and muses. This can be experienced by listening to *The Bill Gibb Line* podcast, which contains all of the poems, or by viewing the short film in which I perform the poems to camera wearing a variety of student-designed garments (as explored in Chapter 14) while code-switching my accent and delivery to match the voice and perspective of each poem.[9] For instance, I take on a more upper-class accent for the poem inspired by Gibb's 1974 Autumn/Winter collection (on p. 142) to be phonetically closer to the voice of fashion journalist Michael Roberts, the reviewer Gibb is said to have sweated most over.[10] On the other hand, I take on a working-class London accent for the 1977 tanka poem to reflect the collection's British inflections such as the broderie anglaise wedding dress and 'dear panties' made of voile and lace. Janet Street-Porter inspired this choice, being a fashion journalist at this time who was in the audience for Gibb's first independent label show at London's Oriental Club in 1972, and who – like Gibb and his fellow designers Ossie Clarke and Zandra Rhodes – was breaking into an industry that had been predominantly run by the upper and middle classes before free tuition fees became available thanks to the Education Act 1962. The simultaneous changing of clothes and voice throughout the film is intended to evoke the altered personas we take on when we wear something unique – the transformative power of clothes as a societal 'language' in and of themselves as French philosopher Roland Barthes argued.[11] Gibb was well aware of these ideas of persona and transformation with him often thinking of an ideal wearer during the design process:

> I design with a discriminating woman in mind, probably a career woman with great style and confidence, a woman on the move and in the know, with a vibrant personality to carry the clothes off. If I see them badly worn I feel a deep and strange pain.[12]

While I was always keen to experiment with changing my voice for performance as I had done in spoken-word projects before, I had not initially planned to wear the student-made garments or film myself in them, but during my RLS Fellowship residency in November 2018 at Grez-sur-Loing, a few seeds were planted which led to this. Firstly, I read about Gibb's involvement in the creation of one of sculptor and performance artist Andrew Logan's famous 'half-n-half' looks combining half an evening dress with half a man's tuxedo, which Logan then wore at the second Alternative Miss World at his Hackney studio in 1973 where Gibb acted as one of the judges.[13] I also visited Grayson Perry's 2018–19 exhibition *Vanité, Identité, Sexualité* at Monnaie de Paris, which featured dresses worn for his alter ego Claire, and I researched other artists who have dressed up and dragged up as other personas specifically on film, such as Cindy Sherman and Rachel Mclean. During my residency, I also met Swedish photographer Lisa Brunzell whose project *Let the World Adore You* had involved taking pictures of ABBA tribute acts from across the UK.[14] Reflecting on artists dressing up as other characters along with the idea of a tribute act – a modern-day re-enactment of people from a specific moment from the past, most pertinently the 1970s – led to the epiphany that wearing and performing in the new garments would be a pivotal part of the project. Filmed in a green-screen room a few months later, the sense of re-enactment and contrivance is further heightened by the green screen remaining in the final film along with a light stand and microphone boom, drawing attention to the staging involved.

The play with voice and code-switching is more explicit in the next poem, which starts and ends with slightly tweaked verbatim originally said by Gibb in a Lesley Ebbet's interview,[15] topping and tailing a central stanza which exposes his potential 'inner' voice with touches of Doric, the North East Scots dialect he was brought up speaking which he continued to speak with his family when home in Aberdeenshire:

Hyde Park Hotel, 12th October 1978

I haven't included the usual embellishments, because I think people believe they're there to hide a designer's lack of shape and line.

See-through
        taps and troosers
in gold and black.
        Buckle
tie belts
        in crepe de chine.
Knot
        overskirts at the waist
and aroon an ankle.
        Expose
bare flesh
        in strapless jersey tops.
Criss-cross
        here and there
wi slivers o material.
        Cut great slits
in the sides
        o skirts.
Wrap
        a silk choker
roon yer neck.

So this time I didn't add anything too fantastic. It's all very 1979 without losing the Bill Gibb line.

Figure 16.5 *Drawing of embroidered dress for Spring/Summer 1979 collection. AAGM Collections: ABDMS035724.*

Once again, I experimented with form to sculpt the central, skeletal stanza, 'inverting' the line from the edges to the centre with alternating negative space to mimic this far more stripped back, strappy collection, very much in contrast to many of the earlier poems such as the long, run-on lines of the 1974 Autumn-Winter poem (on p. 142) which layer up like the cosy garments described. There is also BDSM-esque word choice throughout, reflecting the flesh-baring designs – unexpected given most of Gibb's earlier collections are far more conservative and covered up – while also being suggestive of an underlying violence: Gibb's usual penchant for layers and embellishment had to be stripped away and cut back due to financial troubles with his new investors forcing him to produce cheaper, ready-to-wear garments at this time. This is further emphasized by the use of sound once more: soft, sensuous sibilance ('s' and 'sh') is undercut by the full range of harder plosive consonants ('b', 'd', 'g', 'k', 'p' and 't'). To perform the verbatim quotations in this piece, I thought back to the filmed interviews I had watched of Gibb around this time,[16] and attempted to imitate the somewhat Received Pronunciation accent he had adopted in London which would have been so alien to his mother tongue, in the same way his native language had been alien to his fellow students at St Martin's when he had first arrived in London causing him much distress. I also tried to capture the weariness you can sense from his expression in these interviews, the bright-eyed excitement visible in the 1972 BBC documentary of his first independent label collection now gone.

The intervening time between this stripped back 1979 Spring/Summer collection and his 1985 Bronze Age collection were not quite wilderness years, but the fact Gibb had to switch to working more on private commissions for celebrity brides and Middle-Eastern clients who still sought out his romantic, fantasy looks, alongside design consultancy work for Harrods and 'make-your-own' dress pattern partnerships with newspapers, means that there was no significant collection with a strong theme or narrative to inspire a poem until the Bronze Age collection, which resulted in the final poem of *The Bill Gibb Line*. This poem shifts more into a metaphorical plane than any other by inhabiting the perspective of Gibb's imagined Bronze Age Bride – the climactic garment as is tradition in the fashion world. It is also far more playful with the source material, mainly a review by *The Daily Telegraph*'s Ann Chubb who was sympathetic to Gibb's vision when several other reviewers were not with its descriptions of the collection's rich colours and textures which take on symbolic significance in the final poem: 'There are two major colour spectrums: bronze hues of beaten gold, deep burgundy, pale gold, lichen and grey or pewter shades of amethyst, grey, foxglove and soft fern green.'[17]

While I spent a lot of time with the sketches and pattern cuttings held in RGU Art & Heritage Collections for his unfinished 1986 Spring/Summer collection inspired by flowers, I decided against writing a further poem that would chronologically extend *The Bill Gibb Line* further, especially since the resulting flower collection, although beautiful, has the sense of feeling half-formed due to Gibb's illness. Poignantly, on the reverse of one of the sketches for this collection is an appointment letter from St Stephen's Hospital in London, which adds to this impression of him always being so intently focused on his work, even when very ill.

In going deeper into history, the Bronze Age collection felt like a return to Gibb's design roots, yet the resulting poem also has the sense of an ending, resonating with Gibb's death at only 44 years old less than three years later.

The Apex Room, Olympia, 16th March 1985

Figure 16.6 *Portrait of Bill Gibb in 1966 by Kaffe Fassett, painted in egg tempera. Courtesy of Kaffe Fassett.*

Take me as your Bronze Age bride,
share my dowry of beaten gold.

Whisper to me in silver hues,
unravel tangled scrolls of cord.

Shear my wool by the river, foxglove me on the soft green ferns.

Cave paint me in deep burgundy,
drink me in like liquid cork.

Patch me up with burnished leather,
heal drunkenness with amethyst.

With a touch as rough as tree bark,
let me soften your pewter heart.

Abandon long-held fantasies.
Awake to stark reality.

Now I am grey and dressed in lichen,
bury me in clay and sleep beside me.

Notes

Introduction

1 Jean Rafferty, 'Gentle genius of style was ahead of his time', *Scotland on Sunday*, 6 November 1988: 4. Also: 'Ahead of his time, he was aware of the value of celebrity endorsement and dressed rock stars, actresses and film stars from Rod Stewart to Bianca Jagger and Elizabeth Taylor.' – Iain R. Webb, *Bill Gibb: Fashion and Fantasy* (London: V&A, 2018): jacket cover summary.

2 'In any other country, Bill's talents would have won him more commercial success' – Zandra Rhodes quoted in 'Fashion Star Bill Gibb Dies', *The Times*, 4 Jan 1988. Also: 'he was totally underrated as a designer in this country . . . It was a great mistake for him to choose to go to London. Had he gone to Paris he would have received much wider recognition.' – Glasgow shop-owner Betty Davis quoted in Rafferty.

3 Alice Fisher, 'Fashion Designer Bill Gibb (1943-1988)' in 'A punk, a monkey, a maths genius and our pick of local heroes who deserve a blue plaque', *The Observer*, 10 September 2023. https://www.theguardian.com/culture/2023/sep/10/a-punk-a-monkey-a-maths-genius-our-pick-of-local-heroes-who-deserve-a-blue-plaque (accessed February 2024).

4 Suzy Menkes, 'Bill Gibb: A bittersweet story of a forgotten designer', *The New York Times*, 24 November 2008. https://www.nytimes.com/2008/11/25/style/25iht-fbill.1.18094446.html (accessed 16 September 2024).

5 Colleen Toomey, 'Where are they now?', *The Observer*, 8 January 1984: 28.

6 Menkes, 'Bill Gibb: A bittersweet story of a forgotten designer'.

7 Christine Rew, *Bill Gibb: The Golden Boy of British Fashion* (Aberdeen: Aberdeen City Council, 2003).

Chapter 2

1 British *Vogue*, 1 April 1976: 123.

2 The archive was purchased by Aberdeen City Council with financial contributions from the Art Fund, the Friends of Aberdeen Art Gallery and Museums and the National Fund for Acquisitions. The archive is cared for by Aberdeen Archives, Gallery and Museums and may be accessed by appointment.

3 Brenda Polan, 'Expensive Thrills', *Guardian*, 20 May 1982.

4 'Fraserburgh lad enters the fashion world', *People's Journal*, 19 November 1966: 12.

5   Georgina Howell, *In Vogue: 75 Years of Style* (London: Condé Nast, 1991), 196.

6   Ernestine Carter, 'The Mixture as Never Before', *Sunday Times*, 21 December 1969.

7   Linda Grant, 'The History Boy', *Stella*, 5 October 2008: 50–53.

8   Carter, *Sunday Times*, 21 December 1969.

9   Victoria and Albert Museum, accession number E.529-2015 https://collections.vam.ac.uk/item/O1322369/fashion-illustration-by-veronica-papworth-fashion-illustration-papworth-veronica/ (accessed 26 March 2024).

10 Cally Blackman, *100 Years of Fashion Illustration* (London: Laurence King Publishing, 2007), 240 and 241.

11 For examples of Hillson's designs see Victoria and Albert Museum, accession number E.655-2015 https://collections.vam.ac.uk/item/O1261607/fashion-illustration-bobby-hillson/ (accessed 26 March 2024).

12 Examples of Ossie Clark's sketches are reproduced in Judith Watt, *Ossie Clark 1965|74* (London: V&A Publications, 2003), 105 and 109.

13 British *Vogue*, 15 September 1972: 16.

14 For examples of Jean Muir's designs see Victoria and Albert Museum accession numbers E.129-1978 https://collections.vam.ac.uk/item/O553601/fashion-design-jean-muir/ and E.133-1978 https://collections.vam.ac.uk/item/O553597/fashion-design-jean-muir/ (both accessed 26 March 2024).

15 British *Vogue*, 15 September 1972: 20.

16 British *Vogue*, 1 April 1976.

17 British *Vogue*, 15 September 1972.

18 Emilio Coia, 'Bill Gibb', *Scottish Field*, May 1977: 90.

19 The dress and accessories are held in the collections of Leeds Museums and Galleries. The Fashion Museum Bath also holds a black and white photograph of the dress photographed by Patrick Lichfield for the *Sunday Times*.

20 Bill Gibb, *Designer*, May 1981: 10.

21 Aberdeen, Archives, Gallery and Museums collection, accession number ABDMS070183.

22 Polan, *Guardian*, 20 May 1982.

23 Jackie McGlone, 'The Forgotten Genius', *Herald Magazine*, 3 November 2001: 22.

24 Norman Parkinson, *Vogue*, November 1977: 192.

25 British *Vogue*, April 1976: 123.

26 See drawings in Aberdeen Archives, Gallery and Museums collection, accession numbers ABDMS067195 and ABDMS095708.

27 Ernestine Carter, *Sunday Times*, 23 April 1972: 41.

28 'The Gorizia designer who dressed Lady D has died at the age of 79', Obituary, *Il Piccolo*, 13 August 2015. Available online: https://ilpiccolo.gelocal.it/trieste/cronaca/2012/08/13/news/morta-a-79-anni-la-stilista-gorziana-che-vesti-lady-d-1.11928959 (accessed 2 September 2023).

29 Bill Gibb, *Daily Express*, 30 September 1974: 9.

Chapter 3

1. Marie McLoughlin, '"The textile student needs little Giotto, (or a little will go a long way)" (Pevsner Nov 1968.) The 1970 Coldstream Report in response to the art school unrest of 1968', *Journal of Design History*, Volume 32, Issue 2, May 2019: 170–87.

2. Christine Rew, 'Bill Gibb', *Costume,* Vol 28, No 1 (1994): 81–96.

3. Zandra Rhodes, *The Art of Zandra Rhodes* (London: Michael O'Mara and Zandra Rhodes Publications Ltd, 1984), 9.

4. Max Tilke, *Costumes of Eastern Europe*. First published in 1925 in Berlin; reprinted in English in London: Ernest Benn, 1926.

5. Iain R. Webb, *Bill Gibb: Fashion and Fantasy* (2008). Back cover.

6. Webb, 23.

Chapter 4

1. Yves Saint Laurent, *Dim Dam Dom,* (TV show on fashion) March 10, 1968 quoted in Pierre Bergé, Jéromine Savignon (eds), *Saint Laurent Rive Gauche. Fashion Revolution* (New York: Harry N. Abrams, 2012), 75.

2. Insee: Institut national de la statistique et des études économiques du Ministère de l'Economie et des Finances en France quoted by Florence Brachet-Champsaur in 'Un grand magasin à la pointe de la mode: Les Galeris Lafayette', in Dominique Veillon, Michèle Ruffat (eds), *La Mode des Sixties. L'entrée dans la modernité*, (Paris: Autrement, 2007): 181.

3. Gérald Chevalier, 'La boutique des années 1960: un nouvel espace pour un nouveau mode de consommation', in Ruffat Veillon, *La Mode des Sixties* (Paris: Autrement, 2008), 194–5.

4. *Gazette de Lausanne et Journal Suisse*, no 276, 26 November 1971: 16; (author's translation).

5. François Bon, 'autobiographie des objets | 48, pattes d'eph. L'Internet a été inventé pour qu'on y parle de ses culottes' (2011; author's translation), https://www.tierslivre.net/spip/spip.php?article2663 (accessed August 2024).

6. Jole Rota, 'Swiss couturier in Rome. Heinz W. Riva', *Textiles Suisses*, 1969, no 2, 48–9.

7. Katja Baigger, 'Der Walliseller, der den Minijupe nach Italien brachte', *Neue Zurcher Zeitung*, 28 August 2010.

8. Anon., 'Collections printemps-été 1972. Et que se passe-t-il outre-Manche (Echos de Grande-Bretagne)', *Journal de Genève*, 23 March 1972: 16; (author's translation).

9. Most probably bought at Joel & Son Fabrics in London which sold the Swiss brand, email communication (06.03.2024) by Martin Leuthold, former artistic director of Jakob Schlaepfer. Other shops selling Swiss fabrics were Jason's of Bond St., Jacob Gordon Ltd, Allans of Duke Street, Simmonds at Stanley & Lowe, cf. Beatrice Feisst, 'Meeting Swiss fabric friends: London', *Textiles Suisses*, 1982 no 49, 102–5.

10. Valerie Steele, *Paris Fashion: A Cultural History* (Bloomsbury, 2017), 249.

11. Anne Diatkine, 'Kenzo' interview, in Olivier Saillard et al., eds, *Fashion Mix – Mode d'ici, créateurs d'ailleurs* (Paris: Flammarion, 2014), 123; (author's translation).

12 Quoted in Joel Lobenthal, *Radical Rags* (London: Abbeville Press, 1990), 48.

13 Ibid, 17.

14 French *Vogue*, May 1969, spread reproduced in Bergé et al., *Saint Laurent Rive Gauche*: 144–5.

15 John Urry, Jonas Larsen, *The Tourist Gaze 3.0*, (Sage publications, 3rd edition, 2011), 4.

16 Marie-Claude Treglia, *100 Idées, l'aventure des seventies* (Paris: Hoëbeke, 2015). The magazine, first a quarterly of *Marie-Claire*, became independent in 1973, published monthly till 1988. It was revived in 2023.

17 Caroline Baker in *Nova,* April:77 (1970) quoted in June Marsh, *History of Fashion. New Look to Now* (London: Vivays Publishing, 2012), 130.

18 *Touches d'exotisme, XIVe – XXe siècles* (Paris: Union centrale des arts décoratifs, 1999).

19 Olivier Saillard et al., *Fashion Mix*.

20 Elodie Chazalon, 'A contre-mode? Du vêtement hippie et de son authenticité aux Etats-Unis de 1967 à nos jours', *Modes pratiques. Revue d'histoire du vêtement et de la mode,* no 2 'Sans la mode' (2015), 317.

21 Elizabeth Wilson, *Adorned in Dreams* (Berkeley: University of California Press, 1985), 30.

22 Quoted by Iain R. Webb, *Bill Gibb. Fashion and Fantasy* (London: V&A Publications, 2008), 1.

23 Sarah Kennedy in Kennedy et al. (eds), *Vintage Fashion* (London/Sydney: Welbeck, 2022), 144–207, 154–5 and 164–7.

24 Bill Gibb in *Flair* magazine, September 1972, quoted by Webb, *Bill Gibb. Fashion and Fantasy*, 29.

25 Bill Gibb in an interview with Joan Bakewell for *Radio Times*, 26 April 1973, promoting the BBC programme 'For the Sake of Appearance' aired 1 May 1973, in ibid.

26 Anne Chassagnol, 'Fabuleuse Albion : l'art de fabriquer une identité culturelle hégémonique', *Romantisme,* 4, 170 (2015): 11–22, 21.

27 Amy De la Haye, Valerie Mendes, 'Bill Gibb' in Lydia Kamitsis and Bruno Remaury (eds), *Dictionnaire international de la mode* (Paris: Editions du Regard, 2004), 73; (author's translation).

28 Lauren D. Whitley, *Hippie Chic*, (Boston: MFA Publications, 2013), 45–70.

29 Diatkine in Saillard et al., *Fashion Mix,* 123; (author's translation).

30 Ginette Sainderichin, *Kenzo* (Paris: Du May, 1989), 28.

31 Quoted in ibid., 64; (author's translation).

32 Kathleen (Kate) Franklin, PR agent, quoted by Webb, *Bill Gibb: Fashion and Fantasy*, 39.

33 Ginette Sainderichin, *Kenzo* (Paris: Assouline, 1998), 13; (author's translation).

34 Diatkine in Saillard et al., *Fashion Mix*, 124; (author's translation).

35 Quoted in Sainderichin, *Kenzo* (1989), 34–6; (author's translation).

36 Greta Sitek, 'Top Fashion from London in Top Fabrics from Switzerland' in *Textiles Suisses - Swiss Textiles*, 1977 no 30, 106; https://www.e-periodica.ch/digbib/view?pid=txs-005%3A1977%3A512%3A%3A115#221 (accessed August 2024). The Swiss textile and clothing trade journal, with a worldwide circulation, was published as of 1926 under the aegis of the OSEC (Swiss Office of Commercial Expansion). The multilingual edition ran from 1966 to

1997. The St Gallen Textile museum holds the matching sample of the embroidered wool tartan used by Bill Gibb, produced by Jakob Schlaepfer in 1976, inv. nr 71609, https://emp-web-58.zetcom.ch/eMP/eMuseumPlus. I am grateful to Luba Nurse, Head of Collection + Library of the Textilmuseum St. Gallen, for the reference.

37 Sainderichin, *Kenzo* (1998), 13.

38 Ibid.

39 'Jules François Crahay', Fashion & Lace Museum, https://www.fashionandlacemuseum.brussels/en/triplex/jules-francois-crahay-belgian-first-exhibition-one-of-the-last-geniuses-of-couture-compared-to-christian-dior-haute-couture (accessed August 2024).

40 Pierre-Yves Guillen, Jacqueline Claude, *Le Dé d'Or – Haute Couture Française*, (Editions J.M.G., 1990), 36–7; (author's translation).

41 Khémaïs Ben Lakhdar, 'Folklores et exotismes dans l'œuvre de Jules-François Crahay' in Nicolas Lor (ed.), *Jules-François Crahay: Grand couturier redécouvert* (Brussels: Lanoo, 2024), 194–5; (author's translation).

42 Quoted in the exhibition *L'Asie rêvée d'Yves Saint-Laurent*, Musée Yves Saint-Laurent, Paris, 2018–2019. See https://museeyslparis.com/expositions/asie-revee-yves-saint-laurent, (accessed August 2024; author's translation).

43 Quoted by Marie Ottavi, 'Yves Saint-Laurent. La fièvre voyageuse' in *Libération*, 25 October 2018; (author's translation).

44 Edward Said, *Orientalism: Western Conceptions of the Orient* (Originally published 1978. London: Penguin, 1995), i.

45 Aurélie Samuel, curator Musée Yves Saint-Laurent, quoted by Ottavi in 'Yves Saint-Laurent. La fièvre voyageuse'; (author's translation).

46 Audrey Bartis, 'Atypical' in Pierre Antoine Vettorello, 'On colonial violence in fashion schools', *The Yarn*, no 1 (Antwerp: October 2023), 30–1.

47 Whitley, *Hippie Chic*, 70.

Chapter 6

1 Helena Matheopoulos, 'The art of making history in fashion', *Daily Express*, 12 April 1976: 4.

2 Kevin Almond, 'Fashion in peril: an investigation into how fashion mirrored change in UK society,' *International Journal of Fashion Design, Technology and Education*, No.4 (2011): 21–30.

3 Joanne Turney, *The Culture of Knitting* (New York: Berg Publishing, 2009), 53.

4 Laurel Forster and Sue Harper (eds), *British Culture and Society in the 1970's: The Lost Decade* (Cambridge Scholars Publishing, 2010), 3.

5 Suzy Menkes, *Knitwear Revolution: Designer Patterns to Make* (HarperCollins Publishers Ltd, 1983).

6 Sandy Black, 'A designer's perspective on a creative era in knitwear design: British fashion knitwear 1970–1990', *Creativity in Knitted Textiles – Special Issue TEXTILE* (2023): 875–902.

7 Christine Rew, *Bill Gibb: The Golden Boy of British Fashion* (Aberdeen City Council, 2003), 59.

8. Iain R. Webb, *Bill Gibb: Fashion and Fantasy* (London: V&A Publishing, 2008), 87.

9. Ibid, 3.

10. Ibid, 95.

11. Kaffe Fassett, interview with editors, December 2023.

12. Fully fashioned is a shaping technique where the stitches in a knitted garment are increased and decreased creating no fabric waste. It is symbolic of craftmanship and premium knitwear. Cut and sew is a technique where a blanket of fabric is knitted and the shape of the garment is then cut out and constructed. It is used primarily in mass manufactured knitwear as a more economic and cost effective production method however creates waste fabric.

13. Fassett, interview with editors.

14. Rachael Matthews, *The Mindfulness of Knitting: Meditations on Craft and Calm* (Brighton: Leaping Hare Press, 2016), 9.

15. V&A, 'Interviews with knit designer and textile artists', Patricia Roberts Interview, V&A website, https://www.vam.ac.uk/articles/interviews-with-knit-designers-and-textile-artists (accessed 24 September 2024).

16. Viewable via https://lizeggleston.com/2011/01/14/inspirational-images-alice-ormsby-gore-in-bill-gibb-for-baccarat/ (accessed 1 October 2024).

17. Iain R. Webb, *Bill Gibb: Fashion and Fantasy* (London: V&A Publishing, 2008), 101.

18. Turney, *The Culture of Knitting*, 104.

19. Amy Twigger Holroyd, *Folk Fashion: Understanding Homemade Clothes* (I.B. Tauris & Co. Ltd, 2017), 18.

20. Frédéric Joignot, 'Sonia Rykiel, queen of knitwear', *The Guardian*, 20 October 2013. https://www.theguardian.com/fashion/2013/oct/08/sonia-rykiel-queen-of-knitwear (accessed 24 September 2024).

21. Kitty Dann, 'Small business in the spotlight . . . Wool and the Gang', *The Guardian*, 4 April 2015. https://www.theguardian.com/small-business-network/2015/apr/04/in-the-spotlight-wool-and-the-gang (accessed 24 September 2024).

22. Ravelry, https://www.ravelry.com

23. Webb, *Bill Gibb: Fashion and Fantasy*, 61.

24. Bill Gibb, *Hollywood Knits: Twenty glamorous sweaters to knit* (Pavillion Books Limited. London, 1987).

Chapter 7

1. Anna Piaggi, personal interview with author.

2. Kate Franklin, personal interview with author.

3. Lesley Ebbetts, personal interview with author.

4. Ibid.

5. Hamish Bowles, personal interview with author.

6   Ibid.

7   American *Vogue*, October 2005: 186.

8   Lesley Ebbetts, personal interview with author.

9   British *Vogue*, February 1978: 8.

10 Quoted in interview with Ann Chubb, *The Daily Telegraph*, 7 November 1977: 15.

11 *Draper's Record*, 3 December 1977.

12 Janet Street-Porter, *Evening Standard*, 6 November 1972: 30.

13 Quoted in interview with Shirley Lowe, *Over 21* magazine, February 1973: 38.

14 Kate Franklin, personal interview with author.

15 Ibid.

16 Jackie McGlone, *The Scotsman*, 17 February 1999: 12.

17 Quoted from press release, Kathleen Franklin Publicity, March 1985.

18 Bernadine Morris, *The New York Times*, 19 March 1985.

19 *Washington Times Magazine*, 9 April 1985.

20 Michele Paradise, personal interview with author.

21 Brenda Polan, personal interview with author.

22 Sarah Mower, 'Maison Margiela', *Vogue Runway*, 25 January 2024. https://www.vogue.com/fashion-shows/spring-2024-couture/maison-martin-margiela (accessed August 2024).

23 Quoted in interview with Caroline Baker, *Ritz* magazine, No.1, 1976: 26.

24 *Evening Mail*, Slough, Buckinghamshire, 21 May 1974.

25 Cindy White, personal interview with author.

26 Ibid.

27 Ibid.

28 Kaffe Fassett, personal interview with author.

29 Quoted in interview with Caroline Baker, *Ritz* magazine, No.1, 1976: 25.

30 Manolo Blahnik, personal interview with author.

31 Pam Hogg, personal interview with author.

32 Ibid.

33 Patricia Davidson, personal interview with author.

34 Pam Hogg, personal interview with author.

35 Ian Jack, *The Sunday Times*, 2 November 1980: 38.

36 Ibid.

37 Katy England, personal interview with author.

38 Ibid.

39 *Edinburgh Evening News*, 20 August 1985: 4.

40 Katy England, personal interview with author.

41 Quoted in interview with Mick Rock, *19* magazine, December 1974: 40

42 Interview with Jeff Banks, 'The Clothes Show', BBC TV, 1985.

43 'All in a Day', BBC TV, shooting script, 1972.

44 Kay Tench, personal interview with author.

45 'All in a Day' shooting script.

46 'All in a Day', BBC TV, 1972.

47 'All in a Day' shooting script.

48 Ibid.

49 Quoted in interview with Mick Rock, *19* magazine, December 1974: 41

50 *Women's Wear Daily*, 25 April 1972.

51 Steven Philips, personal interview with author.

52 Ibid.

53 *Aberdeen Press & Journal*, 15 November 1972: 15.

54 Ibid.

55 Jessie Gibb, personal interview with author.

56 Douglas Keay, *Woman* magazine, 18 October 1975.

57 Kaori O'Connor, ed., *The London Fashion Guide for Spring 1975* (London: Farrol Kahn Ltd., 1975): 12.

58 British *Vogue*, November 1977: 193.

59 Ibid.

60 Valerie Webster, *The Journal*, Newcastle-upon-Tyne, 8 November 1972.

61 Lesley Ebbetts, personal interview with author.

62 *Flair*, September 1972.

63 Jasper Conran, personal interview with author.

Chapter 8

1 Interview with Patsy Davidson by author, 2007.

2 Remy Charlip, *Arm in Arm: A Collection of Connections, Endless Tales, Reiterations, and Other Echolalia* (New York: Parents Magazine Press, 1969).

3   Ibid., 32.

4   Christine Rew, *Bill Gibb: The Golden Boy of British Fashion* (Aberdeen: Aberdeen Art Gallery, 2003).

5   Iain R. Webb, *Bill Gibb: Fashion and Fantasy* (London: V&A Publishing, 2008).

6   NJ Stevenson, 'Liberty in Fashion: The Role of Private Collectors Lending to Museums', *Fashion Theory*, 22:4-5 (2018), 545-551, DOI: 10.1080/1362704X.2018.1425530

7   Bethan Bide, 'Signs of Wear: Encountering Memory in the Worn Materiality of a Museum Fashion Collection', *Fashion Theory*, 21:4 (2017): 449-476. DOI: 10.1080/1362704X.2017.1290204

8   Kaat Debo, 'Foreword' in Elisa De Wyngaert et al. (eds), *Echo: Wrapped In Memory* (Lannoo: Tielt 2023), 7.

9   Raphael Samuel, *Theatres of Memory Vol 1: Past and Present in Contemporary Culture* (London: Verso, 1996), 10.

10 Susan Stewart, *On Longing: Narratives of the Miniature, the Gigantic, the Souvenir, the Collection* (Duke University Press: Durham, NC, 1992), 151.

11 Gaynor Kavanagh, *Dream Spaces: Memory and the Museum* (Leicester University Press: Leicester 2000), 98.

12 Stevenson, 'Liberty in Fashion', 546.

13 *All in a Day*: '3. The Collection', directed by Keith Sheather, BBC; first aired 17 January 1973.

14 Stevenson, 2008, Exhibition label, Fashion and Textile Museum.

15 Ibid.

16 Jan De Villeneuve, interview with author, 2007.

17 Sally Pasmore, interview with author, 2008, NB, 'Justin' is Justin de Villeneuve, former manager and boyfriend of Twiggy and later husband of Jan de Villeneuve.

18 Pasmore, interview.

19 Irene Andrae, interview with author, 2008.

20 Patsy Davidson, interview with author, 2008.

21 Tessa Dahl, interview with author, 2008.

22 Rupert De Klee, email correspondence with author, 2008.

23 *The Stud* (dir. 1978), Quentin Masters, Great Britain.

24 Ann Barr, telephone conversation with author, 2008.

25 Olive Campbell, letter to Fashion and Textile Museum, 2008.

26 Liz MacKinnon, conversation with author, 2008.

27 Stacey Williams, conversation with author, 2008.

28 Meg Wynn Owen, interview with author, 2008.

29 Jessie Gibb and Patsy Davidson, conversation with author, 2008

30 Pasmore, interview.

31 Kate Franklin, interview with author, 2008.

32 Charlip, *Arm in Arm*.

Chapter 10

1. Alice Fisher, 'Fashion Designer Bill Gibb (1943-1988)' in 'A punk, a monkey, a maths genius and our pick of local heroes who deserve a blue plaque', *The Observer,* 10 September 2023. https://www.theguardian.com/culture/2023/sep/10/a-punk-a-monkey-a-maths-genius-our-pick-of-local-heroes-who-deserve-a-blue-plaque (accessed February 2024).

2. Mal Burkinshaw, 'Knitwear: Chanel to Westwood review – showcasing the diversity of knitted fashion', *The Conversation,* 2023. https://theconversation.com/knitwear-chanel-to-westwood-review-showcasing-the-diversity-of-knitted-fashion-199335 (accessed February 2024).

3. Iain R. Webb, *Bill Gibb: Fashion and Fantasy* (London: V&A Publishing, 2008).

4. Agnés Rocamora, 'New fashion times: Fashion and digital media' in Sandy Black et al. (eds), *The Handbook of Fashion Studies* (London: Bloomsbury Academic, 2013): 61-77.

5. Mark K. Brewer, 'Slow fashion in a fast fashion world: Promoting sustainability and responsibility', *Laws* 8 no. 4 (2019): 24.

6. Claire Allen, 'Style surfing: changing parameters of fashion communication — where have they gone?', *1st Global conference: Fashion exploring critical issues*, 25–27 September 2009, Mansfield College: Oxford.

7. Scarlett Conlon, 'The fashion guide to Instagram', British *Vogue* (online), 23 February 2016. https://www.vogue.co.uk/gallery/eva-chen-fashion-partnerships-instagram-rules (accessed July 2023).

8. Marco Pedroni, 'Two decades of fashion blogging and influencing: A critical overview', *Fashion Theory* 27, no. 2 (2023): 237–68.

9. Agnés Rocamora, 'Personal fashion blogs: Screens and mirrors in digital self-portraits', in Stella Bruzzi and Pamela Church Gibson (eds) *Fashion Cultures Revisited* (Oxfordshire: Routledge, 2013): 112–27.

10. Crystal Abidin, 'Visibility labour: engaging with influencers' fashion brands and #OOTD advertorial campaigns on Instagram', *Media International Australia* 161, no. 1 (2016): 86–100.

11. Brooke E. Duffy, 'Social media influencers', *The International Encyclopedia of Gender, Media and Communication* 15 (2020): 1–4.

12. Brooke E. Duffy and Elizabeth Wissinger, 'Mythologies of creative work in the social media age: Fun, free, and "just being me"', *International Journal of Communication* 11 (2017): 4652–71.

13. Yu-I Ha et al., 'Fashion conversation data on Instagram', *Proceedings of the International AAAI Conference on Web and Social Media* 11, no. 1 (2017): 418–27.

14. John Brandon 'Instagram is outpacing TikTok for consumer growth. Here's why', *Forbes* (online), 24 June 2023. https://www.forbes.com/sites/johnbbrandon/2023/06/24/instagram-is-outpacing-tiktok-for-user-growth-heres-why/?sh=531508f85dbd (accessed July 2023).

15. Webb, *Bill Gibb: Fashion and Fantasy.*

16. Statistica, 'Distribution of Instagram users worldwide as of April 2024 by age group', 2 May 2024. https://www.statista.com/statistics/325587/instagram-global-age-group/ (accessed September 2024).

17. Sumit Paul-Choudhury, 'Digital legacy: the fate of your online soul', *New Scientist* 210, no. 2809 (2011): 41–3.

18. Cristiano Maciel and Pereira Carvalho Vinicius, *Digital Legacy and Interaction.* (Heidelburg: Springer 2015).

19 Eduardo A., Yamauchi et al., 'Digital Legacy Management Systems: Theoretical, Systemic and User's Perspective', *23rd Annual International Conference on Enterprise Information Systems*, vol.2 (2021): 41–53.

20 Annette Kuhn, 'Photography and cultural memory: a methodological exploration', *Visual Studies* 22, no. 3(2007): 283–92.

21 Caroline Hood and Peter Reid, 'Social media as a vehicle for user engagement with local history: A case study in the North East of Scotland', *Journal of Documentation* 74, no. 4 (2018): 741–62.

22 Antoinette M. Fionda and Christopher. M. Moore, 'The anatomy of the luxury fashion brand', *Journal of brand Management* 16, no. 5 (2009): 347–63.

23 Benjamin G. Voyer et al., 'Co-creating stakeholder and brand identities: A cross-cultural consume perspective', *Journal of Business Research* 70 (2017): 399–410.

24 Venus S. Jin and Ehri Ryu, 'Instagram fashionistas, luxury visual image strategies and vanity', *Journal of Product & Brand Management* 29, no. 3 (2020): 355–68.

25 Christine Vallaster and Sylvia Von Wallpach, 'An online discursive inquiry into the social dynamics of multi-stakeholder brand meaning co-creation', *Journal of Business Research* 66, no. 9 (2013): 1505–15.

26 Bernard Cova and Daniele Dalli, 'Working Consumers: The Next Step in Marketing Theory?', *Marketing Theory* 9, no. 3 (2009): 315–39.

27 Laurence Dessart et al., 'Consumer engagement in online brand communities: a social media perspective', *Journal of Product & Brand Management* 24, no.1 (2015): 28–42.

28 Joseph H. Hancock, *Brand/story: cases and explorations in fashion branding* (New York: Fairchild Books, Bloomsbury 2016).

29 Mette Mortensen et al., 'The iconic image in a digital age', *Nordicom Review* 38, no. 2 (2017): 71–86.

30 Jeffrey C. Alexander, 'The celebrity-icon', *Cultural Sociology* 4, no. 3 (2010): 323–36.

31 Betsy Thomas, 'Representing Twiggy in 1967: Twiggy as a New Icon', in Barbara Brownie et al. (eds), *Fashion: Exploring Critical Issues* (Netherlands: Brill 2012): 25–37.

32 Webb, *Bill Gibb: Fashion and Fantasy*.

33 Lauren Fritz, 'Knolling: the art of material culture', *Art Education* 72 (2018): 50–8.

34 Monica Kass Rogers, 'The flat-lay on knolling', *Communication Arts* (online), 2023: https://www.commarts.com/columns/the-flat-lay-on-knolling (accessed November 2023).

35 Alise Tifentale and Lev Manovich, 'Selfiecity: Exploring photography and self-fashioning in social media', in Dave M Berry and Michael Dieter (eds), *Postdigital Aesthetics: Art, Computation and Design* (London: Palgrave Macmillan, 2015): 109–22.

36 Madeleine Marcella-Hood, 'Augmenting sustainable fashion on Instagram', *Sustainability*, 15, no. 4 (2023): 3609.

37 Anders Gustafsson et al., 'Consumer co-creation in service innovation: a matter of communication?', *Journal of Service Management* 23, no. 3 (2012): 311–27.

38 Azzouz Essamri et al., 'Co-creating corporate brand identity with online brand communities: A managerial perspective', *Journal of Business Research* 96 (2019): 366–75.

39 Alice E. Marwick, "They're really profound women, they're entrepreneurs': Conceptions of authenticity in fashion blogging', *7th international AIII conference on weblogs and social media,* 2013: 1–8.

40 Vivian Hendricksz, 'How the selfie effect is disrupting the industry', *Fashion United* (online), 13 August 2015. https://fashionunited.uk/news/fashion/how-the-selfie-effect-is-disrupting-the-industry/2015081317334 (accessed August 2023).

Chapter 11

1 Rachael King, 'From cookies to cashmere, the comfort economy gains momentum during the coronavirus pandemic', *Fortune*, 21 April 2020, https://fortune.com/2020/04/21/coronavirus-athleisure-comfort-self-care-economy-covid-19/ (accessed 23 April 2020); Helen Palmer, Olivia Barnes, Yvonne Kostiak and Jo Lynch, 'Sustainability & Innovation: Second-Skin Comfort & Innerwear,' *WGSN*, https://www.wgsn.com/fashion/article/91574 (accessed 12 November 2021); McKinsey & Company/Business of Fashion. 'The State of Fashion 2022'. McKinsey & Company/Business of Fashion, 12 January 2022. https://www.mckinsey.com/~/media/mckinsey/industries/retail/our%20insights/state%20of%20fashion/2022/the-state-of-fashion-2022.pdf (accessed 21 October 2024).

2 Maria Skivko, 'The future of outfits after the staying-in trend: Home wear, digitization and cultural shift,' *Clothing Cultures*, no. 7 (2020): 191–202.

3 Lyman Fourt and Norman R.S. Hollies, *Clothing Comfort and Function* (New York, NY: Marcel Decker Inc., 1970).

4 Edwin Kamalha, Yongchun Zeng, Josphat I. Mwasiagi and Salome Kyatuheire, 'The Comfort Dimension; a review of perception in clothing,' *Journal of Sensory Studies*, no. 28 (2013): 423–44.

5 Christine Rew, *Bill Gibb: The Golden Boy of British Fashion* (Aberdeen: Aberdeen City Council, 2003), 49.

6 Valerie Steele, *The Corset: A Cultural History* (New Haven & London: Yale University Press, 2003); Francis Corner, *Why Fashion Matters* (New York, NY: Thames & Hudson, 2014).

7 Rew, *Bill Gibb: The Golden Boy of British Fashion*, 61.

8 Jen G. Baron, 'Curating the Self: A Proposed Intervention for Positive Identity Crafting Through Self-presentation and Clothing' (University of Pennsylvania, 2013), http://repository.upenn.edu/mapp_capstone/51 (accessed 6 June 2015).

9 Kendra Lapolla and Elizabeth B. N. Sanders, 'Encouraging more efficient wardrobes through recirculation of idle apparel,' *Clothing Cultures*, no. 4 (2017): 45–60.

10 Rew, *Bill Gibb*, 49.

11 Carla Buzasi, 'Anatomy of a Trend,' *WGSN* (2017), https://www.modaes.com/files/000_2016/0003centrorecursos/branding/2017%20WGSN%20Anatomy%20of%20a%20trend.pdf (accessed 13 March 2020); Helen Palmer, 'Wellness Textiles,' *WGSN*, https://www.wgsn.com/fashion/article/80539 (accessed 10 March 2021).

12 Christoph-Simon Masuch and Kate Hefferon, 'Understanding the links between positive psychology and fashion: A grounded theory analysis,' *International Journal of Fashion Studies*, no. 1 (2014): 227–46.

13 Rew, *Bill Gibb*, 55.

14 Masuch and Hefferon, 'Understanding the links between positive psychology and fashion: A grounded theory analysis'.

15 Emma Lynas, E., 2010. 'Textiles, connection and meaning,' in *Fashion: Sustainability and Creativity Conference Proceedings* (2010), ed. Commodore Vijay Chaturvedi.

16 Daniel Miller, *The Comfort of Things* (Cambridge, UK: Polity, 2008).

17 Gillian Bennett and Paul Smith, eds, *Contemporary Legend: A Reader* (New York, NY: Routledge, 2011).

18 Linda M. Welters, 'Folklore Look,' *LoveToKnow Corp,* 2020, https://fashion-history.lovetoknow.com/fashion-history-eras/folklore-look (accessed 13 March 2020).

19 European Fashion Heritage Association, 'Bill Gibb: Romantic Fantasy,' *EFHA*, 10 July 2018, https://fashionheritage.eu/bill-gibb-romantic-fantasy/ (accessed 14 March 2020); Aimee Farrell, 'Folk Heroes', *Financial Times,* 26 June 2015. https://www.ft.com/content/951dd9ba-0ac2-11e5-98d3-00144feabdc0 (accessed 13 March 2020).

20 Kathryn McKelvey and Janine Munslow, *Fashion Forecasting* (Oxford: Wiley-Blackwell, 2008).

21 Rosemary Feitelberg, 2018. 'Folklore to Define Fashion, Create New Shapes in Response to Lack of Real Design, Artificial Intelligence,' *Women's Wear Daily*, 29 November 2018. https://wwd.com/eye/people/folklore-to-define-fashion-create-new-shapes-in-response-to-lack-of-real-design-artificial-intelligence-1202916809/ (accessed 20 October 2019).

22 Adam Waytz, 'When customers want to see the human behind the product,' *Harvard Business Review*, 5 June 2019, https://hbr.org/2019/06/when-customers-want-to-see-the-human-behind-the-product (accessed 10 October 2019).

23 Feitelberg, 'Folklore to Define Fashion, Create New Shapes in Response to Lack of Real Design, Artificial Intelligence'.

24 Zygmut Bauman, *Liquid Modernity* (Cambridge, UK: Polity Press, 2012).

25 Environmental Audit Committee, 'Fixing Fashion: Clothing Consumption and Sustainability,' *House of Commons*, 19 February 2019, https://publications.parliament.uk/pa/cm201719/cmselect/cmenvaud/1952/1952.pdf (accessed 10 October 2019).

26 Petr Bogatyrev, *The Functions of Folk Costume in Moravian Slovakia* (The Hague: Mouton, 1971).

27 Irene Vermeulen, 'Lidewij Edelkoort on Folklore,' *Crafts Curator*, 15 February 2019, https://www.craftscurator.com/articles/item/304-lidewij-edelkoort-on-folklore (accessed on 10 March 2021).

28 Svetlana Boym, 'Nostalgia and its discontents,' *The Hedgehog Review, Critical Reflections on Contemporary Culture,* no. 9 (2007).

29 Heike Jens, 'Cross-temporal explorations: Notes on fashion and nostalgia,' *Critical Studies in Fashion & Beauty*, no. 4 (2013): 107–24.

30 Jeffrey K. Olick, Vered Vinitzky-Seroussi and Daniel Levy, *The Collective Memory Reader* (USA: Oxford University Press, 2011).

31 Raluka Creanga, 'Fashion as a tool for the reinterpretation of the past: The case of Romanian folk costume as inspiration for designers and consumers,' *Fashion, Style & Popular Culture*, no. 7(2020): 101–23.

32 Priya Elan, 'Beautiful, dark twisted fantasy: why fashion fell for the folklore image,' *The Guardian*, 7 April 2016, https://www.theguardian.com/fashion/2016/apr/07/beautiful-dark-twisted-fantasy-why-fashion-fell-for-the-folklore-image (accessed 13 March 2020).

33 Feitelberg, 'Folklore to Define Fashion, Create New Shapes in Response to Lack of Real Design, Artificial Intelligence'; Bauman, *Liquid Modernity*.

34 Boym, 'Nostalgia and its discontents'.

35 Feitelberg, 'Folklore to Define Fashion, Create New Shapes in Response to Lack of Real Design, Artificial Intelligence'; Jeffery K. Olick, Vered Vinitzky-Seroussi and Daniel Levy, *The Collective Memory Reader* (USA: Oxford University Press, 2011).

36 Karen Pine, *Mind What You Wear: The psychology of fashion* (UK: Hatfield, 2014); Elan, 'Beautiful, dark twisted fantasy: why fashion fell for the folklore image'.

37 Welters, 'Folklore Look'; Feitelberg, 'Folklore to Define Fashion, Create New Shapes in Response to Lack of Real Design, Artificial Intelligence'; Vermeulen, 'Lidewij Edelkoort on Folklore'.

38 European Fashion Heritage Association, 'Bill Gibb: Romantic Fantasy'.

39 Feitelberg, 'Folklore to Define Fashion, Create New Shapes in Response to Lack of Real Design, Artificial Intelligence'.

40 Rew, *Bill Gibb*, 61.

41 Welters, 'Folklore Look'.

42 Rew, *Bill Gibb*, 14.

43 Welters, 'Folklore Look'.

44 Sarah Mower, 'Fall 2008 Gucci,' *Vogue Runway*, 19 February 2008, https://www.vogue.com/fashion-shows/fall-2008-ready-to-wear/gucci (accessed 13 March 2020).

45 Heike Jens, 'Cross-temporal explorations: Notes on fashion and nostalgia,' *Critical Studies in Fashion & Beauty*, no. 4 (2013): 107.

46 Fred Davis, *Yearning for Yesterday: A Sociology of Nostalgia* (Michigan, USA: Free Press, 1979); Monica D. Guillory, 'Perceived Brand Age and Its Influence on Choice,' *Georgia State University,* 20 December 2012, https://web.archive.org/web/20171012140652id_/http://scholarworks.gsu.edu:80/cgi/viewcontent.cgi?article=1025&context=marketing_diss (accessed 22 March 2020): 23.

47 Bauman, *Liquid Modernity*.

48 Davis, *Yearning for Yesterday: A Sociology of Nostalgia,* 110.

49 Boym, 'Nostalgia and its discontents'.

50 Welters, 'Folklore Look'.

51 Feitelberg, 'Folklore to Define Fashion, Create New Shapes in Response to Lack of Real Design, Artificial Intelligence'.

52 Rew, *Bill Gibb*, 83.

53 Brigitte Vézina, 'Curbing Cultural Appropriation in the Fashion Industry,' *CIGI Papers No. 213*, https://www.cigionline.org/sites/default/files/documents/paper%20no.213.pdf (accessed 30 January 2025).

54 Peter Shand, 'Scenes from the Colonial Catwalk: Cultural Appropriation, Intellectual Property Rights, and Fashion', *Cultural Analysis,* no 3. (2002): 47–8.

55 Barbara Pozzo, 'Fashion between Inspiration and Appropriation', *Laws,* no. 9 (2020): doi:10.3390/laws9010005.

56 Shand, 'Scenes from the Colonial Catwalk: Cultural Appropriation, Intellectual Property Rights, and Fashion', 70.

57 Teresa Sabata, Valeria LaFata and Andrea Torres, 'Cultural Appropriation in the digital context: A comparative study between two fashion cases', *Lecture Notes in Computer Science,* no. 12204 (2020): 504–20.

58 Simon Fraser, 'Think Before You Appropriate. Things to know and questions to ask in order to avoid misappropriating Indigenous cultural heritage', *Intellectual Property Issues in Cultural Heritage Project,* (2015).

59 Pozzo, 'Fashion between Inspiration and Appropriation'.

60 Ben Golik, 'Gucci: the newly inclusive exclusivity', *Shots,* 27 September 2019. https://shots.net/news/view/gucci-the-newly-inclusive-exclusivity (accessed 13 March 2020).

61 Nicole Phelps, 'Spring 2020 Gucci', *Vogue Runway,* 22 September 2019, https://www.vogue.com/fashion-shows/spring-2020-ready-to-wear/gucci (accessed 13 March 2020).

62 Jennifer Craik, *The Face of Fashion* (London: Routledge, 1993).

63 Welters, 'Folklore Look'.

64 Tamison O'Connor, 'Sweatsuits and Yoga Pants are Selling Like Crazy. What Happens when Lockdowns End?' *Business of Fashion*, 20 April 2020, https://www.businessoffashion.com/articles/retail/sweatsuits-and-yoga-pants-are-selling-like-crazy-what-happens-when-lockdowns-end/ (accessed 10 March 2021); Amy De Klerk, 'Will the experience of lockdown change the way we dress forever?' *Harper's Bazaar*, 7 May 2020, https://www.harpersbazaar.com/uk/fashion/fashion-news/a32400342/fashion-post-lockdown/ (accessed 16 July 2020); Sadie Perry, 'Core item updates. Women's loungewear AW 24/25,' *WGSN*, https://www.wgsn.com/fashion/article/641349ee2303463fab681f43 (accessed 18 January 2024).

65 Anat Rafaeli, Jane Dutton, Celia V. Harquail and Stephanie Mackie-Lewis, 'Navigating by Attire: The use of dress by administrative employees,' *Academy of Management Review*, no. 40 (1997): 19–45.

66 Anna Kessel, 'The rise of the body neutrality movement: If you're fat, you don't have to hate yourself,' *The Guardian*, https://www.theguardian.com/lifeandstyle/2018/jul/23/the-rise-of-the-body-neutrality-movement-if-youre-fat-you-dont-have-to-hate-yourself (accessed 21 March 2020); Independent, 'What is modest fashion and why is it becoming mainstream?' *Independent*, 18 April 2019, https://www.independent.co.uk/life-style/fashion/modest-fashion-asos-hijab-range-design-islam-religion-a8875636.html (accessed 23 July 2019).

67 Barbara L. Fredrickson and Tomi-Ann Roberts, 'Objectification Theory: Towards Understanding Women's Lived Experiences and Mental Health Risks,' *Psychology of Women Quarterly*, no. 21 (1997): 172–206.

68 Amy Brown and Helga Dittmar, 'Think thin and feel bad: the role of appearance schema activation, attention level, and thin-ideal internalization for young women's responses to ultra-thin media ideals,' *Journal of Social and Clinical Psychology*, no. 24 (2005): 1088–1113; Ellen E. Fitzsimmons-Craft, Megan B. Harney, Laura G. Koehler, Lauren E. Danzi, Margaret K. Riddell and Anna M. Bardone-Cone, 'Explaining the relation between thin ideal internalisation and body dissatisfaction among college women: the roles of social comparison and body surveillance,' *Body Image*, no. 9 (2011): 43–9.

69 Independent, 'What is modest fashion and why is it becoming mainstream?'; Pip Usher, 'The Multi Billion-Dollar Modest Fashion Industry That's Gone Global,' *Conde Nast*, https://www.vogue.co.uk/article/the-multibillion-dollar-modest-fashion-industry-thats-gone-global (accessed 24 July 22019).

70 Sarah Mower, 2018. 'Gucci Fall 2018 Ready-to-wear,' *Conde Nast*, https://www.vogue.com/fashion-shows/fall-2018-ready-to-wear/gucci (accessed 11 March 2021).

71 Marjolein Stormezand, 'Lidewij Edelkoort: "Folklore is becoming a trend; the tunic is a universal piece of clothing"', *Fashion United*, 15 November 2018, https://fashionunited.uk/news/fashion/lidewij-edelkoort-folklore-is-becoming-a-trend-the-tunic-is-a-universal-piece-of-clothing/201811153997 (accessed 10 March 2021).

72 Feitelberg, 'Folklore to Define Fashion, Create New Shapes in Response to Lack of Real Design, Artificial Intelligence'.

73 Miller, *The Comfort of Things*, 91.

74 Pozzo, 'Fashion between Inspiration and Appropriation'.

75 Stormezand, 'Lidewij Edelkoort: "Folklore is becoming a trend; the tunic is a universal piece of clothing"'.

76 Brown and Dittmar, 'Think thin and feel bad: the role of appearance schema activation, attention level, and thin-ideal internalization for young women's responses to ultra-thin media ideals'; Fitzsimmons-Craft, Harney, Koehler, Danzi, Riddell and Bardone-Cone, 'Explaining the relation between thin ideal internalisation and body dissatisfaction among college women: the roles of social comparison and body surveillance'.

77 Fredrickson and Roberts, 'Objectification Theory: Towards Understanding Women's Lived Experiences and Mental Health Risks'.

78 Kessel, 'The rise of the body neutrality movement: If you're fat, you don't have to hate yourself'.

79 Independent, 'What is modest fashion and why is it becoming mainstream?'.

80 Lois M. Gurel and Marianne S. Beeson, *Dimensions of Dress and Adornment* (US: Kendall/Hunt Publishing Company, 1979).

81 Stormezand, 'Lidewij Edelkoort: "Folklore is becoming a trend; the tunic is a universal piece of clothing"'.

82 Masuch and Hefferon, 'Understanding the links between positive psychology and fashion: A grounded theory analysis'.

83 Rew, *Bill Gibb*, 45.

Chapter 12

1 Tonya Blazio-Licorish and Obi Anyanwu, 'How Cultural Appropriation Became a Hot-button Issue for Fashion', *Women's Wear Daily*, 3 November 2020. See https://wwd.com/feature/how-cultural-appropriation-became-a-hot-button-issue-for-fashion-1234579968/ (accessed August 2024).

2 Flavia Piancazzo, 'Developments of Cultural Appropriation in Fashion: An In-Progress Research', in Nadzeya Sabatini *et al.* (eds) *Fashion and Communication in the Digital Age* (Springer, 2023), 136–43, 137.

3 Jeena Sharma, 'Four things you didn't know about cultural appropriation in fashion', *South China Morning Post*, 7 November 2017. See https://www.scmp.com/magazines/style/fashion-beauty/article/2118724/four-things-you-didnt-know-about-cultural (accessed August 2024).

4 The Museum at FIT online exhibition, 'The Roaring 20s and Swinging 60s: Cultural Appropriation'. See https://exhibitions.fitnyc.edu/roaring-20s-and-swinging-60s/cultural-appropriation/ (accessed August 2024).

5 Jessica R. Metcalfe, 'Just Another Pocahontas Fantasy Story: Critiquing Galliano', *Beyond Buckskin: About Native American Fashion*, 12 October 2012. See https://www.beyondbuckskin.com/2012/10/just-another-pocahontas-fantasy-story.html (accessed August 2024).

6 Anna Battista, 'Occasions to Learn for a Fashion Conglomerate: From The Faux Pas that Led a Fashion House on the Di(s)orient Express (Again) To a Young Designer Bringing Hope to the Scene', *Irenebrination*, 4 September

2019. See https://www.irenebrination.com/irenebrination_notes_on_a/2019/09/dior-thebe-magugu.html (accessed August 2024).

7   John Galliano quoted in Iain R. Webb, *Bill Gibb: Fashion and Fantasy* (V&A, 2008), 68.

8   Brenda Polan, 'Expensive Thrills', *The Guardian*, 20 May 1988, 11.

9   Christine Rew, *Bill Gibb: The Golden Boy of British Fashion* (Aberdeen City Council, 2003), 59–61.

10 Jeena Sharma, 'When does cultural inspiration become appropriation in the fashion world?', *South China Morning Post*, 6 November 2017. See https://www.scmp.com/magazines/style/fashion-beauty/article/2118609/when-does-cultural-inspiration-become-appropriation?module=hard_link&pgtype=article (accessed August 2024).

11 Edward Said, *Orientalism* (1978; London: Penguin Classics, 2019).

12 Chloe Mac Donnell, 'Pharrell Williams showcases American western for Louis Vuitton Collection', *The Guardian*, 17 January 2024, https://www.theguardian.com/fashion/2024/jan/17/pharrell-williams-showcases-american-western-louis-vuitton-collection-paris (accessed August 2024).

13 For more on the history of the 'Paisley print' in Britain see Suchitra Choudhury's *Textile Orientalisms: Cashmere and Paisley Shawls in British Literature and Culture* (Ohio University Press, 2023).

14 Shane Strachan, 'Taking Inspiration from Bill Gibb's Tana Dress', V&A Dundee, October 2020, https://www.vam.ac.uk/dundee/articles/taking-inspiration-from-bill-gibbs-tana-dress (accessed 21 October 2024). See also Dr Bashabi Fraser, 'The Transformational Power of Design', V&A Dundee, October 2020, https://www.vam.ac.uk/dundee/articles/the-transformational-power-of-design (accessed 21 October 2024).

15 Excerpts from a phone interview with Asha Puthli by author, 26 April 2024.

16 Michael Roberts, *The Sunday Times*, 3 April 1977.

17 Ann Chubb, 'Gibb of India. . .', *The Telegraph*, 21 May 1979.

Chapter 13

1   Kerrice Bailey et al., 'The Environmental Impacts of Fast Fashion on Water Quality: A Systematic Review', *Water*, vol. 14(7), 1073 (2022): 1.

2   Steven Markowitz, 'Barry Commoner and the Current Environmental Crisis', *American Journal of Public Health*, Vol. 108, Supplement 2 (2018): S53.

3   Earth Day, 'Our History' (2024), https://www.earthday.org/history/ (accessed January 2024).

4   The Anthropocene Working Group, 'The Anthropocene', *Global Change Newsletter* 41 (2000): 17–18.

5   Christine Rew, 'Bill Gibb', *Costume*, No. 28 (1994): 81–96.

6   National Honey Monitoring Scheme, https://honey-monitoring.ac.uk/ (accessed 4 January 2024).

7   Lynn Wilson, '"Private sufficiency, public luxury": an exploration of consumer clothing circularity', in Marylyn Carrigan et al. (eds), *Research Handbook on Ethical Consumption* (Edward Elgar Publishing, 2023): 312–26.

8   Holly McQuillan, 'Hybrid zero waste design practices: Zero waste pattern cutting for composite garment weaving and its implications', *The Design Journal*, 22 (2019): 803–19.

9   Shrestha Ramkalaon and Abu S.M. Sayem, 'Zero-Waste Pattern Cutting (ZWPC) to tackle over sixty billion square metres of fabric wastage during mass production of apparel', *The Journal of the Textile Institute*, vol. 112 (2021): 809–19.

10 Sophia Luu, and Ellen Mckinney, 2021. 'Kimono: elucidating meanings of Japanese textile artifacts for a museum audience', *Anais do Museu Paulista: História e Cultura Material*, vol. 29, e9 (2021).

11 Lynn Wilson, 'Circular Economy Wardrobe: Exploring Circular Economy Textile Models in Japan', The Churchill Foundation. Circular Economy Wardrobe (2016): 23. https://www.churchillfellowship.org/ideas-experts/ideas-library/exploring-circular-economy-textile-models-in-japan/ (accessed 13 October 2024).

12 Rew, 'Bill Gibb', *Costume*.

13 Osman Ahmed, 'The Impact of John Galliano's A/W 94 Japonisme Collection', *AnOther Magazine* (online), 16 May 2016. https://www.anothermag.com/fashion-beauty/8687/the-impact-of-john-gallianos-a-w94-japonisme-collection (accessed 15 October 2023).

14 Holly McQuillan and Timo Rissanen, *Zero Waste Fashion Design* (London: Bloomsbury Publishing, 2016).

15 Holly McQuillan, 'MAKE/USE' (2024): https://hollymcquillan.com/portfolio/make-use/ (accessed 4 January 2024).

16 Anonymous, 'Just A Little Something I Ran Up Myself', *Cosmopolitan*, January 1978: 73–9.

17 Ibid., p.76.

18 Iain R. Webb, *Bill Gibb: Fashion and Fantasy* (London: V&A, 2008).

19 City of Aberdeen Arts Department, *Bill Gibb: a Tribute to the Fashion Designer of the 70s*. (Aberdeen: City Arts Department, 1990 – ISBN: 0900017252), 9.

20 Lin Gardner, 'From Underwear to Outerwear: The Influence of Machinery on Creativity and Garment Styling in the Scottish Knitwear Industry, 1920s-1970s', *Textile: The Journal of Cloth and Culture*, vol.21, iss.4 (2023): 853–7.

21 City of Aberdeen Arts Department, *Bill Gibb*, 8.

22 Barrie, 'The House of Barrie' (2024). https://www.barrie.com/en/pages/house-of-barrie (accessed 28 December 2023).

23 Wilson, 'Circular Economy Wardrobe: Exploring Circular Economy Textile Models in Japan'.

24 Webb, *Bill Gibb: Fashion and Fantasy*, 78.

25 Ann Chubb, 'Gibb of India …', *The Telegraph*, 21 May 1979: 71.

26 Elvan Ozkavruk Adanir et al., 'An Ethical Approach to Sericulture: Production of Peace Silk in Hatay/Turkey', *Textile: The Journal of Cloth and Culture*, vol.22, iss.1 (2022): 20–30.

27 Jessica Iredale, 'Stella McCartney Partners with Bolt Threads: The biotech lab specializes in luxury sustainable materials, such as yeast-based silk', *Women's Wear Daily*, 20 July 2017. https://wwd.com/feature/stella-mccartney-partners-with-bolt-threads-on-sustainable-material-development-10949591/ (accessed September 2024).

28 Bolt Threads, 'Bolt Technology – Meet B-SILK Protein' (2024). https://boltthreads.com/technology/silk-protein/ (accessed 3 January 2024).

29 Jack Moss, 'How a Hermes silk scarf comes to life', *Wallpaper*, 22 July 2023. https://www.wallpaper.com/fashion-beauty/hermes-silk-scarf-factory-lyon (accessed 24 May 2024).

30 PETA, 'PETA's Milestones for Animals'. https://www.peta.org/about-peta/milestones/ (accessed 21 May 2024).

31 Janaina Alves Klein, et al., 'Textile sustainability: A Brazilian etiquette issue', *Environmental Science & Policy*, vol. 109 (2020): 125–30.

32 Gustav Sandin and Greg M. Peters, 'Environmental impact of textile reuse and recycling – A review', *Journal of Cleaner Production*, vol. 184 (2018): 353–65.

33 Alice Hazlehurst et al., 'Investigating the influence of yarn characteristics on microfibre release from knitted fabrics during laundering', *Frontiers in Environmental Science,* Vol. 12 (2024): 1–13.

34 Stella McCartney, 'Vegea' (2024), https://www.stellamccartney.com/gb/en/sustainability/vegea-grape-based-alternative-to-animal-leather.html (accessed 21 May 2024).

35 Webb, *Bill Gibb: Fashion and Fantasy*, 2.

36 Rew, 'Bill Gibb', *Costume*.

37 Jonathan Chapman, *Emotionally Durable Design: Objects, Experiences and Empathy*, Second edn, (London: Routledge, 2015), 21

38 Webb, *Bill Gibb: Fashion and Fantasy*, viiii.

39 Chapman, *Emotionally Durable Design*, 112.

40 Wendy Fraser, 'Inside Steven Philip's costume collection: a treasure trove of Bill Gibb's designs', *The Costume Society*, 30 January 2022. https://costumesociety.org.uk/blog/post/inside-steven-philips-costume-collection-a-treasure-trove-of-bill-gibbs-designs (accessed January 2024).

41 1st Dibs, 'Bill Gibb Clothing', https://www.1stdibs.com/creators/bill-gibb/fashion/clothing/ (accessed 3 January 2024).

42 Webb, *Bill Gibb: Fashion and Fantasy*.

43 Sara Semic, 'Hermès takes the reins in upcycling', *Financial Times* (online), 27 December 2023. https://www.ft.com/content/9ae2631f-f933-4279-b015-4803f6f960b8 (accessed 21 May 2024).

44 *Fashion Reimagined* (dir. Becky Hutner, 2022), https://www.fashionreimaginedfilm.com/ (accessed 15 December 2023).

45 Mother of Pearl, 'We Create Without Compromise', https://motherofpearl.co.uk/pages/sustainability-landing-page (accessed 15 December 2023).

46 Wilson, '"Private sufficiency, public luxury"'.

47 Emma Johnson and Andrius Plepys, 'Product-Service Systems and Sustainability: Analysing the Environmental Impacts of Rental Clothing', *Sustainability*, vol. 13, no. 4, 2118 (2021): 1–29.

48 Lena Library, https://lena-library.com/ (accessed 4 January 2024).

49 Fraser, 'Inside Steven Philip's costume collection'.

50 Kumari Medha et al., 'A comprehensive review on moth repellent finishing of woolen textiles', *Journal of Cultural Heritage*, vol. 49.1 (2021): 260–71.

51 Lynn Wilson et al., 'Evidencing the Need for a National Citizens Clothing Circularity Strategy (NCCCS)', White Paper Scottish Parliament (University of Glasgow, 2023).

52 Kim Willsher, 'Stitch in time: France to help pay for clothes to be mended to cut waste', *The Guardian*, 12 July 2023. https://www.theguardian.com/environment/2023/jul/12/stitch-in-time-france-to-help-pay-for-clothes-to-be-mended-to-cut-waste (accessed 4 January 2024).

53 Susan Strasser, 'Complications and Complexities: Reflections on Twentieth-Century European Recycling', *Contemporary European History*, vol. 22, no. 3 (2013): 517–26.

54 Chubb, 'Gibb of India …', 71.

Chapter 15

1 Fiona Dieffenbacher, *Fashion Thinking*. Bloomsbury Publishing 2020.

2 Ernestine Carter, 'Top Billing', *The Sunday Times*, 23 April 1972.

3 Anon., 'Bill Gibb Shows Winter Collection', *Press and Journal*, 22 October 1977: 3.

4 For instance, Christine Rew wrote an Art & Design Fashion and Textile Design unit on Gibb for a previous SQA Higher Still qualification for 16–18 years old students which primarily focused on his knitwear collections: https://web.archive.org/web/20150923233923/http:/www.educationscotland.gov.uk/Images/BillGibbLoRes_tcm4-374586.pdf (last accessed July 2024)

5 A 2010 project at Gray's School of Art (Robert Gordon University) saw two students, Fiona McLeod and Eilidh Neilson, develop an owl print skirt and waistcoat inspired by Gibb: https://emuseum.aberdeencity.gov.uk/objects/121582/nocturnal-owl-print-skirt-and-waistcoat (last accessed July 2024)

6 A creative unit based at Gray's School of Art, Robert Gordon University, which hosts a range of events and exhibitions throughout the year all designed to connect, highlight and strengthen the creative sector and community in North East Scotland: https://lookagainaberdeen.co.uk/ (accessed 5 October 2024).

7 Leanne Luce, *Artificial Intelligence for Fashion: How AI is Revolutionizing the Fashion Industry* (Apress, 2018).

8 Zandra Rhodes, interview with editors, October 2023.

9 Morna Annandale, interview with editors, April 2024.

10 As discussed further in Elizabeth Fischer's chapter in this book.

11 Fiona Godfrey, interview with editors, September 2024.

12 Lucie Shilton, 'Archival Digital Garment Solution', University of the Arts London, June 2024, https://ualshowcase.arts.ac.uk/project/518850/cover (last accessed 21 October 2024).

13 Lucie Shilton, interview with editors, July 2024.

Chapter 16

1 'Bill Gibb, 1972' in *Out There* (Freight, 2018): 211–21.

2 The original: 'Ce n'est pas d'où tu prends les choses – c'est où tu veux les amener'. Quoted in 'Jean-Luc Godard – Legendary Filmmaker and Master of French New Wave – Dies', *The Wire*, 13 September 2022, https://thewire.in/film/jean-luc-godard-dies-filmmaker-french-new-wave (accessed 20 December 2023).

3 Anonymous, 'Istanbul' editorial, British *Vogue*, November 1971, alongside images by Barry Lategan.

4 Anonymous, 'Peru' editorial, British *Vogue*, August 1971, alongside images by Bailey.

5 The poem is inspired by 'Oriental Touch from N.E. Designer', *The Press and Journal*, 29 October 1976, and 'Now here comes the Victorian look …', *Scottish Daily Express*, 29 October 1976, both anonymous.

6 Edward Said, *Orientalism* (London: Penguin Classics, 2019). First published 1978.

7 Valerie Wallace, excerpt from 'Bespoke' in *House of McQueen* (New York City: Four Way Books, 2018), 22. © 2018 by Valerie Wallace. Appears with permission of Four Way Books. All rights reserved.

8 Brenda Polan, 'Expensive thrills', *The Guardian*, 20 May 1982.

9 *The Bill Gibb Line* podcast is available on both Apple Music and Spotify. The short film can be viewed on YouTube at https://www.youtube.com/watch?v=JkT8e1PlZmk (accessed 23 October 2024).

10 Iain R. Webb, *Bill Gibb: Fashion and Fantasy* (London: V&A, 2008), 81.

11 'It seems to be extremely useful, by way of an analogy to clothing, to identify an institutional, fundamentally social, reality, which, independent of the individual, is like the systematic, normative reserve from which the individual draws their own clothing, and which, in correspondence to Saussure's *langue*, we propose to call *dress*.' – Roland Barthes, 'History and Sociology of Clothing: Some Methodological Observations' (1957) translated by Andy Stafford in Roland Barthes, *The Language of Fashion* (Sydney: Bloomsbury, 2013): 3–19, 3.

12 Bill Gibb quoted in Helena Matheopoulous, 'The art of making history in fashion', *Daily Express*, 12 April 1976: 4.

13 This is explored further in Shane Strachan, 'Sculptor Andrew Logan's alternative take on the world', *Art UK* (online), 10 February 2020. https://artuk.org/discover/stories/sculptor-andrew-logans-alternative-take-on-the-world (accessed 5 October 2024).

14 Lisa Brunzell, *Let the World Adore You* (Gothenburg, 2024).

15 Lesley Ebbets, 'The Fall and Rise of Bill Gibb', *Daily Mirror*, 12 October 1978: 16–17.

16 Such as David Mills (Director), *Inside Business: The Fall and Rise of Bill Gibb*, 1978, for Thames Television.

17 Ann Chubb, 'Back in the Bronze Age', *Daily Telegraph*, 10 March 1985.

Selected References

Archives and collections

Aberdeen Archives, Gallery and Museums (AAGM), Aberdeen

CSM Museum & Study Collection, Central Saint Martins, UAL, London

Fashion Museum Bath

V&A Dundee

Victoria and Albert Museum (V&A), London

Secondary sources

City of Aberdeen Arts Department. *Bill Gibb: a Tribute to the Fashion Designer of the 70s*. Aberdeen: City Arts Department, 1990 – ISBN: 0900017252.

Gibb, Bill. *Hollywood Knits: Twenty glamorous sweaters to knit*. London: Pavilion Books Limited, 1987.

Rew, Christine. *Bill Gibb: The Golden Boy of British Fashion*. Aberdeen: Aberdeen Art Gallery, 2003.

Rew, Christine. 'Bill Gibb'. *Costume*, Vol 28, No 1 (1994): 81–96.

Webb, Iain R. *Bill Gibb: Fashion and Fantasy*. London: V&A Publishing, 2008.

List of Contributors

Figure 0.9 *Lynn Wilson, Josephine Steed, Morna Annandale, Shane Strachan, Karen Cross, Madeleine Marcella-Hood and Christine Rew viewing the Bill Gibb archive at AAGM's Treasure Hub.*

Karen Cross

Dr Karen Cross studied textile design and worked as a knitwear designer, before moving into education. She is currently Associate Dean for Academic Development and Student Experience at Gray's School of Art, Robert Gordon University, and leads the Fashion Management subject area. Karen's research focuses on the positive impacts of fashion, whether through the preservation of culture, heritage and artisan fashion and textile practices, sustainable fashion practices, or the role of fashion in providing a sense of identity, community, comfort and well-being to the individual. She is also interested in the use of immersive technologies within the fashion industry, to tell stories of place, provenance and people.

Elizabeth Fischer

Elizabeth Fischer is Associate Professor HES-SO in the cultural history of dress and fashion at the University of Art and Design HEAD – Genève (Switzerland). She was dean of the Jewellery and accessory design department from 2009 to 2021, as well as of Fashion design from 2015 to 2021. Holder of an MA in Art History, she specializes in the meaning of dress, textiles and jewellery in painting and photography. Her current research, led in partnership with Magali Le Mens, PhD (University of Rennes 2), focuses on the subversion of binary gender codes in Western fashion from 1850 to today. She has collaborated with museums and universities for over twenty-five years in Switzerland and internationally and published numerous essays in French and English. She is a member of the scientific board of MuMode, the Swiss Fashion Museum in Yverdon.

Marie McLoughlin

Dr Marie McLoughlin is an Honorary Research Fellow in the School of Art and Media at the University of Brighton. Research into wartime clothing led to *Paris Fashion and World War 2: Global Diffusion and Nazi Controls* (Bloomsbury 2020), co-edited with Lou Taylor, which won the Association of Dress Historians Book of Year award for 2021. She is a founding member of the Women's Tailoring Research Interest Group of the European body ACORSO (Appearances, Bodies and Societies) based at Rennes 2, France and has presented various research papers in connection with the group. A publication of the group's research is forthcoming. Her chapter on Gibb's education is informed by Marie's PhD research into fashion and the art school, especially the founding influence of Muriel Pemberton at St Martin's and the development of the art school fashion degree. Gibb arrived at St Martin's during this period of upheaval, his talent spotted and nurtured by Pemberton. Marie herself followed in Gibb's footsteps a few years later and was one of the last intake of students taught by Pemberton.

Madeleine Marcella-Hood

Dr Madeleine Marcella-Hood is a senior lecturer at Gray's School of Art, Robert Gordon University. She is head of year 1 for the BA (Hons) Fashion Management and teaches a range of subjects including fashion business, research methods and creative project management. Her main research interests are Scottish fashion, visual media and identity. Much of her published work focuses on Instagram, which she recognizes for its significance in shaping visual culture and its impact on human behaviour.

Christina Reid

Christina Reid is the course leader for BA (Hons) Digital Marketing and BA (Hons) Digital Marketing and Business Analytics at Aberdeen Business School, Robert Gordon University. She lectures in research methods and digital marketing, including digital marketing strategy, brand management, and social media marketing. Following her undergraduate degree in Fashion Design for Industry at Heriot-Watt University she completed a MSc in Fashion Management at Robert Gordon University where she is currently undertaking a PhD in brand co-creation and online brand management.

Professor Peter Reid

Professor Peter Reid is professor at the School of Law and Social Science, Robert Gordon University. His work is centred around cultural heritage with a strong emphasis on the narratives of the North and North East of Scotland. He has a particular interest in uncovering neglected or forgotten stories, community identity and how it intersects with local culture and heritage, as well as the gathering, interpreting and disseminating of stories. He has recently been involved in projects connected with the creation of an historic film archive for Fraserburgh, Bill Gibb's hometown, and one examining stories of Scandinavian wartime exiles in North East Scotland.

Christine Rew

Former manager of Aberdeen Archives, Gallery and Museums Service, Christine Rew is a decorative arts specialist who has curated several contemporary craft, jewellery and fashion exhibitions including 'Bill Gibb' in 1990 and 'Bill Gibb – the Golden Boy of British Fashion' in 2003, the year that would have marked his sixtieth birthday. At Aberdeen Art Gallery she developed a significant collection of Gibb's work including archival material, fashion drawings, knitwear, daywear and couture garments, creating the most comprehensive collection of Gibb's creative output in the UK.

Jeena Sharma

Jeena Sharma is a fashion journalist, editor and a former student at Central Saint Martins where she wrote a paper on Gibb's body of work as part of her coursework. She currently lives in New York City covering the business and cultural aspects of fashion as a senior reporter at *Morning Brew*. She has previously also been a Beauty Editor at *Paper Magazine*, and has had her writing around the cultural analysis of fashion appear in *South China Morning Post*, *The Guardian*, *Observer* and *Vogue*.

Josephine Steed

Josephine Steed studied Constructed Textiles, specializing in Fashion Knitwear at the University of Middlesex and has a broad range of experience of fashion and textiles from designer/maker practice to textile design for mass-manufacture. She is currently Associate Dean for Research and formerly Course Director for BA (Hons) Fashion & Textile Design at Gray's School of Art, Robert Gordon University. Josephine has a particular interest in the role and relevance of traditional hand skills in contemporary textiles and the value and status of craft making. She was a co-organizer and co-chair of the online symposium 'Fashion, Fantasy, and Collaboration: The Legacy of Bill Gibb' in partnership with Aberdeen Art Gallery in 2021.

NJ Stevenson

Former fashion journalist and stylist, NJ Stevenson began her fashion curatorial career in 2009, with the major monographic exhibition of designer Bill Gibb at the Fashion and Textile Museum, London. She has since worked on many projects with venues including the Fashion and Textile Museum, University of the Arts London and The Southbank Centre, where she curated Cloud, an exhibition and live performance event with costume designer and filmmaker Tim Yip. Publications include, *The Chronology of Fashion* (A&C Black, 2010), an American edition as *Fashion: A Visual History from Regency & Romance to Retro & Revolution* (Griffin, 2012), and contributions to journals *Fashion Theory* (Taylor and Francis) and *Fashion, Film and Consumption* (Intellect). She has recently contributed to *Kaffe Fassett: The Artist's Eye* (Yale University Press, 2022) and to *ReFocus: The Films of Ken Russell* (Edinburgh University Press, 2022). She was Fashion Director of Port Eliot Festival of the Arts and is a lecturer and member of the Centre for Fashion Curation at London College of Fashion. Stevenson's doctoral research on the relationship between historical film costume and fashion revivalism in the 1960s and 1970s informed 'Do A Ruby Keeler: The Boy Friend: Period film and retro fashion in 1971' at the Fashion and Textile Museum (22 March 2023 to 8 September 2024). With Martin Green and David Cabaret, she then co-curated 'Outlaws: Fashion Renegades of 80s London' at the museum from 4 October 2024 to 9 March 2025, and with Martin Green is author of *Outlaws: Fashion Renegades of Leigh Bowery's 1980s London* (Scala Arts and Heritage 2024).

Shane Strachan

Originally from Bill Gibb's hometown of Fraserburgh, Shane Strachan is a writer, performer and academic based in Aberdeen. His spoken word project *The Bill Gibb Line* is available online and was exhibited at Aberdeen Art Gallery, followed by further Bill Gibb-related work for V&A Dundee and in his debut poetry collection, *DWAMS* (Tapsalteerie), nominated for Best Poetry Book in the 2024 Saltire Book Awards. He was the 2022–23 National Library of Scotland's Scots Scriever writer in residence for which he was awarded Scots Champion at the 2023 Scots Language Awards. He holds a PhD in Creative Writing from the University of Aberdeen where he now lectures.

Iain R. Webb

Iain R. Webb is a fashion writer, curator and academic. He is Professor of Fashion & Design at Kingston School of Art and associate lecturer at CSM and Bath Spa University. During his career he has been fashion editor of *BLITZ, The Evening Standard, Harpers & Queen, The Times* and *Elle*. Publications include *Bill Gibb - Fashion and Fantasy, As Seen in BLITZ, Vogue Colouring Book, John Galliano for Dior* and *Rebel Stylist: Caroline Baker, The Woman Who Invented Street Fashion*. He has curated exhibitions at ICA, RCA, Somerset House, Fashion Museum, Bath, The Bowes Museum and The Holburne Museum. Latest projects: chapter contributions to *Little Black Dress* (NMS), *Cracked Actor* (Red Planet), *Outlaws* (Scala Arts & Heritage), and curating *The Fashion Show: Everything But The Clothes* exhibition at V&A Dundee (June 2023 to January 2024).

Lynn Wilson

Lynn Wilson is an award-winning academic researcher, educator and entrepreneur in the field of circular fashion and textiles. Originally trained in Fashion and Textiles at Dundee University (1992) and Nottingham Trent (1994), Dr Wilson gained a PhD (Management), from University of Glasgow, 2022. Her research interests include consumer household experiences of clothing dirt, contamination and hygiene, which leads to clothing being kept in circulation or disposed of. Her consultancy company Circular Design Synergy provides training, mentoring and research to businesses transitioning to the circular economy. Prior to academia, Dr Wilson was the Sector Manager – Textiles, Circular Economy team at Zero Waste Scotland, contributing to the Scottish Government's Making *Things Last – A Circular Economy Strategy for Scotland*. In 2015, she was awarded a Churchill Fellowship, visiting Japan, and researching textile heritage, technology and clothing retail systems that could support a circular economy, and is a Fellow of the Royal Society for Arts, Commerce and Manufacturing (FRSA). From 1996 to 2000, she worked in Botswana developing textile projects with indigenous people of the Kalahari Desert, a seminal experience that drives her commitment to ethical and sustainable production and consumption for a fairer, environmentally sustainable world.

Index

Aberdeen Archives, Gallery and Museums (AAGM), 3, 4, 115–118, 131–137, 174, 176–178, 186
Aberdeen Art Gallery, 36, 42, 44, 73, 104, 106, 113, 116, 119, 174, 177–178, 181
Aberdeen Treasure Hub, 176–179
Aberdeenshire, 19, 23, 103, 186
access (digital vs. physical), 176–178
Adriaan, John, 107–108, 114
AI (Artificial Intelligence), 177
Air France in-flight fashion show, 95, 171
Alice Paul Boutique, 4, 21–22, 28–29, 33, 66, 110
All in a Day (BBC documentary), 98–99, 106
Allen, Katie, 161–162
Alternative Miss World, 195
Amies, Hardy, 39, 50
Andrae, Irene, 109
animal fibres, 157, 163–164
Anthropocene, 157
archives, 114, 174, 176–179
Arm in Arm (Charlip), 103, 104, 114
Arnau, Brenda, 94
Arnott, Janet (née Gibb), 11–18
Arrowsmith, Clive, 5, 123
Art deco, 112
artisan making, 71, 80
Ashley, Bob and Ellen, 33
Austin Reed, 6
Austria, 55
authenticity in design, 172

Babani, 52
Baccarat (fashion house), 5, 22, 28, 32, 106, 109, 148
Baker, Caroline, 95, 99
Baker, Maureen, 25
Banks, Jeff, 97
Barr, Ann, 110

Barthes, Roland, 195
Bartis, Audrey, 61
Bates, John, 5, 7, 25
Bath, Fashion Museum, 48
batwing, 170
Bauman, Zygmunt, 135
Beatles, The, 50, 64
Beaton, Cecil, 99
Beattie, Willa, 110
Bedford, Duchess of, 115
bees in design, 3, 30–31, 104, 114, 116, 157, 163
Bendel, Henri, 4, 21, 110
Biba, 24, 100, 110
Bill Gibb Limited (company), 5, 27, 32, 106, 111
Billy: Bill Gibb's Moment in Time (exhibition), 104–114
Bishop, Amanda, 20
Black, Monty, 5, 22
Black, Sandy, 78
Blahnik, Manolo, 96
Blender software, 183–184
bloggers, rise of, 120
Blotter, Arnold, 55
Boboli, Piero, 33
body image, 138–140
body positivity, 141
bohemian fashion, 136
Bon, François, 50
Bond Street showroom, 5, 67
Bosch, Herman, 55
Bosch, Hieronymus, 53
Boulton, Mildred, 66, 71, 73–74, 76, 80, 161
Boursnell, Clive, 111, 112
Bovan, Matty, 99
Bowles, Hamish, 89–90
Bradfield, Erika, 114

braid, 46–47, 53, 57, 69
branding, 121–122, 182
Bray, Natalie, 42
bricolage, 35, 48, 136
British Caledonian Airways, 94
British Embassy (Paris), 94
British Fashion Council, 165
British fashion industry, 107–108, 110
British Museum, 53
British Overseas Trade Board, 5
Brittain, Judy (Judith), 23, 43, 66, 74
Bronze Age collection, 7, 31, 92, 198–199
Brocklehurst, Jo, 40
Brunzell, Lisa, 196
Bruyère, Luc (Lucky Love), 94
Byzantine collection, 5, 7, 27, 73, 81

Callot Soeurs, 52
camouflage, 138–140
Campbell, Naomi, 192
Campbell, Olive, 110
Campbell, Sarah, 33
carbon emissions, 157, 164
Cardin, Pierre, 42, 50
Carnaby Street, 49
Carroll, Annette, 6
Carter, Ernestine, 23, 31, 32
Carven boutique, 20
casualization of dress, 130, 138
celebrities, 89, 91, 146, 152–153
Central Saint Martins (CSM), 7, 20, 25, 35, 182
Chanel, 145, 161
Charlip, Remy, 103, 104, 114
Chatsworth House, 6, 92
Chen, Eva, 120
Chopova, Lowena, 99
Chubb, Ann, 81, 112, 156, 161, 198
Clark, Ossie, 1, 23, 25, 47, 51, 63, 181, 195
climate change, 157, 158, 167
clothing history/studies, 35–36, 40
co-creation, 121–122, 127
Coddington, Grace, 99
code technique, 187
collaboration, 63–64, 66, 71, 73–76, 171, 174, 181–182, 185
collectors, 115–117
Collier, Susan, 33

Collins, Joan, 1, 6, 110
colonial gaze, 60
colonialism, 145, 191
comfort, 130–132
commercialization of design, 67–69
Conran, Jasper, 102
conservation practices, 178
construction techniques, 158–161, 170–171
Contemporary Dance Theatre, London, 114
content creators, 120
contextual research, 175–176
Cooper, Gary, 81
costume, 45, 53, 55–56, 101, 132–134, 139
cotton, 23, 46, 54, 56, 157, 163
Courrèges, André, 50–51
Courtaulds Show (1981), 161
Courtelle, 6, 75
Cowdray Hall show (1977), 173–174
crafts, 52, 66, 71, 80, 173, 185
Crahay, Jules-François, 53, 58–59, 61
CSM Museum and Archive, 45
cultural appropriation, 44, 46, 53, 60–61, 68, 136, 138–139, 145–146, 149–151, 160, 180–181
cultural referencing, 173, 180–181

Dahl, Tessa, 6, 109
Davidson, Patricia (Patsy) (née Gibb), 11–18, 96, 103, 106
De Klee, Charlotte, 110
de Villeneuve, Jan, 103–104, 106–107, 114
de Villeneuve, Justin, 123, 186
Deacon, Giles, 1, 3, 53, 99, 169–172
Deacon knitwear, 161
decoration vs. structure, 67
Delevoryas, Lillian, 71
design development, 97 175–176
design inspiration, 64, 66–67, 146–155
digital garment simulation, 182–184
digital legacy, 120–121, 123, 129, 165–167
digitization of archives, 178–179
Dior, Christian, 35, 36, 42, 146
diversity in fashion, 171
DIY fashion, 78–79
Dolce & Gabbana, 145
draping, 34, 42
Dsquared, 151
Duthie, Bob (Robert), 4, 12, 36, 39

Ebbetts, Lesley, 89–91, 102
eccentricity, 171
eco-friendly materials, 163–165
Edelkoort, Li, 132–133, 139–140
education (fashion), 35–36, 38–39, 41, 97, 171, 173–185
Education Act 1962 (Butler), 38, 195
Egyptian interest, 64
Emcar, 36
Emelle, 33
emotional connection to clothing, 131–132
emotionally durable design, 165
embroidery, 42, 47–48, 55, 57, 124, 168
Embroidery Industry of Vorarlberg, 55
England, Katy, 97
environmental concerns, 120, 124, 129
Equal Pay Act (1970), 72
Ernestine Carter, 99
escapism, fashion as, 97
ethics of materials, 164–165
ethnic dress, 133–134
ethnic fashion inspirations, 52–53, 60–61
ethnic motifs, 145–146, 149
eudaimonic wellbeing, 132, 141
European Fashion Heritage Association, 7
experimental fashion techniques, 180–181
exoticism, 52–53, 58–61, 133, 191

Fair Isle knitting, 65, 73–74
Falaise, Loulou de la, 51
fantasy fashion, 53–54
Fashion Aid (1985), 92
Fashion and Textile Museum, 2, 7, 104–106, 108, 110–115
fashion design education, 35–36, 38–39, 41, 97, 171, 173–185
fashion industry critiques, 145–146, 155–156
fashion influencers, 120
fashion journalism, 186–187
fashion law, 149
fashion resale, 165, 167
fashion shows, 92, 95, 170–171
Fassett, Kaffe,
 – artistic influence and colour use, 22–23, 32–33, 63–65
 – collaborations with Bill Gibb, 3–5, 63–70, 73–76, 106, 113, 181, 187
 – design style and philosophy, 63–70, 73–78
 – legacy and impact, 95, 112–113, 147–148, 157, 200
fast fashion, 78, 132, 140
faux leather, 164
feminism and fashion, 72
fibre innovation, 68, 162–165
Fielding, Fenella, 102
financing, fashion business and, 96
fine art influences, 168
flat-lay photography, 124
Flowers and Lace collection, 6
Foale and Tuffin, 50–51
Foale, Marion, 23
folk dress, 45, 52–55, 80, 132–136, 141
Fortuny, 52
foundation course, 39
Fox, Alfred and Philip, 6
Fraserburgh Academy, 4, 12, 20, 36, 38, 147, 186
Fraserburgh Heritage Centre, 106, 119, 175
Franklin, Kathkleen (Kate), 5, 89, 92–93, 99, 104, 106–107, 108, 114–115, 148
Freidan, Betty, 72
French haute couture, 49–50
fur, 33–34, 57, 133–136, 163

Gainsbury, Sam, 97
Galliano, John, 1, 2, 11, 48, 93–94, 99, 145–150, 160, 165
Garland, Judy, 81
Garment simulation, 183–184
George, Susan, 32
Gibb family, 39
Gibb, Bill
 – artistic integrity and struggle, 68, 96–97
 – business practices and struggles, 74, 76, 96, 107–108, 156
 – childhood and early life, 1, 4, 11–13. 19–20, 36, 38, 64–65, 101, 186
 – collaborations, 32–33, 73–76, 106, 113, 181–182
 – creative leadership, 66–67
 – death and illness, 1, 7, 199
 – design style and philosophy, 35, 48, 63–69, 71, 73, 91–92, 102, 123–127, 171–171, 195
 – design process, 14–16, 53–54, 61–62
 – drawing and design process, 12, 15, 19, 24–31, 158–165, 168–170

- education, 12–13, 20–21, 24, 35–40, 45, 97, 110, 147–148
- influence and inspirations, 1–3, 11–12, 14, 19–20, 23, 44–45, 61–62, 102 146–148
- legacy, 1–3, 7, 11, 17–18, 80–82, 103–114, 120–121, 123, 154, 173–185
- materials used, 162–165
- posthumous exhibitions and events, 2, 3, 7
- Scottish roots, 64–65, 71, 73
- travels, 68–70, 95

Gibb, Evelyn Reid (grandmother), 19
Gibb, Marlyn, 11–18
Gitana/Romani styles, 134–135
Godard, Jean-Luc, 187
Godfrey, Fiona, 182
Gould's (Leicester), 75–76, 80
Grant, Evie, 111
Grant, Linda, 23
Gray, Keith, 180
Gray's School of Art (Robert Gordon University), 2, 173–185
Green, Harry, 161
Groom, Avril, 79
Grumbach, Didier, 50
Gucci, 134–140
Gudrun, 22

H&M, 158
hand drawing, 176–177
hand skills vs. digital, 177
hand-knitting, 71, 77–78
handmade, 157, 161, 168
Harden, Rosemary, 104
Harper & Queen magazine, 106, 110, 117
Harris Tweed, 7, 33
Harrods, 5, 6, 20, 31, 33, 198
Hartnell, Norman, 39, 50
Harvey Nichols, 107–108
hedonic wellbeing, 131
Henry VIII, 36
heritage fashion, 152, 155, 173, 182
heritage knitting, 74
heritage preservation, 141
Herschelle, 33
Hillson, Bobby, 24–25
hippie fashion, 64, 68
historic dress references, 64, 132–133, 170–171

historical textiles, 64
Historicism, 35, 48, 97, 179
Hockley, Philip, 33–34
Hodin, Annabel, 95
Hogger, Lesley, 33
Hollywood Knits, 7, 17, 82
Holroyd, Amy Twigger, 80
homogenized fashion, 171
Honey magazine, 36
Hong Kong, 6
Hogg, Pam, 96
Hot Gossip (dance troupe), 89
House of McQueen, 192
Howell, Georgina, 23

Identity London Ltd., 100
illustration, fashion, 24, 36, 40, 168, 178
inclusivity, 171, 181
India, as inspiration, 52, 59–60, 147–148, 153–154
India Imports, 156
Indian manufacturing, 163
Indian miniatures, 64
individuality in fashion, 170–171
Instagram, 120–121, 124, 127–128
Intarsia knitting, 74
interdisciplinary collaboration, 174, 185
internet-era challenges, 176
Inverness, 74, 111
Iranian influences, 152–153
Ironside, Janey, 4, 64

Jagger, Bianca, 1, 14, 118, 148
Japan, influence of, 50, 56, 59, 154–155, 158–160
Jeffrey, Charles, 99

Kagan, Sasha, 78
Katinka School, 42
Kelly (Kellie Wilson), model, 98–99
Kemp, Sue, 33, 173
Kensington, Alice Paul Boutique, 110
Kenzo (Takada), 50, 53–57, 59–61
kimono, 52, 56, 154–155, 158–161, 191
King's Road, London, 51, 64
Knitting patterns (published), 79
knitwear, 23, 27, 31, 33, 65–67, 74–76, 106, 113, 126, 161, 170, 181
knolling, 124

lace, 74, 133
Lacroix, Christian, 90
lamé fabric, 92
language of fashion, 186
Lanvin, 59
Laura Ashley, 47
Leach, Rachel, 31
leather, 27, 32–33, 112, 117, 163–164, 168, 171
Lelong, Lucien, 42
Les Ambassadeurs Club, 5
Liberty's of London, 6, 33, 47–48
Lichfield, Patrick, 23
lingerie collection, 91
liquid modernity, 135
lockdown dressing, 130, 137
London, 63, 168, 170
London College of Fashion, 41, 104
London fashion industry, 105–106, 113
London fashion scene, 48–49, 51
London's Oriental Club, 195
Look Again Aberdeen, 2, 174–175, 181
Loopy Ewe, 162
Louis Vuitton, 151
Lovable, company, 5
Lulu, 5
loungewear, 137–138
lurex, 75, 115, 163
luxury fashion, 162–165

McCartney, Stella, 145, 163–164
MacCorkindale, Simon, 32
Macdonald, Catherine, 180
Macdonald, Samantha, 180
Maclean, Rachel, 195
McDowell, Colin, 92
McGlone, Jackie, 30
McKinley, Barry, 117
MacKinnon, Liz, 110
MacLachlan, Sally, 33, 71, 163, 168
McQueen, Lee Alexander, 11, 48, 90, 96–98
Madison Avenue, New York, 6
Maison Margiela, 90, 94
Maja styles, 135
make-up and hair styling, 99
map dresses, 101
Marriot, Steve, 106
mass production issues, 67–68

mass-manufacturing vs slow fashion, 71, 75, 77
Matheopoulas, Helena, 6, 71
maximalism, 136
Menkes, Suzy, 2, 72, 186
Michele, Alessandro, 136, 138
Middle Eastern influences, 181
Middle-Eastern clients, 198
Milgrim, Sally, 145–146
Miller, Beatrix, 5, 23, 48, 74, 99
Miller, Daniel, 141
miniskirt, 23, 42, 49–50, 67
Missoni, 77, 80
Modefest, Yugoslavia, 5
models, 89–90, 95, 98–99
modesty, cultural constructs of, 138–141
Montgomery, David, 109
Moon and Buddha collection, 5, 76–77
Moon, Sarah, 23, 48
Morocco, influence of, 68
Morris, May, 35
Morris, William, 35
Morrison, Bryan, 5
Moss, Kate, 1, 100
motifs, 116, 146–153, 157, 166
museum research, 64

Nailoid, nail varnish, 5
narrative design, 168–170
National Art Library, 43
National Design Diploma (NDD), 39
Native American designs, 146, 149–151
natural fibres, 157, 163
natural landscapes, 127–128
needlepoint, 63
New Pitsligo, 103, 104, 186
New York, 6, 14, 21, 94
Newham College of Further Education, 111
Noble, Kirstie, 181
nostalgia, 133–136
Nothdruft, Dennis, 106, 110, 112, 113
Nutter, Tommy, 172
nylon, 164

objectification, 138–140
Oklahoma, 70
Oldfield, Bruce, 92
Olympia London, 186

Ora, Rita, 1, 7, 81
organic materials, 157
Oriental Club show, 5, 98–99, 106, 112, 148, 154, 168
Orientalism, 150, 191
Ormesby-Gore, Alice, 78
Otterburn Mills, 71
Otway, John, 89
Over 21 (magazine), 92
Owen, Meg Wynn, 112, 131
ownership and attribution, 123

Pahlavi, Farah Diba, 153
Paisley pattern, 27, 66, 152–153
Papworth, Veronica, 24
Park Lane Hotel, 92
Parkinson, Norman, 30
Parsons, Pauline, 33
Pasmore, Sally, 107–108, 114
pattern cutting, 36, 42, 158, 182–184
pattern mixing, 14, 64, 66
peasant fashion, 52, 54, 59, 133–134, 137
Pemberton, Muriel, 9, 13, 35–36, 40–42, 44, 48, 147
Perry, Grayson, 195
Persian miniatures, 64
Pevsner, Nikolaus, 40
Philip Hockley (label), 100
Philip, Steven, 100, 166, 170
Phillips, Arlene, 89
physical vs. digital access, 176–179
picture books (as design source), 60
plaids, 66, 113
plant-based materials, 164
pleats, 23, 42, 48, 56, 89, 109, 116, 139–140, 180
poems (chronological order)
    – '15 February 1967', 8
    – 'January 1970', 83
    – 'August – December 1971', 188
    – '26 April 1972', 87–88
    – '30 April 1974', 142
    – '18 November 1977', 193–194
    – '12 October 1978', 197
    – '28 October 1976', 190
    – '16 March 1985', 200
poetry
    – form and techniques, 189–190, 198
    – narrative poetry, 192
    – shape in poetry, 187–189
    – use of persona, 195–196
    – use of sound, 190–191
Poiret, Paul, 52, 146
Polan, Brenda, 19, 147, 192
poncho, 52, 74, 133, 139–140, 161
Porcelain collection, 5
Porter, Thea, 47, 107
postmodernism in design, 187
Powney, Amy, 165–166
Pre-Raphaelite influences, 53
Prince Albert, 42
print design and techniques, 23, 27, 33, 47, 71, 90, 107, 110, 136, 148, 154, 157, 163 168, 171
private collections, 104, 106
provenance, 115
Puthli Asha, 5, 153–154

Qiana jersey, 33, 89–90, 106, 108, 110, 131
Quant, Mary, 23, 50

Rabanne, Paco, 50
Rampling, Charlotte, 106, 117
Ravelry, 81
Read, Suzannah, 78
recycled fashion, 181
reimagination of designs, 125–127
repair and maintenance, 158, 166–167
reproduction of imagery, 121–123
retrospective exhibitions, 104–114
Rhodes, Dame Zandra, 1, 5, 6, 23, 45, 104, 106, 113, 159–160, 177, 181
Rigg, Diana, 99
Renaissance collection, 2, 5, 19
Renaissance influence, 53, 55, 147
reusability, 158, 166
RGU (Robert Gordon University), 174–181
RGU Art & Heritage Collections, 2, 198
Ricci, Nina, 59
Rigg, Diana, 99
Riva, Heinz W., 49
Rive Gauche (YSL line), 50–51
Roberts, Michael, 99, 155, 186, 195
Roberts, Patricia, 72, 78
Rock, Mick
Romanian blouses, 52, 55
Romanticism in fashion, 53, 166

Roosevelt, Eleanor, 146
Rose collection, 7
Rowan Yarns, 78
Royal Albert Hall retrospective show, 2, 6, 14–15, 89–90, 92, 102, 110, 173, 192–194
Royal College of Art (RCA), 4, 13, 20–21, 22, 24, 36, 42, 45, 63, 110
Royal Darroch Hotel, 5, 100–101
Russell, Annie and Alice, 22, 110, 65–66
Russell, Ken, 50
Russian/Cossack style, 133–135
Russophilia, 134
Rykiel, Sonia, 80

Sackville-West, Vita, 171
Saint Laurent, Yves, 50–51, 53, 59–61, 69, 134
Samuel, Raphael, 105
Sanquhar patterns, 74
sarafan, 139
Scafidi, Susan, 149–151
Schiaparelli, 51
Schlaepfer, Jakob, 50, 57
Scotland, 100–101, 103, 113
Scottish collection, 6, 27
Scottish heritage, 53, 57, 64–65, 146, 152, 155
Scottish manufacturing, 161–162
Scottish textiles, 71, 73–74, 119
Scoular, Charlotte Rose, 179
screen printing, 163
second-hand fashion, 110
selfie (as aesthetic), 124
sentimentality in dress, 135
sequins, 33, 57, 68, 106, 159, 161
Sex Discrimination Act (1975), 72
Shaw, Sandie, 152
Sheather, Keith, 98
Sherman, Cindy, 195
Shilton, Lucie, 182–184
silk, 33, 110, 131, 148, 159–160, 162–164, 167, 178
simulation (3D digital), 182–184
Singapore, 54
Sleep, Wayne, 89, 102
slow fashion, 71, 77–80, 132, 141
social media, 120
South, Vera, 42
St Martin's School of Art, 4, 20, 35–36, 39–40, 41, 168–170

Steinem, Gloria, 72
Stella magazine, 23
Steven Phillip Design Consultancy, 170
Stevenson, Pauline, 41
storytelling in fashion, 71, 106, 114, 145, 155, 165, 168–169
Street Porter, Janet, 99, 195
student project, 175–181
supply chain, 162, 165
Susan Small, 25
sustainability, 68, 71, 80
sustainability in dress, 130, 141
sustainable design, 157, 162–165, 158–161
synthetic fibres, 163–164

Tangye, Howard, 39
tartan, 47, 64, 113, 152, 155, 180
Taylor, Elizabeth, 2, 5, 107
Taylor, Janet, 33, 71, 110, 155, 187
technology, digital fashion, 182–184
textile choices, 68
textile conservation, 178
textile heritage, 141
textile innovation, 162–165
theatricality in design, 168, 170
The Bill Gibb Line, 2, 7, 174, 179, 181–182
The Boyfriend (film), 50
The Stud (film), 108
thin-ideal, 138, 141
Tilke, Max Karl, 45, 55–56
Timeless Vixen, 128
toile production, 33, 176
traditional techniques, 158, 163
travel as inspiration, 52, 55, 59, 64, 68–70
Tuffin, Sally, 23, 51
Turney, Joanne, 72, 80
tweed, 33, 57, 106
Twigger Holyroyd, Amy, 80
Twiggy, 1, 2, 5, 7, 14–15, 50, 99, 102, 107, 113, 118, 122–123, 146, 186, 194

upcycling, 167, 181
user-generated content, 120–121
Uzbekistan textiles, 134

V&A Dundee, 7, 47–48, 152–153, 155
Vanhee, Nadege, 165

Vegea, 164
Victoria & Albert Museum (V&A), 25, 35, 40, 42–45, 53, 64, 78, 119, 147–148, 152, 155
Vidal Sassoon, 99
vintage fashion, 100, 136, 124–126, 165–167
visual storytelling, 121, 168–169
volume in design, 168, 170
Vogue, 2, 5–6, 19, 23, 25–26, 30, 43, 48, 65, 74, 78, 79, 83, 90, 102–103, 109, 123, 165, 189, 191
Vogue Designer of the Year (1970), 157
Vogue Knitting, 74, 79

Wainwright, Janice, 23
Walker, Douglas, 128
Walker, Sarah, 180
Wallace, Valerie, 192
Wan, Barney, 109
Warhol, Andy, 67
waste reduction, 158–161
Wella (promotion), 33

Westwood, Vivienne, 1, 72
White, Cindy, 91, 95
Wholegarment, 161
Williams, Pharrell, 151
Williams, Stacey, 112
Wilson, Ronald, 41
Winter 1974 collection, 31
Womersley, Richard, 71
wool, 27, 48, 74–75, 103, 115–116, 133, 136–137, 157, 163
Wool and the Gang, 81
Woollybear Yarns, 78
Wright, Peter, 32–33, 107
Wynn Owen, Meg, 100, 112

Yamamoto, Kansai, 107
Yardley 'London Look Award', 4, 21
Yorston, Valerie, 71

zero waste, 158–161

Figure 0.10 *Detail from woollen printed scarf with Bill Gibb signature, mid-1970s. AAGM Collections: ABDMS093606.*